Munnings, Sir Alfred *An Artist's Life* (1956)

Rawcliffe C. & Wilson, R. (eds) *Norwich Since 1550* (2004)

Press, C. A. Manning *Norfolk Notabilities* (1893)

Preston, H. *Early East Anglian Banks and Bankers* (1994)

Sparkes, W. L. *The Story of Shoemaking in Norwich* (1949)

Symes Scutt, G. P. *The History of the Bank of Bengal: an epitome of 100 years of Banking in India* (1904)

Vaughan, A. *Samuel Morton Peto: A Victorian Entrepreneur* (2009)

Vaughan, A. *Railwaymen, Politics and Money – the Great Age of Railways in Britain (1997)*

Wheldon, F. W. *A Norvic Century* (1946)

Wright, T. *The Romance of the Shoe* (1922)

Journals & Academic Papers

Barney, J. 'Death & Disgrace in Victorian Norwich' (*'The Annual'* - the bulletin of the Norfolk Archaeological & Historical Research Group, No. 17, 2008)

Church, Roy & Clark, Christine 'Cleanliness next to Godliness: Christians in the Victorian Starch Industry' (*Business and Economic History*, Vol. 28 1999)

Doyle, Professor B. M. 'Through the Windows of A Baptist Meeting House' (*Baptist Quarterly* 1996, Volume 36)

Doyle, Professor B. M. 'Education and the Liberal Rank and File in Edwardian England; the case of Sir George White' (*Liberal Democrat History Group Newsletter*, September 1996)

Jones, D. 'Business, Tact and Thoroughness- a History of the Norvic Shoe Company' (*Journal of the Norfolk Industrial Archaeological Society*, 1986)

Jones, Diana K. 'Jeremiah James Colman (1830-1898) and the Protestant Work Ethic Thesis' (*Bulletin of the John Rylands Library*)

Ryan R. *A History of the Norwich Union Fire and Life Societies from 1797 to 1914* (PhD Thesis submitted to the University of East Anglia 1983)

Virgoe, Norma & Williamson, T. (eds) 'Religious Dissent in East Anglia' (*Norfolk Archaeological and Historical Research Group/Centre of East Anglian Studies, University of East Anglia 1993*)

East Anglian Studies: The Nineteenth Century (Open University Press 1984)

'Bloomsbury Chapel and the Mercantile Majority: the case of Sir Morton Peto' (*Baptist Quarterly*, January 1984)

Trade and Company Press

Southwell, E. B. 'J & J Colman Ltd :Early Days at Stoke Holy Cross' (*Carrow Works Magazine*, 1925)

the ultimate FENDER book

PAUL DAY & DAVE HUNTER

ILEX

ILEX

Published in the United Kingdom by The Ilex Press Ltd.
210 High Street
Lewes, East Sussex
BN7 2NS
www.ilex-press.com

For ILEX:
Publisher: Alastair Campbell
Managing Editor: Nick Jones
Senior Editor: Ellie Wilson
Art Director: Julie Weir

British Library Cataloguing-in-Publication Data
A catalogue record for this book is available
from the British Library.

ISBN: 978-1-907579-85-1

COMMISSIONING EDITOR: Nigel Osborne
ART DIRECTOR: Paul Cooper Design
DESIGN: Elizabeth Owens

10 9 8 7 6 5 4 3 2 1

Printed and bound in China

Colour Origination by Ivy Press Reprographics

CONTENTS

"He gave us the weapons."

KEITH RICHARDS ON LEO FENDER

INTRODUCTION

Back in the 40s, Leo Fender and his team ran a small business in California making a handful of steel guitars and amplifiers. Soon, however, they turned an avant-garde idea into the world's first commercial solidbody electric guitar, and in the process began to make musical history.

A great new run of instruments began to tumble from Fender's workshop – the Telecaster in 1950, Stratocaster in 1954, the Jazzmaster in 1958, and more – just in time for rock'n'roll. Ever since, guitarists hungry for stylish and playable instruments have lined up to use them.

Everyone from Jimi Hendrix and Kurt Cobain to Eric Clapton and John Mayer has played a Fender guitar. But it is the millions of unknown guitarists regularly drawn to these instruments who have ensured that today Fender remains the leading modern electric-guitar brand.

This book is designed to show and describe all the electric guitars that Fender has made since 1950, with an accompanying DVD to demonstrate the classics.

In the book, the overall organization is chronological, with main model types dealt with individually as they appear in the story. Within each broad model type, the various model variations are listed chronologically, and then alphabetically within each year.

Each entry for an individual model variation shows its name and its production dates, a single-line identification, and then specifications for neck, body, electronics, and hardware. Unless stated, models are made in the U.S.: MIM indicates a model made in Fender's Mexico factory; MIJ indicates one made in Japan; and MIK indicates a model made in Korea.

The DVD in this package features Dave Hunter and Carl Verheyen, who have teamed up to take you on a tour of the Brian Fischer collection of vintage Fender guitars (and a few classic amplifiers, too). Dave is a guitarist, journalist, and author, and Carl is a guitarist, lecturer, and teacher. Together in this special show, they demonstrate exactly what it is that gives the classic Fender models their timeless appeal.

The Ultimate Fender Book is a unique journey through the fascinating history and the present-day greatness of Fender guitars. We hope you enjoy it.

"I didn't really think about revolutionizing the industry or anything of that sort. We were spending all of our time thinking about doing a better job for the musician."

LEO FENDER

THE PLANK THAT ROCKED THE WORLD

By the late 1940s, Leo Fender saw the need for an entirely new breed of electric guitar. He was intimately acquainted with the requirements of the professional musicians he served and knew that the hollowbody archtops with added pickups played by most country and dance-band guitarists weren't right for the job. The problems with these instruments kept many players at the back of the stage, while the singers, fiddle players, and more recently steel-guitar players were in the spotlight.

Of course, even these hollowbody electrics had been a revelation just a little over a decade before, enabling players of Spanish-style guitars to be heard amid a big-band at least, but they were boomy sounding, prone to feedback, and didn't maximize the potential of the available amplification.

Leo Fender devised a plan for a solidbody electric guitar that, as he saw it, needed to satisfy a number of performance criteria. It should have a bright, cutting, sustaining sound; be resistant to feedback; be relatively simple and economical to manufacture; and should be easy for a player or repairer to fix on the road. To achieve these goals, Fender totally redrew the blueprint for the six-string. The guitar that we now know as the Telecaster – first named the Esquire, and then the Broadcaster – lived up to its billing so successfully that it has remained a staple of rock, pop, and country music for nearly 60 years.

■ **1951** press advertisement

The sound of the Telecaster's twangy, fat, well-defined single-coil bridge pickup has virtually single-handedly defined the sound of country lead guitar, while the guitar's alluring simplicity and fast-playing neck have remained eternally appealing to a diverse camp of players. Rickenbacker and Bigsby had some years before developed solidbody guitars, which they built in limited numbers, but Fender's successful effort would become the first mass-produced solidbody electric guitar. Many musical instrument retailers and others in the industry derided the Fender electric guitar as a 'plank' and a 'canoe paddle', but hey – they began selling in decent numbers nevertheless.

In early 1951, Fender removed the Broadcaster name from the guitar's decal after Gretsch objected to the use of a name too similar to its established 'Broadkaster' drums. For a few months, the Fender model became what is now known as the Nocaster, before the Telecaster name hit the headstock in the early months of 1951. The Esquire name, which had briefly designated both the early one-pickup and two-pickup guitars, now became the name of the standard one-pickup model.

BROADCASTER 1950–51

Model name on headstock, 21 frets, slab single-cutaway body, two single-coils, three-saddle bridge.

- **Neck:** fretted maple; truss-rod adjuster at body end; one string-guide.
- **Body:** slab single-cutaway; originally blonde only, later sunburst or colors.
- **Electronics:** one plain metal-cover pickup (at neck) and one black six-polepiece pickup (angled in bridgeplate); two controls (volume, pickup blender) and three-way selector, all situated on the metal plate that adjoins the pickguard; side-mounted jack.
- **Hardware:** five-screw black fiber pickguard; three-saddle raised-sides bridge with through-body stringing (strings anchored at bridgeplate and not through body 1958–60).

BROADCASTER became TELECASTER in 1951, but some transitional examples have no model name on the headstock and are unofficially known as NOCASTERS (see later listing).

BROADCASTER

1950-1951

■ **1950** Broadcaster

7

ESQUIRE 1950–69

Model name on headstock, 21 frets, slab single-cutaway body, one pickup.

- **Neck:** fretted maple (1950–59 and 1969), maple with rosewood fingerboard (1959–69), maple fingerboard official option (1967–69); truss-rod adjuster at body end; one string-guide.
- **Body:** slab single-cutaway; originally blonde only, later sunburst or colors.
- **Electronics:** one black six-polepiece pickup (angled in bridgeplate); two controls (volume, tone) and three-way selector, all situated on the metal plate that adjoins the pickguard; side-mounted jack.
- **Hardware:** five-screw (eight-screw from 1959) black plastic pickguard (white plastic from 1954; white laminated plastic from 1963); three-saddle bridge with through-body stringing (strings anchored at bridgeplate, not through body, 1958–60).

Very few of the earliest 'pre-production' examples were without a truss-rod, and some have a second pickup at the neck.

■ **1952** Esquire

ESQUIRE 1950-1959

■ **1953** Esquire

■ **1955** Esquire

■ **1959** Esquire

THE WORLD'S MOST INFLUENTIAL ELECTRIC GUITAR

The name of Fender's first solid electric six-string may have been amended more than once during its incubation period, but by the time manufacture commenced in earnest, the company had settled on the final name: Telecaster. Reflecting the new age of television, it was coined by Don Randall, head of Fender's sales team and one of the main motivators behind the new two-pickup model.

Unlike the marketing amendments, the basic design had stayed more or less the same, although there were some improvements. One major change was the inclusion of an adjustable truss-rod. From the outset, Leo Fender was adamant that his guitar's rock maple neck did not need such a device, but he soon had to concede its commercial benefits, again at the insistence of Randall.

Despite being derided as a 'plank' or 'canoe paddle' by many manufacturers and others in the music industry, the Telecaster began to gain ground among guitarists, particularly country players. One of the earliest converts to the new Fender was the hot-picking Jimmy Bryant, and he boosted the Tele's popularity with high-profile exposure on television shows and numerous live performances.

The Telecaster name certainly had a futuristic ring, but it was bestowed on a six-string that, while certainly innovative and advanced for the era, was far from sleek and streamlined. The hard-edged body, with its abundance of straight lines and right angles, echoed an engineering-based design ethos that suited the instrument's no-nonsense image. Fender's target market was the straightforward working musician rather than the flashy entertainer, so this perception did not exactly impede sales to any great degree. However, some players voiced complaints about the Telecaster's comparatively minimal level of comfort. These criticisms and much more would be answered by Fender's next creation, which followed a few years later.

The Telecaster had barely become established in the guitar world when Fender began to plan a new, more versatile design. The Fender Stratocaster has become known particularly as a prime choice of rock and blues players, but it's the world's most imitated electric guitar design, and arguably the most popular.

The instrument has been used for every conceivable style of amplified music. That said, Leo Fender was still catering primarily to the country, western swing, and dance-band scenes in the early 1950s, and his revolutionary three-pickup model was still aimed squarely at the requirements of these players. Fender had apparently recognized the need for a guitar with a vibrato tailpiece back in 1952 or even 1951. Many local guitarists, Bill Carson included, had consulted with Fender regarding a solidbody electric with more versatile pickup selections and, it seems, a more comfortable, form-fitting body.

The Stratocaster hit the market in the spring of 1954, embodying all of these advances and more. It had an extremely well-engineered vibrato tailpiece that allowed greater pitch-bend than the popular Bigsby unit while also permitting individual intonation of the strings. Its three pickups provided three very different but usable sounds, from bright and twangy to warm and throaty, yet all with good clarity and definition. Finally, it had heavily contoured curves at the bodyedges that usually dug into a player's right forearm and ribcage on other guitars but here offered a more comfortable playing experience.

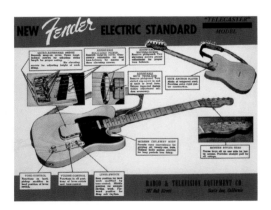

Ironically, although the Stratocaster was taken up by a number of country players, it never became the staple of the genre that the Telecaster continued to dominate. The Strat did, however, receive a more immediate and resounding welcome than its older sibling four years before and, with rock'n'roll waiting in the wings, the new guitar blazed forward to enormous success.

■ **1950** flyer

10

NOCASTER 1951

*Model name on headstock, 21 frets, slab single-cutaway
body, two single-coils, three-saddle bridge.*

• **Neck:** fretted maple; truss-rod adjuster at body end;
one string-guide.
• **Body:** slab single-cutaway; originally blonde only,
later sunburst or colors.
• **Electronics:** one plain metal-cover pickup (at neck)
and one black six-polepiece pickup (angled in
bridgeplate); two controls (volume, pickup blender)
and three-way selector, all situated on the metal
plate that adjoins the pickguard; side-mounted jack.
• **Hardware:** five-screw black fiber pickguard;
three-saddle raised-sides bridge with through-body
stringing (strings anchored at bridgeplate and not
through body 1958–60).

BROADCASTER *became* TELECASTER *in 1951, but some
transitional examples have no model name on the
headstock and are unofficially known as* NOCASTERS

■ 1951 Nocaster

11

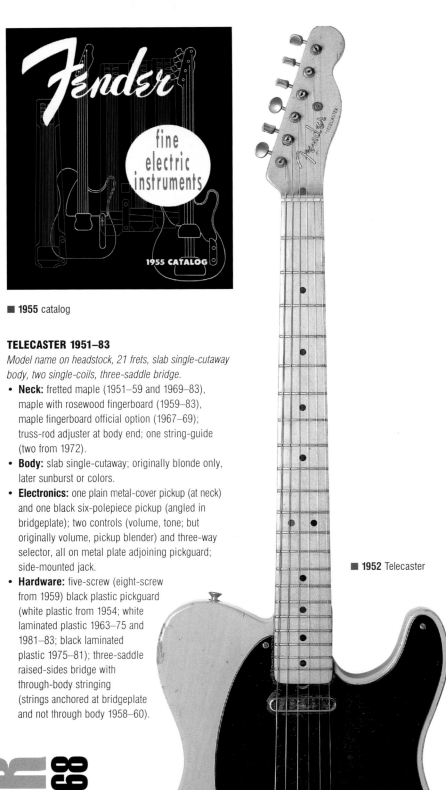

■ **1955** catalog

TELECASTER 1951–83

Model name on headstock, 21 frets, slab single-cutaway body, two single-coils, three-saddle bridge.

- **Neck:** fretted maple (1951–59 and 1969–83), maple with rosewood fingerboard (1959–83), maple fingerboard official option (1967–69); truss-rod adjuster at body end; one string-guide (two from 1972).
- **Body:** slab single-cutaway; originally blonde only, later sunburst or colors.
- **Electronics:** one plain metal-cover pickup (at neck) and one black six-polepiece pickup (angled in bridgeplate); two controls (volume, tone; but originally volume, pickup blender) and three-way selector, all on metal plate adjoining pickguard; side-mounted jack.
- **Hardware:** five-screw (eight-screw from 1959) black plastic pickguard (white plastic from 1954; white laminated plastic 1963–75 and 1981–83; black laminated plastic 1975–81); three-saddle raised-sides bridge with through-body stringing (strings anchored at bridgeplate and not through body 1958–60).

■ **1952** Telecaster

TELECASTER 1951-1968

■ **1957** Telecaster

■ **1963** Telecaster

■ **1968** Telecaster

13

1957 press advertisement

1959 press advertisement

■ **1969** Telecaster

TELECASTER
1969-1972

■ **1969** Telecaster

■ **1970** Telecaster

■ **1972** Telecaster

15

BINDING THE BODY AND BENDING THE 'B'

Introduced in 1959, the Custom Telecaster represented Fender's first fiddle with their earliest electric six-string. It was launched when Leo and his team decided to inject some cosmetic class into the bare-bones Tele. They achieved this by adding body-edge binding to contrast a smart three-tone sunburst color scheme, which was the only finish offered. These visual enhancements warranted the more upscale 'Custom Telecaster' logo on the model's headstock and an extra $30 on the $229 price tag. Although the binding process may seem comparatively simple, at first it proved tricky for the company to master, and Fender sought the assistance of acoustic masters Martin to ensure it was done properly.

The Custom Telecaster was among the earliest Fenders to employ a rosewood fingerboard on a maple neck, a combination that would soon replace the all-maple neck across the line. The model remained unaltered in the catalog until 1972, when it was superseded by a more radical revision, the Telecaster Custom. The name was somewhat confusing: although the change involved a simple word switch, the two guitars were in fact very different. The new Telecaster Custom was the second 70s Fender to feature the new Wide Range staggered-polepiece humbucker, designed by Seth Lover, the man responsible for Gibson's original twin-coil design. It emulated a popular upgrade that some players made at the time: replacing the regular Tele pickup at the neck, which many found too feeble. A common method of injecting more muscle was to swap this small single-coil for a higher-power humbucker that could deliver desirably fatter sounds.

The Telecaster Custom made this aftermarket modification official, combining it with the standard single-coil pickup mounted in the bridgeplate. In contrast, the Custom was the first Fender solid to employ Gibson-style circuitry, with twin volume and tone controls plus a three-way toggle-type selector, as on a Les Paul and on a necessarily enlarged pickguard.

As usual by this time, Fender offered rosewood or maple fingerboard options, while the choice of finish initially spanned sunburst, black, blonde, natural, or white. However, another significant departure from standard

Tele spec came with the Custom's use of Fender's recently introduced bullet-type truss-rod adjuster, located at the headstock, as well as a three-bolt neck-fixing method, complete with built-in tilt mechanism.

Despite the advantages of the added humbucker, the Custom's additional Gibson-like features didn't sit too well with Fender fans – although Rolling Stone Keith Richards' high-profile handling of this particular Tele did help convert a few players to the Custom cause. Production ceased in 1981. Along with its humbucker-equipped stablemates, the Thinline and Deluxe, the Custom Telecaster made a comeback during the next decade, and this forgotten Fender threesome has in recent years been elevated to fashionable status by a new generation of players. Fender has naturally cashed in on the new-found appeal of these previously undesirable designs, offering an increasing number of new Telecaster Customs that range from accurate reissues to modified interpretations.

■ **1959** flyer

■ **1964** rear of 'B Bender' Telecaster

CUSTOM ESQUIRE 1959–69

*Same as Esquire (see earlier listing)
other than bound body.*

CUSTOM TELECASTER 1959–72

*Model name on headstock, 21 frets, slab single-cutaway
body, two single-coils, three-saddle bridge.*

- **Neck:** fretted maple (1951–59 and 1969–83),
  maple with rosewood fingerboard (1959–83),
  maple fingerboard official option (1967–69);
  truss-rod adjuster at body end;
  one string-guide (two from 1972).
- **Body:** slab single-cutaway; bound body
- **Electronics:** one plain metal-cover pickup
  (at neck) and one black six-polepiece pickup
  (angled in bridgeplate); two controls (volume,
  tone; but originally volume, pickup blender)
  and three-way selector, all on metal plate
  adjoining pickguard; side-mounted jack.
- **Hardware:** five-screw (eight-screw from 1959)
  black plastic pickguard (white plastic from 1954;
  white laminated plastic 1963–75 and 1981–83;
  black laminated plastic 1975–81); three-saddle
  raised-sides bridge with through-body stringing
  (strings anchored at bridgeplate and not through
  body 1958–60).

■ **1963** Custom Telecaster

PAISLEY RED TELECASTER 1968–69

Model name on headstock, 21 frets, slab single-cutaway body, two single-coils, three-saddle bridge.

- **Neck:** fretted maple (1951–59 and 1969–83), maple with rosewood fingerboard (1959–83), maple fingerboard official option (1967–69); truss-rod adjuster at body end; one string-guide (two from 1972).
- **Body:** slab single-cutaway; with red paisley-pattern body finish and clear plastic pickguard.
- **Electronics:** one plain metal-cover pickup (at neck) and one black six-polepiece pickup (angled in bridgeplate); two controls (volume, tone; but originally volume, pickup blender) and three-way selector, all on metal plate adjoining pickguard; side-mounted jack.
- **Hardware:** five-screw (eight-screw from 1959) black plastic pickguard (white plastic from 1954; white laminated plastic 1963–75 and 1981–83; black laminated plastic 1975–81); three-saddle raised-sides bridge with through-body stringing (strings anchored at bridgeplate and not through body 1958–60).

BLUE FLOWER TELECASTER 1968-69

As TELECASTER of the period (see 1951 listing) but with blue floral-pattern body finish and clear plastic pickgouard.

■ **1968** Paisley Telecaster

TELECASTER 1968

COUNTRY STANDARD GETS CREATIVE

While the Stratocaster settled into a format that remained largely unchanged (other than in a handful of details, largely unseen) from 1965 to late 1971, the Telecaster became the subject of a lot of modification and experimentation in the late 60s.

Deluxe appointments had already visited twang-town in 1959 in the form of the Custom Telecaster (and Esquire), which had a bound body, sunburst finish – and later other colors too – and a triple-ply pickguard. (A sunburst finish was considered 'custom' on the normally blonde Telecaster, while a blonde finish was 'custom' on a normally sunburst Stratocaster – and collectors still pay a premium when they find them in this condition.)

In 1968, Fender offered a model with far more significant modifications: the Thinline Telecaster. Stocks of ash and alder timber had been growing heavier and heavier, and Fender found a means to lighten the load by partially routing the body of a Telecaster. This offered the cosmetic bonus of presenting a 'thinline' semi-acoustic appearance, with a stylish f-hole.

Rather than putting a cap on a semi-hollow body, Fender sliced the back from slabs of solid ash or mahogany, routed out chambers on the bass and treble sides of the lower bout, cut an f-hole on the bass side (the pickguard would cover the other side), and glued the fillet of wood back on to the back of the guitar. The technique has provided an enduring alternative look for the Telecaster virtually ever since.

In the same year, Fender made a bid to appeal to the hippie scene with the Paisley Red and Blue Flower Telecasters. These were standard Teles (although fitted with maple-cap necks rather than rosewood) decorated with stick-on pink paisley or blue floral wallpaper front and back, sprayed around the edges in a pinkish-red or bright blue finish, and topped off with a plexiglass pickguard.

The ploy was far too obvious to appeal to many genuine flower children, but the Paisley model in particular was taken up by a handful of country players (notably James Burton, back in the day, and more recently Brad Paisley, naturally).

The tail-end of 1968 also witnessed Fender's presentation of a specially-made solid rosewood Telecaster to George Harrison of The Beatles. A now ultra-rare Rosewood Telecaster model was available on and off as a regular production model between 1969 and 1972.

■ **1959** press advertisement

■ **1968** flyer

19

■ **1968** press advertisement

THINLINE TELECASTER (first version) 1968–71
F-hole body, two single-coils, 12-screw white pearl pickguard.

- **Neck:** maple with maple fingerboard (fretted maple or maple with rosewood fingerboard from 1969); truss-rod adjuster at body end; one string-guide.
- **Body:** semi-solid slab single-cutaway with f-hole; sunburst or colors.
- **Electronics:** one plain metal-cover pickup with visible height-adjustment screws (at neck) and one black six-polepiece pickup (angled in bridgeplate); two controls (volume, tone) and three-way selector, all on pickguard; side-mounted jack.
- **Hardware:** 12-screw pearl laminated plastic pickguard; three-saddle raised-sides bridge with through-body stringing.

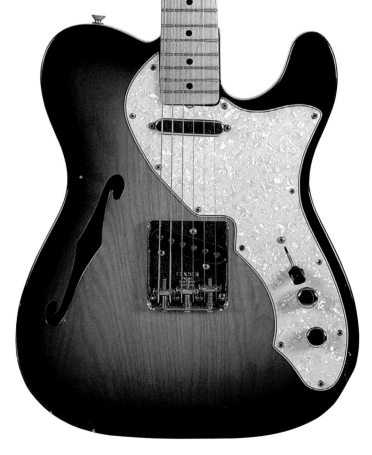

■ **1968** Thinline Telecaster

TELECASTER 1968-1971

■ **1969** Thinline Telecaster

■ **1971** Thinline Telecaster

■ **1971** Thinline Telecaster

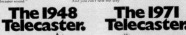

■ **1971** press advertisement

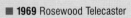
■ **1969** Rosewood Telecaster

TELECASTER
1969-1972

ROSEWOOD TELECASTER 1969–72

Model name on headstock, 21 frets, slab single-cutaway body, two single-coils, three-saddle bridge.

- **Neck:** fretted rosewood neck (1951–59 and 1969–83), maple with rosewood fingerboard (1959–83), maple fingerboard official option (1967–69); truss-rod adjuster at body end; one string-guide (two from 1972).
- **Body:** slab single-cutaway; solid (later semi-solid) rosewood body.
- **Electronics:** one plain metal-cover pickup (at neck) and one black six-polepiece pickup (angled in bridgeplate); two controls (volume, tone; but originally volume, pickup blender) and three-way selector, all on metal plate adjoining pickguard; side-mounted jack.
- **Hardware:** five-screw (eight-screw from 1959) black plastic pickguard (white plastic from 1954; white laminated plastic 1963–75 and 1981–83; black laminated plastic 1975–81); three-saddle raised-sides bridge with through-body stringing (strings anchored at bridgeplate and not through body 1958–60).

THINLINE TELECASTER (second version) 1971–79

F-hole body, two humbuckers.

Similar to THINLINE TELECASTER FIRST VERSION (see 1968 listing) except:

- **Neck:** fretted maple only; 'bullet' truss-rod adjuster at headstock; three-screw neckplate.
- **Electronics:** two metal-cover split-polepiece humbuckers.
- **Hardware:** 12-screw black, white or white pearl laminated plastic re-styled pickguard; six-saddle small bridge with through-body stringing.

■ **1972** Thinline Telecaster (second version)

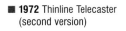

23

TELECASTER CUSTOM 1972–81

One humbucker and one single-coil, four controls.

- **Neck:** fretted maple, or maple with rosewood fingerboard; 'bullet' truss-rod adjuster at headstock end; two string-guides; three-screw neckplate.
- **Body:** slab single-cutaway; sunburst or colors.
- **Electronics:** one metal-cover split-polepiece humbucker (at neck) and one black six-polepiece pickup (angled in bridgeplate); four controls (two volume, two tone) and three-way selector, all on pickguard; side-mounted jack.
- **Hardware:** 16-screw black laminated plastic pickguard; six-saddle raised-sides bridge with through-body stringing.

Earliest examples with 15-screw pickguard and/or three-saddle raised-sides bridge.
For Custom Telecaster (with bound body) see 1959 listing.

■ **1977** Telecaster Custom

TELECASTER 1972-1976

■ **1973** press advertisement

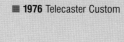
■ **1976** Telecaster Custom

TELECASTER DELUXE 1973-81

Two covered humbuckers, normal Tele body.

- **Neck:** fretted maple; 'bullet' truss-rod adjuster at headstock end; two string-guides; large Stratocaster-style headstock; three-screw neckplate.
- **Body:** contoured single-cutaway; sunburst or colors.
- **Electronics:** two metal-cover split-polepiece humbuckers; four controls (two volume, two tone) and three-way selector, all on pickguard; side-mounted jack.
- **Hardware:** 16-screw black laminated plastic pickguard; six-saddle small bridge with through-body stringing.

Some examples with Stratocaster-type six-pivot bridge/vibrato unit.

ANTIGUA TELECASTER 1977–79

As TELECASTER of the period (see 1951 listing) but with white/brown shaded body finish and matching-color laminated plastic pickguard.

ANTIGUA TELECASTER CUSTOM 1977–79

As TELECASTER CUSTOM (see 1972 listing) but with white/brown shaded body finish and matching-color laminated plastic pickguard.

ANTIGUA TELECASTER DELUXE 1977–79

As Telecaster Deluxe (see 1973 listing) but with white/brown shaded body finish and matching-color laminated plastic pickguard.

■ **1976** Telecaster Deluxe

TELECASTER 1976

A HUMBUCKER FOR THE TWANG CROWD

By the start of the 70s, Gibson's Les Paul was back in fashion, with humbuckers succeeding single-coils as the pickups of choice for many players. Until this time, Fender had never offered a dual-coil design on any of its six-strings, but now the company felt obliged to follow fashion and offer the trendy alternative of fatter sounds. To achieve this aim, Fender had enlisted the services of electronics engineer Seth Lover, luring him away from rival Gibson in 1967. Lover was the brains behind Gibson's groundbreaking no-noise design that had first appeared on Gibson models during the late 50s. Fender wanted him to repeat this feat without incurring any legal problems concerning the patents still in force.

Three years later, Lover came up with an appropriate new variation on his original hum-canceling creation. Known as the Wide Range humbucking pickup, it provided the required extra output and was about the same size as his original Gibson design. However, the internal construction was very different. It employed magnets made of cunife (an alloy of copper, nickel, and iron) rather than alnico. Lover also made changes to coils, wire, and the number of windings, contributing to a deliberately brighter sound, which Lover felt was more in keeping with the recognized Fender tonality.

His new humbucker was mounted on four screws, a method that allowed the player to alter the tilt as well as the height of the pickup, and Lover even managed to make the new unit look different to anything else on the market at the time. Rather than a single line of screw-type polepieces, his new Fender humbucker's plated metal cover split the polepieces into two rows of three, with those for the lower strings offset from the treble trio. Although it was a new idea for a six-string, this apparently novel arrangement echoed the layout featured on Fender's revised Precision bass pickup, introduced back in 1957. That pickup employed two separate, small single-coil pickups wired as one humbucker, but back then Fender chose not to draw too much attention from Gibson or anyone else to this presumably coincidental configuration.

The Thinline Telecaster was the first guitar with Fender's new humbucker, and the model proudly boasted a brace of them as part of a major makeover for the Thinline from 1971. The following year saw one employed at the neck on the new Telecaster Custom, partnered with a standard single-coil in the bridge position. Completing a trio of distinct variations on the standard Tele theme, the Telecaster Deluxe, introduced in 1973, included a pair of the new humbuckers to accompany yet further departures from traditional Tele design.

"You get there faster on a Fender."

Play it from the top
Fender

Debuting during 1976, the semi-acoustic Starcaster was similarly equipped and proved to be the final Fender to feature this particular pickup. The model proved far from popular and has yet to be revived. The various Telecaster variations were also relatively unsuccessful at the time, but they have since gone on to enjoy far greater fashionable appeal in recent years, and Fender has of course reissued all three humbucker-equipped versions.

Fender's own humbucker disappeared at the start of the 80s, and although subsequently the company tended to concentrate on single-coils, it has also continued to cater for those players who require more pickup power. Fender has achieved this either by using twin single-coils wired to produce the same results, or with conventional humbuckers. Humbuckers have been employed on numerous Telecaster and Stratocaster variations and on a smattering of all-new instruments, with some pickups made by Fender itself while others have been supplied by specialist makers such as DiMarzio, Lace, and Seymour Duncan.

■ **1974** press advertisement

BLACK & GOLD TELECASTER 1981–83

Normal Tele pickup layout, 21 frets, black body, gold hardware.

Similar to 1981-period TELECASTER (see 1951 listing) except:

- **Neck:** black-face headstock.
- **Body:** black only.
- **Hardware:** gold-plated brass; black laminated plastic pickguard; six-saddle heavy-duty small bridge with through-body stringing.

SQUIER SERIES '52 TELECASTER (MIJ) 1982–83

Replica of 1952-period U.S. original (see TELECASTER 1951 listing) with small Squier Series logo on headstock 1982–83. Known as 50s TELECASTER 1990 onward. Sold under the Squier brandname (1983–85) and new Fender version introduced in 1990, although Japanese market manufacture continuous since 1982. Also Foto Flame fake figured wood finish option (1994).

ELITE TELECASTER 1983–84

Two white plain-top humbuckers.

- **Neck:** fretted maple, or maple with rosewood fingerboard; truss-rod adjuster at headstock end; two string-guides.
- **Body:** slab single-cutaway bound; sunburst or colors.
- **Electronics:** two white plain-top humbuckers; four controls (two volume, two tone) and three-way selector, all on body; side-mounted jack; active circuit.
- **Hardware:** white laminated plastic optional mini pickguard; re-designed six-saddle bridge/tailpiece.

GOLD ELITE TELECASTER 1983–84

As ELITE TELECASTER listing this year but with pearl tuner buttons and gold-plated hardware.

■ **1983** Gold Elite Telecaster

TELECASTER 1983

TELECASTER STANDARD 1983–84

21 frets, slab single-cutaway body, two single-coils, six-saddle bridge/tailpiece.

- **Neck:** fretted maple; truss-rod adjuster at headstock end; two string-guides.
- **Body:** slab single-cutaway; sunburst or colors; also in red, yellow, or blue streaked finish, unofficially known as BOWLING BALL or MARBLE TELECASTER (1984).
- **Electronics:** one plain metal-cover pickup at neck and one black six-polepiece pickup (angled in bridgeplate); two controls (volume, tone) and three-way selector, all on metal plate adjoining pickguard; side-mounted jack.
- **Hardware:** five-screw (originally eight-screw) white plastic pickguard; six-saddle flat bridge/tailpiece (no through-body stringing).

WALNUT ELITE TELECASTER 1983–84

As ELITE TELECASTER listing this year but with walnut neck and ebony fingerboard, walnut body, pearl tuner buttons, and gold-plated hardware.

'52 TELECASTER 1983–84, 86–98

Replica of 1952-period original (see 1951 listing).

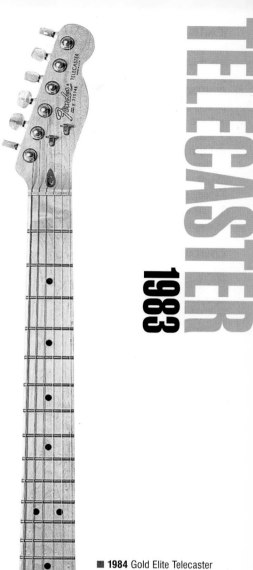

TELECASTER 1983

■ **1984** Gold Elite Telecaster

BOWLING BALL TELECASTER 1984

Also known as Marble Telecaster.
See TELECASTER STANDARD 1983 listing.

CONTEMPORARY TELECASTER (MIJ) (first type) 1985–87

Black neck, two humbuckers.
- **Neck:** maple neck with rosewood fingerboard; 22 frets; truss-rod adjuster at headstock end; string clamp; black neck.
- **Body:** slab single-cutaway body; various colors.
- **Electronics:** two black coverless humbuckers; two controls (volume, tone), three-way selector and coil-switch, all on body; side-mounted jack.
- **Hardware:** black-plated; no pickguard; two-pivot bridge/ vibrato unit.

CONTEMPORARY TELECASTER (MIJ) (second type) 1985–87

Black neck, two single-coils and one humbucker.
Similar to CONTEMPORARY TELECASTER FIRST TYPE
(see previous listing) except:
- **Electronics:** two black six-polepiece pickups and one black coverless humbucker (at bridge); two controls (volume, tone) and three mini-switches, all on body.

CUSTOM TELECASTER '62 (MIJ) 1985–onward

Replica of 1962-period U.S. original with bound-body (see 1959 listing). Foto Flame fake figured wood finish option (1994–96).

BLUE FLOWER TELECASTER (MIJ) 1986–onward

Replica of 1969-period U.S. original with blue floral pattern-finish body (see 1968 listing).

AMERICAN STANDARD TELECASTER first version 1986-2000

PAISLEY TELECASTER 1986–onward

Replica of 1969-period U.S. original with paisley-pattern body finish (see 1968 listing).

ROSEWOOD TELECASTER (MIJ) 1986–onward

Replica of 1969-period U.S. original with rosewood neck and body (see 1969 listing).

TELECASTER CUSTOM '72 (MIJ) 1986–onward

Replica of 1972-period U.S. original with humbucker and single-coil (see 1972 listing).

■ **1985** Contemporary Telecaster

TELECASTER 1984-1985

■ **1984** Telecaster Standard Bowling Ball

■ **1984** Telecaster Standard Bowling Ball

■ **1984** Telecaster Standard Bowling Ball

CUSTOM SHOP GUITARS, REISSUED AMPLIFIERS

After their Corona factory was up and running from 1986, Fender set about establishing a Custom Shop next door in 1987 under the supervision of master luthiers John Page and Michael Stevens. This facility concentrated at first on one-offs, extremely limited runs, and major artist models but soon began to manufacture lines of 'standard' Custom Shop models. Such production would expand considerably through the course of the '90s, with the introduction of numerous Custom Shop Signature Models based on the guitars of famous artists and the popular distressed-look Relic models.

The Custom Shop currently produces general catalog models, which are noted in the main U.S. listing here and indicated as 'Custom Shop production'. The Shop also makes limited-edition instruments, which over the years have variously been called Builder Select, Custom Team Built, Dealer Select, Limited Edition, Limited Release, Master Builder, Master Built, Master Design Limited Edition, Stock Team Built, Tribute Series, and probably more besides.

The year 2010 saw Fender celebrating 60 years since the Telecaster first appeared. Naturally enough, the Custom Shop was well placed to make the most of this special event and offered several appropriate additions to the Limited Collection line. One was an accurate reproduction of Fender's original prototype, and this partnered an Esquire in its original pre-Tele two-pickup guise as well as the more familiar single-pickup form. A two-pickup Broadcaster and similarly equipped Nocaster completed the birthday celebrations.

Other recent newcomers include the Custom Deluxe production instruments, and yet more Limited Collection examples. One of these was a model that Fender maybe should have made: the La Cabronita Espesial again hinted at an old-time Tele but came equipped with Gretsch-style pickups.

These limited editions are clearly still big business, with the majority ordered by distributors or stores worldwide. Quantities of each item can range from tens to hundreds, and the number of models so far is considerable – making it impossible to identify and itemize all of them here, especially as Fender cannot supply complete records. Regardless of order size, all official Custom Shop instruments carry an identifying logo on the back of the headstock. Originally oval, the logo was later amended to the current 'V' shape.

Dreams-Come-True

■ **1994** catalog

THINLINE TELECASTER '69 (MIJ) 1986–onward
Replica of 1969-period U.S. original with two single-coils
(see 1968 listing).

THINLINE TELECASTER '72 (MIJ) 1986–onward
Replica of 1972-period U.S. original with two
humbuckers (see 1971 listing).

AMERICAN STANDARD TELECASTER 1988–2000
*22 frets, slab single-cutaway body, two single-coils,
six-saddle bridge.*
- **Neck:** fretted maple, or maple with rosewood
  fingerboard; 22 frets; truss-rod adjuster at headstock
  end; one string-guide.
- **Body:** slab single-cutaway; finished in sunburst
  or colors.
- **Electronics:** one plain metal-cover pickup with
  visible height-adjustment screws (at neck) and one
  black six-polepiece pickup (angled in bridgeplate);
  two controls (volume, tone) and three-way
  selector, all on metal plate adjoining pickguard;
  side-mounted jack.
- **Hardware:** eight-screw white laminated plastic
  pickguard; six-saddle flat bridge with through-body
  stringing (earliest examples with raised-sides type).
*Also with anodized aluminum hollow body option
(1994–95).Succeeded by* AMERICAN TELECASTER
(see 2000 listing).

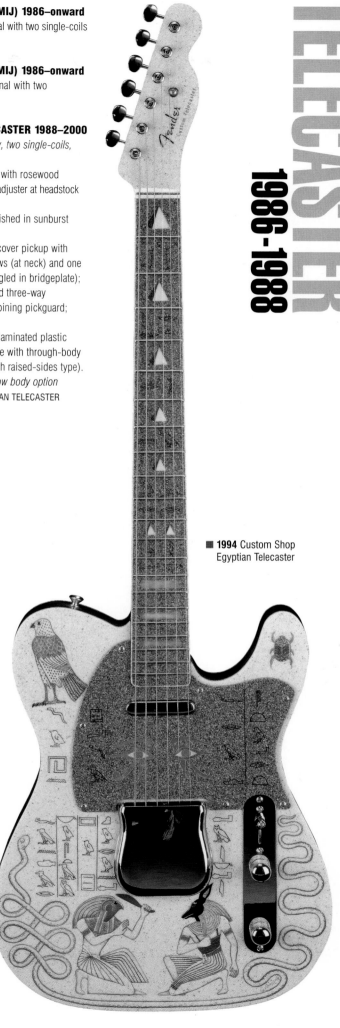

■ **1994** Custom Shop
Egyptian Telecaster

STANDARD TELECASTER (MIJ) 1988–91

Two string-guides, five-screw pickguard, six-saddle bridge/tailpiece with no through-body stringing.

- **Neck:** fretted maple; truss-rod adjuster at body end; two string-guides.
- **Body:** slab single-cutaway; black or blonde.
- **Electronics:** one plain metal cover pickup (at neck) and one black six-polepiece pickup (angled in bridgeplate); two controls (volume, tone) and three-way selector, all on metal plate adjoining pickguard; side-mounted jack.
- **Hardware:** five-screw white plastic pickguard; six-saddle flat bridge/tailpiece with no through-body stringing.

Previously marketed under the Squier brandname (1985–88). Later, production moved to Mexico (see 1991 listing).

■ **1991** American Standard Telecaster

TELECASTER 1988

1988 catalog

1989 Telecaster
40th Anniversary

ALBERT COLLINS TELECASTER 1990–current

Signature on headstock.

- **Neck:** maple with maple fingerboard; truss-rod adjuster at body end; one string-guide; Albert Collins signature on headstock.
- **Body:** slab single-cutaway bound; natural only.
- **Electronics:** one metal-cover six-polepiece humbucker (at neck) and one black six-polepiece pickup (angled in bridgeplate); two controls (volume, tone) and three-way selector, all on metal plate adjoining pickguard; side-mounted jack.
- **Hardware:** eight-screw white laminated plastic pickguard; six-saddle raised-sides bridge with through-body stringing.

Custom Shop production.

DANNY GATTON TELECASTER 1990–current

Signature on headstock.

- **Neck:** fretted maple; 22 frets; truss-rod adjuster at body end; one string-guide; Danny Gatton signature on headstock.
- **Body:** slab single-cutaway; blonde or gold.
- **Electronics:** two black twin-blade humbuckers (bridge pickup angled); two controls (volume, tone) and three-way selector, all on metal plate adjoining pickguard; side-mounted jack.
- **Hardware:** five-screw cream plastic pickguard; modified three-saddle raised-sides bridge with through-body stringing.

Custom Shop production.

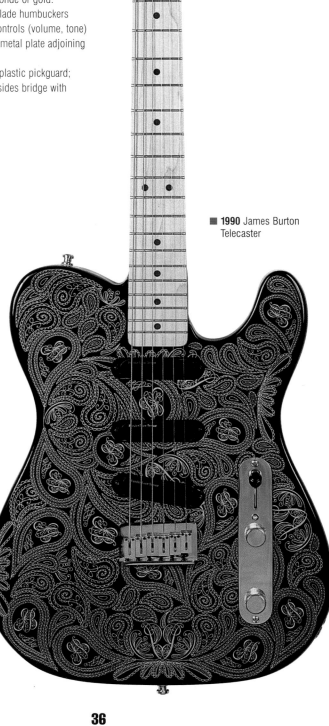

■ **1990** James Burton Telecaster

TELECASTER 1990

JAMES BURTON TELECASTER (first version) 1990–2005

Signature on headstock.
- **Neck:** fretted maple; truss-rod adjuster at body end; one string-guide; pearl tuner buttons; James Burton signature on headstock.
- **Body:** slab single-cutaway; black with gold or red paisley-pattern, red or white.
- **Electronics:** three black plain-top Lace Sensor pickups (bridge pickup angled); two controls (volume, tone) and five-way selector, all on metal plate; side-mounted jack.
- **Hardware:** black-plated or gold-plated; no pickguard; six-saddle small bridge with through-body stringing.

TELE PLUS (first version) 1990–95

Three Lace Sensor pickups (two at bridge).
- **Neck:** fretted maple, or maple with rosewood fingerboard; 22 frets; truss-rod adjuster at headstock end; one string-guide.
- **Body:** slab single-cutaway; sunburst or colors.
- **Electronics:** three black plain-top Lace Sensor pickups (two in single separate surround at bridge); two controls (volume, tone), three-way selector and coil-switch, all on metal plate adjoining pickguard; side-mounted jack.
- **Hardware:** eight-screw white laminated plastic pickguard; six-saddle small bridge with through-body stringing.

50s TELECASTER (MIJ) 1990–onward

Replica of 1952-period U.S. original (see 1951 listing). Previously known in UK as SQUIER SERIES '52 TELECASTER, with small Squier Series logo on headstock (1982–83). Sold under the Squier brandname (1983–85) and new Fender version introduced in 1990, although Japanese market manufacture continuous since 1982. Foto Flame fake figured wood finish option (1994).

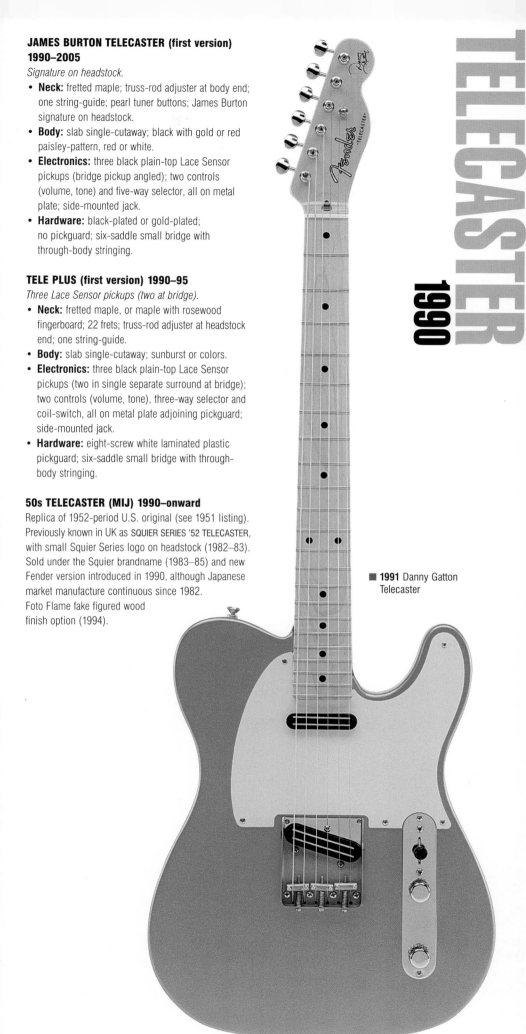

■ **1991** Danny Gatton Telecaster

HMT ACOUSTIC-ELECTRIC (first version) (MIJ) 1991–94

Stratocaster-style headstock, wooden-base bridge.

- **Neck:** maple with rosewood fingerboard; 25.1-inch scale, 22 frets; truss-rod adjuster at headstock end; one string-guide; large Stratocaster-style headstock with black-face.
- **Body:** enlarged semi-solid slab single-cutaway bound; f-hole; sunburst or colors.
- **Electronics:** one black plain-top Lace Sensor (angled at neck) and piezo pickup (in bridge); three controls (volume, tone, pan), all on body; side-mounted jack; active circuit.
- **Hardware:** no pickguard; single-saddle wooden-base bridge.

HMT TELECASTER (first version) (MIJ) 1991–92

Stratocaster-style headstock, F-hole body, two humbuckers.

- **Neck:** maple with rosewood fingerboard; 25.1-inch scale, 22 frets; truss-rod adjuster at headstock end; Stratocaster-style black-face headstock.
- **Body:** larger semi-solid slab single-cutaway bound; f-hole; sunburst or colors.
- **Electronics:** two black coverless humbuckers; two controls (volume, tone), three-way selector and coil-switch, all on body; side-mounted jack.
- **Hardware:** no pickguard; six-saddle small bridge with through-body stringing.

■ **1991** HMT Acoustic Electric Telecaster

TELECASTER 1991

HMT TELECASTER (second version) (MIJ) 1991–92

Drooped headstock with long 'streamlined' Fender logo, f-hole body, angled Lace Sensor and humbucker.
Similar to HMT TELECASTER FIRST VERSION
(see previous listing) except:
- **Neck:** split-triangle markers; locking nut; long 'streamlined' Fender logo on drooped black-face headstock.
- **Electronics:** one black plain-top Lace Sensor pickup (angled at neck) and one black coverless humbucker (at bridge).
- **Hardware:** two-pivot locking bridge/vibrato unit.

SET NECK TELECASTER 1991–95

Two coverless humbuckers, glued-in neck.
- **Neck:** mahogany glued-in with rosewood fingerboard (pao ferro from 1993); 22 frets; truss-rod adjuster at headstock end; two string-guides; neck and headstock face match body color.
- **Body:** semi-solid slab single-cutaway bound; various colors.
- **Electronics:** two black coverless humbuckers; two controls (volume, tone), three-way selector and coil-tap, all on body; side-mounted jack.
- **Hardware:** no pickguard; six-saddle small bridge with through-body stringing.
Custom Shop production.

SET NECK TELECASTER FLOYD ROSE 1991–92

Two coverless humbuckers and one single-coil, glued-in neck, locking vibrato system.
Similar to SET NECK TELECASTER
(see previous listing) except:
- **Neck:** ebony fingerboard; locking nut.
- **Electronics:** two black coverless humbuckers and one black six-polepiece pickup (in center); two controls (volume, tone), five-way selector and coil-tap, all on body; side-mounted jack.
- **Hardware:** two-pivot locking bridge/vibrato unit.
Custom Shop production.

SET NECK TELECASTER PLUS 1991–92

Two coverless humbuckers, glued-in neck, vibrato.
Similar to SET NECK TELECASTER
(see earlier listing this year) except:
- **Neck:** ebony fingerboard; locking tuners; roller nut.
- **Hardware:** two-pivot bridge/vibrato unit.
Custom Shop production.

■ **1991** press advertisements

STANDARD TELECASTER (MIM) 1991–current

Modern-style 'thick' Fender headstock logo in silver, two single-coils.

- **Neck:** fretted maple; truss-rod adjuster at headstock end; one string-guide.
- **Body:** slab single-cutaway; sunburst or colors.
- **Electronics:** one plain metal-cover pickup with visible height-adjustment screws (at neck) and one black six-polepiece pickup (angled in bridgeplate); two controls (volume, tone) and three-way selector, all on metal plate adjoining pickguard; side-mounted jack.
- **Hardware:** eight-screw white laminated plastic pickguard; six-saddle flat bridge/tailpiece (no through-body stringing).

TELE PLUS DELUXE 1991–92

Three Lace Sensor pickups (two at bridge), vibrato.
Similar to TELE PLUS FIRST VERSION
(see 1990 listing) except:

- **Neck:** no string-guide; locking tuners; roller nut.
- **Hardware:** two-pivot bridge/vibrato unit.

BAJO SEXTO TELECASTER baritone 1992–98

Model name on headstock, long-scale neck.

- **Neck:** fretted maple; 30.2-inch scale; 24 frets; truss-rod adjuster at body end; one string-guide; Bajo Sexto on headstock.
- **Body:** slab single-cutaway; sunburst or blonde.
- **Electronics:** one plain metal-cover pickup (at neck) and one black six-polepiece pickup (angled in bridgeplate); two controls (volume, tone) and three-way selector, all on metal plate adjoining pickguard; side-mounted jack.
- **Hardware:** five-screw black plastic pickguard; three-saddle raised-sides bridge with through-body stringing.

Custom Shop production.

■ **1993** Standard Telecaster

TELECASTER 1991-1992

40

JD TELECASTER (MIJ) 1992–99

'JD' on headstock, black six-polepiece pickup at neck.

- **Neck:** fretted maple; truss-rod adjuster at body end; one string-guide; Jerry Donahue initials on headstock.
- **Body:** slab single-cutaway bound; sunburst or colors.
- **Electronics:** two black six-polepiece pickups (bridgeplate pickup angled); two controls (volume, tone) and five-way selector, all on metal plate adjoining pickguard; side-mounted jack.
- **Hardware:** eight-screw black laminated plastic pickguard; three-saddle raised-sides bridge with through-body stringing.

Based on signature model of U.S. Custom Shop (see next listing).

■ **1995** Standard Telecaster (left hand)

TELECASTER
1991-1992

41

JERRY DONAHUE TELECASTER 1992–2001

Signature on headstock.
- **Neck:** fretted maple; truss-rod adjuster at body end; one string-guide; Jerry Donahue signature on headstock.
- **Body:** slab single-cutaway; sunburst, blue or red.
- **Electronics:** two black six-polepiece pickups (bridgeplate pickup angled); two controls (volume, tone) and five-way selector, all on metal plate adjoining pickguard; side-mounted jack.
- **Hardware:** gold-plated; five-screw black laminated plastic pickguard; three-saddle raised-sides bridge with through-body stringing.

Custom Shop production.

SET NECK TELECASTER COUNTRY ARTIST 1992–95

One humbucker and one single-coil, glued-in neck.
Similar to SET NECK TELECASTER (see 1991 listing) except:
- **Electronics:** one black coverless humbucker (at neck) and one black six-polepiece pickup (angled in bridgeplate).
- **Hardware:** five-screw tortoiseshell laminated plastic small pickguard.
- **Hardware:** gold-plated; six-saddle flat bridge with through-body stringing.

Custom Shop production.

SPARKLE TELECASTER 1992–95

Colored sparkle finish on body.
- **Neck:** fretted maple, or maple with rosewood fingerboard; truss-rod adjuster at body end; one string-guide.
- **Body:** slab single-cutaway; sparkle colors.
- **Electronics:** one plain metal-cover pickup (at neck) and one black six-polepiece pickup (angled in bridgeplate); two controls (volume, tone) and three-way selector, all on metal plate adjoining pickguard; side-mounted jack.
- **Hardware:** eight-screw white laminated plastic pickguard; three-saddle raised-sides bridge with through-body stringing.

Custom Shop production.

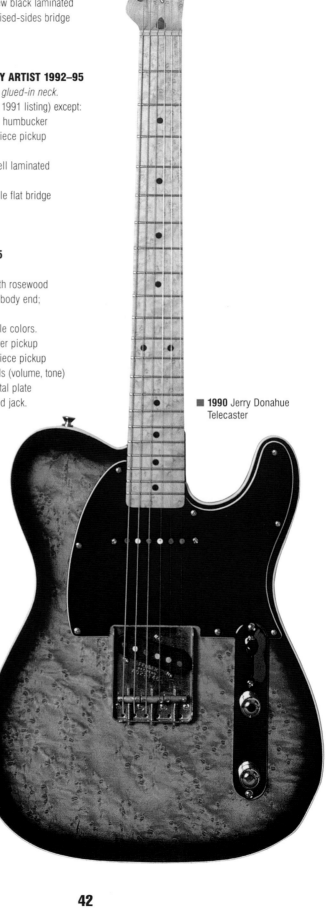

■ **1990** Jerry Donahue Telecaster

TELECASTER 1992-1993

42

■ **1992** Set Neck Telecaster
Country Artist

■ **1993** Clarence White Telecaster

SQUIER SERIES STANDARD TELECASTER (MIK)
1992–94

Modern-style 'thick' Fender headstock logo in black, two single-coils.
Similar to vintage-style Telecaster except:
• **Neck:** fretted maple; truss-rod adjuster at headstock end; one string-guide.
• **Body:** slab single-cutaway; black, red or white.
• **Electronics:** one plain metal-cover pickup with visible height-adjustment screws (at neck) and one black six-polepiece pickup (angled in bridgeplate); two controls (volume, tone) and three-way selector, all on metal plate adjoining pickguard; side-mounted jack.
• **Hardware:** eight-screw white laminated plastic pickguard; six-saddle flat bridge/tailpiece (no through-body stringing).
Later made in Mexico, with small Squier Series logo on headstock (see 1994 listing), then name changed to TRADITIONAL STRATOCASTER *(see 1996 listing).*

CLARENCE WHITE TELECASTER 1993–2001

Signature on headstock.
• **Neck:** fretted maple; truss-rod adjuster at body end; Scruggs Peg banjo-style de-tuners for 1st and 6th strings; Clarence White signature on headstock.
• **Body:** slab single-cutaway; sunburst only.
• **Electronics:** one white six-polepiece pickup (at neck) and one black six-polepiece pickup (angled in bridgeplate); two controls (volume, tone) and three-way selector, all on metal plate adjoining pickguard; side-mounted jack.
• **Hardware:** eight-screw tortoiseshell laminated plastic pickguard; three-saddle raised-sides bridge with through-body stringing; factory-fitted B-Bender built-in bending device for 2nd string.

ALUMINUM-BODY TELECASTER 1994–95

Anodized aluminum hollow-body option for
AMERICAN STANDARD TELECASTER (see 1988 listing).

JAMES BURTON STANDARD TELECASTER (MIM)
1995–current

Signature on headstock.
Similar to STANDARD TELECASTER (see 1991 listing)
except:
- **Neck:** James Burton signature on headstock.
- **Hardware:** eight-screw white plastic pickguard;
  six-saddle raised-sides bridge with through-body
  stringing.

SPECIAL EDITION 1994 TELECASTER 1994

Commemorative neckplate.
Similar to AMERICAN STANDARD TELECASTER
(see 1988 listing) except:
- **Body:** black or blonde.
- **Hardware:** eight-screw gray pearl or tortoiseshell
  laminated plastic pickguard; commemorative neckplate.

SQUIER SERIES STANDARD TELECASTER (MIM)
1994–96

Another name for TRADITIONAL TELECASTER
(see 1996 listing).

TELE SPECIAL (MIM) 1994–96

Humbucker at neck, black pickguard.
Similar to STANDARD TELECASTER
(see 1991 listing) except:
- **Electronics:** one metal-cover six-polepiece
  humbucker (at neck) and one black six-polepiece
  pickup (angled in bridgeplate); two controls
  (volume, tone) and five-way selector.
- **Hardware:** eight-screw black laminated plastic
  pickguard; six-saddle raised-sides bridge
  with through-body stringing.

■ **1995** James Burton
Standard Telecaster

TELECASTER 1994-1995

AMERICAN CLASSIC TELECASTER
(first version) 1995–99

Three single-coils (two white, one black), inverted control plate, five-way selector.

Similar to AMERICAN STANDARD TELECASTER (see 1988 listing) except:

- **Electronics:** two white six-polepiece pickups and one black six-polepiece pickup (angled in bridgeplate); two controls (volume, tone) and five-way selector, all on inverted control plate adjoining pickguard.
- **Hardware:** gold-plated option; eight-screw white pearl or tortoiseshell laminated plastic pickguard.

Custom Shop production.

AMERICAN STANDARD B-BENDER TELECASTER
1995–97

Standard Tele pickup layout, 22 frets, B-Bender string-bending device installed.

Similar to AMERICAN STANDARD TELECASTER (see 1988 listing) except:

- **Neck:** fretted maple only.
- **Hardware:** factory-fitted B-Bender (built-in bending device for 2nd string).

HMT ACOUSTIC-ELECTRIC
(second version) (MIJ) 1995–97

Telecaster headstock, wooden-base bridge.

Similar to HMT ACOUSTIC-ELECTRIC FIRST VERSION (see 1991 listing) except:

- **Neck:** Telecaster headstock.
- **Body:** sunburst or black.
- **Electronics:** one black plain-top pickup (angled at neck) and piezo pickup (in bridge).

■ **1995** American Classic Telecaster

TELE JNR 1995–2000

Two large black rectangular pickups.

- **Neck:** mahogany glued-in, with pao ferro fingerboard; 22 frets; truss-rod adjuster at headstock end; one string-guide; neck and headstock face match body color.
- **Body:** semi-solid slab single-cutaway; sunburst or colors.
- **Electronics:** two large black six-polepiece pickups; two controls (volume, tone) and three-way selector, all on inverted metal plate adjoining pickguard; side-mounted jack.
- **Hardware:** small tortoiseshell plastic, or white pearl, tortoiseshell or black laminated plastic pickguard; six-saddle small bridge with through-body stringing.

Custom Shop production.

TELE PLUS (second version) 1995–98

Three Lace Sensor pickups
(one angled in bridgeplate).

- **Neck:** fretted maple, or maple with rosewood fingerboard; 22 frets; truss-rod adjuster at headstock end; one string-guide.
- **Body:** slab single-cutaway bound; sunburst or colors.
- **Electronics:** three plain-top Lace Sensor pickups (bridgeplate pickup angled); two controls (volume, tone) and three-way selector, all on metal plate adjoining pickguard; side-mounted jack.
- **Hardware:** eight-screw white pearl or tortoiseshell laminated plastic pickguard; six-saddle flat bridge with through-body stringing.

■ **1995** Telecaster Junior

TELECASTER 1995-1996

46

TELECASTER XII 12-string 1995–98

Model name on 12-string headstock.
- **Neck:** fretted maple, or maple with rosewood fingerboard; truss-rod adjuster at headstock end; one 'bracket' string-guide; six-tuners-per-side headstock.
- **Body:** slab single-cutaway; sunburst or colors.
- **Electronics:** one plain metal-cover pickup (at neck) and one black six-polepiece pickup (angled in bridgeplate); two controls (volume, tone) and three-way selector, all on metal plate adjoining pickguard; side-mounted jack.
- **Hardware:** five-screw black or white plastic, or white pearl laminated plastic pickguard; 12-saddle bridge with through-body stringing.

Custom Shop production.

WAYLON JENNINGS TRIBUTE TELECASTER 1995–2003

Signature on headstock.
- **Neck:** fretted maple; truss-rod adjuster at body end; one string-guide; pearl tuner buttons; Scruggs Peg banjo-style de-tuner for 6th string; 'W' inlay at 12th fret and Waylon Jennings signature on headstock.
- **Body:** slab single-cutaway bound; black only with white leather inlay.
- **Electronics:** one plain metal-cover pickup with visible height-adjustment screws (at neck) and one black six-polepiece pickup (angled in bridgeplate); two controls (volume, tone) and three-way selector, all on metal plate adjoining pickguard; side-mounted jack.
- **Hardware:** eight-screw white laminated plastic pickguard; six-saddle flat bridge with through-body stringing.

Custom Shop production.

90s TELECASTER CUSTOM (MIJ) 1995–98

Black or white bound body with matching headstock face, pearl pickguard, gold-plated hardware.
- **Neck:** maple with rosewood fingerboard; truss-rod adjuster at body end; one string-guide; black- or white-face headstock.
- **Body:** slab single-cutaway bound; black or white.
- **Electronics:** one plain metal cover pickup (at neck) and one black six-polepiece pickup (angled in bridgeplate); two controls (volume, tone) and three-way selector, all on metal plate adjoining pickguard; side-mounted jack.
- **Hardware:** gold-plated; eight-screw grey or white pearl laminated plastic pickguard; six-saddle flat bridge with through-body stringing.

90s TELECASTER DELUXE (MIJ) 1995–98

Contoured body, three six-polepiece pickups, reversed control plate.
- **Neck:** maple with rosewood fingerboard; truss-rod adjuster at body end; one string-guide.
- **Body:** single-cutaway; sunburst or colors.
- **Electronics:** two white six-polepiece pickups (neck and center) and one black six-polepiece pickup (angled in bridgeplate); two controls (volume, tone) and five-way selector, all on reversed metal plate adjoining pickguard; side-mounted jack.
- **Hardware:** eight-screw white pearl laminated plastic pickguard; six-saddle flat bridge with through-body stringing.

Foto Flame' fake figured wood finish option (1995–96).

NOKIE EDWARDS TELECASTER (MIJ) 1996

Signature on headstock, two twin-blade humbuckers.
- **Neck:** maple with ebony fingerboard; 22 frets; truss-rod adjuster at body end; brass nut; optional Scruggs Peg banjo-style de-tuner for 6th string; Nokie Edwards signature on headstock.
- **Body:** Single-cutaway with figured front; natural only.
- **Electronics:** two black twin-blade humbucker pickups; two controls (volume, tone) and three-way selector, all on body, side-mounted jack.
- **Hardware:** gold-plated; no pickguard; six-saddle small bridge with through-body stringing.

Optional Nokie Edwards logo for body.

■ **1995** press advertisement

RELIC 50s NOCASTER 1996–98

Distressed-finish replica of 1950s-period original with no model name on headstock (see BROADCASTER 1950 listing). Custom Shop production.

TRADITIONAL TELECASTER (MIM) 1996–98

Modern-style 'thick' Fender headstock logo in black, two single-coils.
Similar to vintage-style Telecaster except:
- **Neck:** fretted maple; truss-rod adjuster at headstock end; one string-guide.
- **Body:** slab single-cutaway; black, red, or white.
- **Electronics:** one plain metal-cover pickup with visible height-adjustment screws (at neck) and one black six-polepiece pickup (angled in bridgeplate); two controls (volume, tone) and three-way selector, all on metal plate adjoining pickguard; side-mounted jack.
- **Hardware:** eight-screw white laminated plastic pickguard; six-saddle flat bridge/tailpiece (no through-body stringing).

Previously known as SQUIER SERIES STANDARD TELECASTER, with small Squier Series logo on headstock (see 1994 listing).

50s TELECASTER 1996–98

Replica of 1950s-period original
(see TELECASTER 1951 listing).
Gold-plated hardware option.
Custom Shop production.

50th ANNIVERSARY TELECASTER 1996

Commemorative neckplate.
Similar to AMERICAN STANDARD TELECASTER
(see 1988 listing) except:
- **Neck:** fretted maple; commemorative neckplate.
- **Body:** sunburst only.
- **Hardware:** gold-plated.
Numbered factory production run of 1,250.

60s TELECASTER CUSTOM 1996–98

Replica of 1960s-period original
(see TELECASTER 1951 listing).
Gold-plated hardware option.
Custom Shop production.

CALIFORNIA FAT TELE 1997–98

*'California Series' on headstock, one humbucker
and one single-coil.*
- **Neck:** fretted maple; truss-rod adjuster at
  headstock end; one string-guide;
  'California Series' on headstock.
- **Body:** slab single-cutaway; sunburst or colors.
- **Electronics:** one metal-cover six-polepiece
  humbucker (at neck) and one black six-polepiece
  pickup (angled in bridgeplate); two controls
  (volume, tone) and three-way selector, all on metal
  plate adjoining pickguard; side-mounted jack.
- **Hardware:** eight-screw white laminated plastic
  pickguard; six-saddle raised-sides bridge with
  through-body stringing.

■ **1997** 50s Telecaster

TELECASTER 1997

CALIFORNIA TELE 1997–current

'California Series' on headstock, two single-coils.
Similar to CALIFORNIA FAT TELE (see 1997 listing) except:
• **Neck:** fretted maple, or maple with rosewood fingerboard.
• **Electronics:** one white six-polepiece pickup (at neck) and one black six-polepiece pickup (angled in bridgeplate).

DELUXE NASHVILLE TELE (MIM) 1997–current

White six-polepiece pickup in center position.
Similar to STANDARD TELECASTER (see 1991 listing) except:
• **Neck:** fretted maple, or maple with rosewood fingerboard.
• **Body:** sunburst or colors.
• **Electronics:** one plain metal-cover pickup with visible height-adjustment screws (at neck), one white six-polepiece pickup (in center) and one black six-polepiece pickup (angled in bridgeplate); white six-polepiece pickup (in center); two controls (volume, tone) and five-way selector.
• **Hardware:** eight-screw tortoiseshell laminated plastic pickguard; six-saddle raised-sides bridge with through-body stringing.

MERLE HAGGARD TELE 1997–current

Signature on headstock.
• **Neck:** fretted maple; 22 frets; truss-rod adjuster at body end; one string-guide; pearl tuner buttons; 'Tuff Dog Tele' inlay and Merle Haggard signature on headstock.
• **Body:** slab single-cutaway bound; sunburst only.
• **Electronics:** one plain metal-cover pickup (at neck) and one black six-polepiece pickup (angled in bridgeplate); two controls (volume, tone) and four-way selector, all on metal plate adjoining pickguard; side-mounted jack.
• **Hardware:** gold-plated; seven-screw cream plastic re-styled pickguard; six-saddle flat bridge with through-body stringing.

Custom Shop production.
Catalog name varies: Merle Haggard Tribute Tuff Dog Tele (1997–2000); Merle Haggard Tribute Tele (2001–03); Merle Haggard Signature Telecaster (2004–current).

TEX-MEX TELE SPECIAL (MIM) 1997

Humbucker at neck, white pickguard.
Similar to STANDARD TELECASTER (see 1991 listing) except:
• **Electronics:** one metal-cover six-polepiece humbucker (at neck) and one black six-polepiece pickup (angled in bridgeplate); two controls (volume, tone) and five-way selector.
• **Hardware:** six-saddle raised-sides bridge with through-body stringing.

90s TELE THINLINE 1997–2001

f-hole body, 22 frets.
• **Neck:** fretted maple, or maple with rosewood fingerboard; 22 frets; truss-rod adjuster at headstock end; one string-guide.
• **Body:** semi-solid slab single-cutaway bound; sunburst or colors.
• **Electronics:** one plain metal-cover pickup with visible height-adjustment screws (at neck) and one black six-polepiece pickup (angled in bridgeplate); two controls (volume, tone) and three-way selector, all on pickguard; side-mounted jack.
• **Hardware:** 12-screw white pearl or tortoiseshell laminated plastic pickguard; six-saddle flat bridge with through-body stringing.

■ **1997** Deluxe Nashville Tele

WILL RAY JAZZ-A-CASTER (MIJ) 1997–98

Signature and model name on headstock,
two large white pickups.

- **Neck:** maple with rosewood fingerboard, triangle markers; 22 frets; truss-rod adjuster at headstock end; one string guide; locking tuners; 'Hellecasters' inlay at 12th fret; Will Ray signature on small Stratocaster-style headstock.
- **Body:** slab single-cutaway; gold foil leaf only.
- **Electronics**: two large white rectangular six-polepiece pickups (bridge pickup angled); two controls (volume, tone) and four-way selector, all on metal plate adjoining pickguard; side-mounted jack.
- **Hardware:** eight-screw white pearl laminated plastic pickguard; modified six-saddle bridge with through-body stringing; Hipshot bending device on 2nd string.

AMERICAN DELUXE TELECASTER
(first version) 1998–99

Contoured bound body, 22 frets,
additional center pickup.

Similar to AMERICAN STANDARD TELECASTER
(see 1986 listing) except:

- **Body:** contoured single-cutaway, bound.
- **Electronics:** one plain metal-cover pickup with visible height-adjustment screws (at neck), one white six-polepiece pickup (in center) and one black six-polepiece pickup (angled in bridgeplate); two controls (volume, tone), five-way selector and mini-switch, all on metal plate adjoining pickguard.
- **Hardware:** eight-screw white or tortoiseshell laminated plastic pickguard.

■ **1997** Will Ray Jazz-A-Caster

TELECASTER 1997-1998

50

AMERICAN VINTAGE '52 TELECASTER
1998–current
Replica of 1952 original (see TELECASTER 1951 listing).

BUCK OWENS TELECASTER (MIJ) 1998
Signature on headstock, red, silver and blue sparkle striped body front.

CLASSIC '69 TELECASTER THINLINE (MIM)
1998–current
Replica of 1969-period original
(see THINLINE TELECASTER FIRST VERSION 1968 listing).

NASHVILLE B-BENDER TELE 1998–current
Additional center pickup, B-Bender string-bending device installed.
Similar to AMERICAN STANDARD B-BENDER TELECASTER
(see 1995 listing) except:
- **Electronics:** one plain metal-cover pickup with visible height-adjustment screws (at neck), one white six-polepiece pickup (in center) and one black six-polepiece pickup (angled in bridgeplate); two controls (volume, tone) and five-way selector, all on metal plate adjoining pickguard.
- **Hardware:** eight-screw white pearloid laminated plastic pickguard.

Known as AMERICAN NASHVILLE B-BENDER TELE
(see 2000 listing).

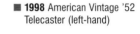

■ **1998** American Vintage '52
Telecaster (left-hand)

TELE-SONIC 1998–2004

Model name on headstock.

- **Neck:** maple with rosewood fingerboard; 24.75-inch scale, 22 frets; truss-rod adjuster at headstock end; one string-guide; black-face headstock.
- **Body:** semi-solid slab single-cutaway; sunburst or red.
- **Electronics:** two black-top six-polepiece pickups; four controls (two volume, two tone) and three-way selector, all on body; side-mounted jack.
- **Hardware:** six-screw black laminated plastic pickguard; two-section wrapover bridge/tailpiece (six-saddle wrapover bridge/tailpiece from 2003).

U.S. FAT TELE 1998–2000

One humbucker and one single-coil, five-way selector.
Similar to AMERICAN STANDARD TELECASTER (see 1988 listing) except:

- **Electronics:** one metal-cover humbucker (at neck) and one black six-polepiece pickup (angled in bridgeplate); two controls (volume, tone) and four-way selector, all on metal plate adjoining pickguard.

Known as AMERICAN FAT TELE (see 2001 listing).

■ **1999** American Vintage '52 Telecaster

TELECASTER 1998-1999

■ **1999** Will Ray Telecaster

WILL RAY TELECASTER 1998–2001
Signature on headstock, skull markers.
- **Neck:** maple with rosewood fingerboard, skull markers; 22 frets; truss-rod adjuster at headstock end; one string-guide; locking tuners; Will Ray signature on small Stratocaster-style headstock.
- **Body:** slab single-cutaway; gold foil leaf on various colors.
- **Electronics:** two large rectangular white six-polepiece pickups (bridge pickup angled); three controls (volume, two tone) and three-way selector, all on metal plate adjoining pickguard; side-mounted jack.
- **Hardware:** eight-screw white pearl laminated plastic re-styled pickguard; modified three-saddle bridge with through-body stringing; optional Hipshot bending device on second string.
Custom Shop production.

1998 COLLECTORS EDITION TELECASTER 1998
Commemorative fingerboard inlay and neckplate.
Similar to 50s TELECASTER (see 1996 listing) except:
- **Neck:** fretted maple with commemorative inlay at 12th fret; commemorative neckplate.
- **Body:** sunburst only.
- **Hardware:** gold-plated; five-screw white plastic pickguard.
Numbered factory production run of 1,998.

AMERICAN CLASSIC TELECASTER
(second version) 1999–2000
Two single-coils, inverted control plate, three-way selector.
Similar to AMERICAN CLASSIC TELECASTER FIRST VERSION (see 1995 listing) except:
- **Electronics:** one plain metal-cover pickup with visible height-adjustment screws (at neck) and one black six-polepiece pickup (angled in bridgeplate); two controls (volume, tone) and three-way selector, all on inverted metal plate adjoining pickguard.
- **Hardware:** eight-screw white laminated plastic pickguard.
Custom Shop production.

AMERICAN DELUXE POWER TELE 1999–2001
Contoured bound body, two dual-concentric controls.
Similar to AMERICAN DELUXE TELECASTER SECOND VERSION (see next listing) except:
- **Electronics:** two dual-concentric controls (volume, tone for magnetic and piezo pickups), three-way selector and mini-switch, all on metal plate adjoining pickguard.
- **Hardware:** Fishman Power Bridge with six piezo-pickup saddles.

■ **1991** flyer

AMERICAN DELUXE TELECASTER
(second version) 1999–2003
Contoured bound body, 22 frets, two single-coils.
Similar to AMERICAN DELUXE TELECASTER FIRST VERSION (see 1998 listing) except:
- **Electronics:** one plain metal-cover pickup with visible height-adjustment screws (at neck) and one black six-polepiece pickup (angled in bridgeplate); two controls (volume, tone) and three-way selector, all on metal plate adjoining pickguard.

AMERICAN VINTAGE '52 TELE SPECIAL
1999–2001

Replica of 1952-period original
(see TELECASTER 1951 listing).
Body sunburst only, gold-plated hardware.

AMERICAN VINTAGE '62 CUSTOM TELECASTER
1999–current

Replica of 1962-period original with bound body
(see TELECASTER 1951 listing).

CLASSIC 50s TELECASTER (MIM) 1999–2006

Replica of 1950s-period original
(see TELECASTER 1951 listing).

CLASSIC '72 TELECASTER CUSTOM (MIM)
1999–current

Replica of 1972-period original
(see entry in 1972 listing).

CLASSIC '72 TELECASTER THINLINE (MIM)
1999–current

Replica of 1972-period original
(see entry in 1971 listing).

■ **1999** American Vintage
'62 Custom Telecaster

TELECASTER 1999

■ **1999** Classic '72 Telecaster Custom

■ **1999** Classic 50s Custom

■ **1999** Deluxe Nashville Power Tele

DELUXE NASHVILLE POWER TELE (MIM)
1999–current
White six-polepiece pickup in center position,
one dual-concentric control.
Similar to DELUXE NASHVILLE TELE
(see 1997 listing) except:
- **Electronics:** one dual-concentric control
  (volume, tone for magnetic pickups),
  one regular control (volume for piezo pickups)
  plus one five-way selector.
- **Hardware:** Fishman Power Bridge with six
  piezo-pickup saddles.

'51 NOCASTER 1999–current
Replica of 1951-period original with no model
name on headstock
(see TELECASTER 1951 listing).
Offered with three finish distress degrees:
N.O.S., Closet Classic and Relic.
Custom Shop production.

'63 TELECASTER 1999–current
Replica of 1963-period original
(see TELECASTER 1951 listing).
Offered with three finish distress degrees:
N.O.S., Closet Classic, and Relic.
Custom Shop production.

AMERICAN NASHVILLE B-BENDER TELE
2000–current
Another Name For NASHVILLE B-BENDER TELE
(see 1998 listing).
- **Hardware:** 11-screw white pearl or
  tortoiseshell laminated plastic pickguard.
Fitted with different-specification but visually
similar pickups.

■ **2000** Standard Telecaster
(left-hand)

TELECASTER 1999-2000

■ **2000** '51 Nocaster Relic

■ **2000** American Nashville B-Bender Tele

■ **2000** Telecaster Relic

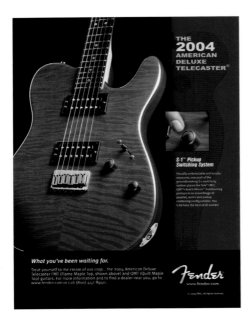

THE
2004
AMERICAN
DELUXE
TELECASTER®

*S-1™ Pickup
Switching System*

Visually undetectable and tonally awesome, one push of the groundbreaking S-1 switching system places the Tele® FMT/ QMT's Dual Enforcer™ humbucking pickups in an assemblage of parallel, series and pickup-combining configurations. You CAN have the best of all worlds!

What you've been waiting for.

Treat yourself to the cream of our crop... the 2004 American Deluxe Telecaster FMT (Flame Maple Top, shown above) and QMT (Quilt Maple Top) guitars. For more information and to find a dealer near you, go to www.fender.com or call (800) 447-8940.

Fender
www.fender.com

■ **2003** press advertisement

AMERICAN TELECASTER 2000–current
Succeeded AMERICAN STANDARD TELECASTER
(see 1988 listing).

CUSTOM CLASSIC TELECASTER 2000–08
Two single-coils, inverted control plate, four-way selector.
Similar to AMERICAN CLASSIC TELECASTER SECOND VERSION
(see 1999 listing) except:
• **Electronics:** two controls (volume, tone) and four-way
   selector, all on inverted metal plate adjoining pickguard.
Custom Shop production.

AMERICAN TELECASTER 2000-07
*22 frets, slab single-cutaway body, two single-coils,
six-saddle bridge, staggered height tuners.*
Similar to AMERICAN STANDARD TELECASTER
first version (see previous listing), except:
• **Neck:** vintage-style Fender
   logo on headstock.
• **Hardware:** staggered
   height tuners.
Succeeded AMERICAN STANDARD
TELECASTER first version
(see previous listing).

■ **2000** Leo Fender
Broadcaster

TELECASTER
2000-2001

■ **2004** press advertisement

AMERICAN FAT TELE 2001–03
Another name for U.S. FAT TELE (see 1998 listing).

CLASSIC 60s TELECASTER (MIM) 2001–current
Replica of 1960s-period original
(see TELECASTER 1951 listing).

SUB-SONIC TELE baritone 2001–05
Sub-Sonic on headstock, long-scale neck.
- **Neck:** fretted maple; 27-inch scale, 22 frets;
  truss-rod adjuster at body end; one string-guide;
  Sub-Sonic on headstock.
- **Body:** slab single-cutaway; sunburst or colors.
- **Electronics:** one plain metal cover pickup
  (at neck) and one black six-polepiece
  pickup (angled in bridgeplate);
  two controls (volume, tone) and
  four-way selector, all on metal
  plate adjoining pickguard;
  side-mounted jack.
- **Hardware:** eight-screw white
  laminated plastic pickguard;
  six-saddle bridge with
  through-body stringing.
Custom Shop production.

■ **2001** Classic 60s Telecaster

59

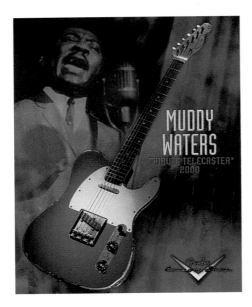

MUDDY WATERS TELECASTER (MIM) 2001–09

Custom Telecaster on headstock, amplifier-type black plastic control knobs.

Similar to CLASSIC 60S TELECASTER (see 1999 listing) except:

• **Neck:** 'Custom Telecaster' on headstock.
• **Body:** red only.
• **Hardware:** nine-screw white plastic pickguard; amplifier-type black plastic control knobs.

HIGHWAY ONE TELECASTER (first version) 2002–06

Satin finish, 22 frets, five-screw pickguard.

• **Neck:** fretted maple, or maple with rosewood fingerboard; 22 frets; truss-rod adjuster at headstock end; one string-guide.
• **Body:** slab single-cutaway; sunburst or colors, satin finish.
• **Electronics:** one plain metal-cover pickup (at neck) and one black six-polepiece pickup (angled in bridgeplate); two controls (volume, tone) and three-way selector, all of which are situated on the metal plate that adjoins the pickguard; side-mounted jack.
• **Hardware:** five-screw white plastic pickguard; three-saddle raised-sides bridge with through-body stringing.

■ **2001** Muddy Waters Telecaster

AMERICAN ASH TELECASTER 2003–07
Five-screw pickguard, 22 frets.
Similar to AMERICAN TELECASTER (see 2000 listing) except:
- **Neck:** fretted maple only.
- **Body:** sunburst or blonde.
- **Hardware:** five-screw white or black plastic pickguard.

AMERICAN TELECASTER HH (first version) 2003–04
Two black coverless humbuckers, no pickguard.
Similar to AMERICAN TELECASTER HS
(see following listing) except:
- **Electronics:** two black coverless humbuckers.
- **Hardware:** six-saddle small bridge with through-body stringing.

AMERICAN TELECASTER HS (first version) 2003–04
Coverless black humbucker at neck, no pickguard.
- **Neck:** fretted maple, or maple with rosewood fingerboard; 22 frets; truss-rod adjuster at headstock end; one string-guide.
- **Body:** slab single-cutaway; various colors.
- **Electronics:** one black coverless humbucker (at neck) and one black six-polepiece pickup (angled in bridgeplate); two controls (volume, tone) and three-way selector, all on metal plate; side-mounted jack.
- **Hardware:** no pickguard; six-saddle flat bridge with through-body stringing.

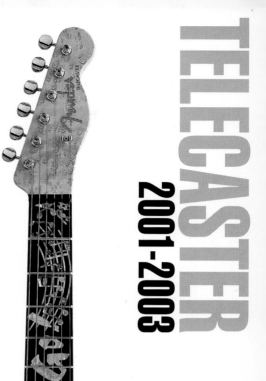

■ **2001** Go Cat Go
Telecaster Custom Shop

CUSTOM TELECASTER FMT HH (MIK)
2003–current

Glued-in neck, bound body with figured top.
- **Neck:** maple glued-in, with bound rosewood fingerboard; 22 frets; truss-rod adjuster at headstock end; two string-guides.
- **Body:** single-cutaway bound; figured top; various colors.
- **Electronics:** two black coverless humbuckers; two controls (volume, tone with pull switch) and three-way selector, all on body; side-mounted jack.
- **Hardware:** smoked-chrome-plated; no pickguard; six-saddle small bridge with through-body stringing.

ESQUIRE CUSTOM CELTIC (MIK) 2003

Celtic design inlay at 12th fret, single-cutaway body.
- **Neck:** mahogany glued-in, with rosewood fingerboard; 22 frets; truss-rod adjuster at headstock end; two string-guides; no front markers except Celtic design inlay at 12th fret.
- **Body:** single-cutaway, contoured; silver only, satin finish.
- **Electronics:** one black coverless humbucker (at bridge); one control (volume) on body; side-mounted jack.
- **Hardware:** black-plated; no pickguard; six-saddle small bridge with through-body stringing.

ESQUIRE CUSTOM GT (MIK) 2003

Center striped single cutaway body.
- **Neck:** mahogany glued-in, with bound rosewood fingerboard; 22 frets; truss-rod adjuster at headstock end; two string-guides.
- **Body:** single-cutaway, contoured, bound; blue, red, or silver, with center stripes.
- **Electronics:** one black coverless humbucker (at bridge); one control (volume) on body; side-mounted jack.
- **Hardware:** black-plated; no pickguard; six-saddle small bridge with through-body stringing.

ESQUIRE CUSTOM SCORPION (MIK) 2003

Scorpion inlay at 12th fret, single-cutaway body.
- **Neck:** mahogany glued-in, with bound rosewood fingerboard; 22 frets; truss-rod adjuster at headstock end; two string-guides; no front markers except Scorpion inlay at 12th fret.
- **Body:** single-cutaway, contoured, bound; black only.
- **Electronics:** one black coverless humbucker (at bridge); one control (volume) on body; side-mounted jack.
- **Hardware:** black-plated; no pickguard; six-saddle small bridge with through-body stringing.

HIGHWAY ONE TEXAS TELECASTER 2003–current

Satin finish, 21 frets.
Similar to HIGHWAY ONE TELECASTER FIRST VERSION (see 2002 listing) except:
- **Neck:** fretted maple only; 21 frets.
- **Body:** sunburst or blonde, satin finish.

FLAT HEAD TELECASTER 2003–04

Name on headstock, 22 frets, one humbucker, single-cutaway body.
- **Neck:** maple with ebony fingerboard; 22 frets; truss-rod adjuster at headstock end; staggered height locking tuners; no position markers except 'crossed pistons' inlay at 12th fret; 'Flat Head' on headstock.
- **Body:** single-cutaway slab; various colors.
- **Electronics:** one black coverless humbucker; one control (volume) on body; side-mounted jack.
- **Hardware:** black-plated; no pickguard; six-saddle small bridge that incorporates through-body stringing.
Custom Shop production.

JIMMY BRYANT TELECASTER 2003–05

Decorative tooled leather pickguard overlay.
- **Neck:** fretted maple; truss-rod adjuster at body end; one string-guide.
- **Body:** slab, single-cutaway; blonde only.
- **Electronics:** one plain metal-cover pickup (at neck) and one black six-polepiece pickup (angled in bridgeplate); two controls (volume, tone) and three-way selector, all on metal plate adjoining pickguard; side-mounted jack.
- **Hardware:** five-screw black plastic pickguard with decorative tooled leather overlay; three-saddle raised sides bridge with through-body stringing.
Custom Shop production.

J5:BIGSBY 2003–current

Headstock with three tuners each side, Bigsby vibrato tailpiece.
Similar to J5:HB TELECASTER (see following listing) except:
- **Electronics:** one plain metal-cover pickup with visible height-adjustment screws (at neck) and one black six-polepiece pickup (angled in bridgeplate); two controls (volume, tone) on metal plate adjoining pickguard.
  Hardware: six-saddle bridge, 'F' logo Bigsby vibrato tailpiece.
Custom Shop production.

J5:HB TELECASTER 2003–current

Headstock with three tuners each side, humbucker at bridge.
- **Neck:** maple with rosewood fingerboard; 22 frets; truss-rod adjuster at headstock end; no string-guide; black-face three tuners-per-side headstock.
- **Body:** slab, single-cutaway; bound; black only.
- **Electronics:** one plain metal-cover pickup with visible height adjustment screws (at neck) and one black coverless humbucker (in bridgeplate); two controls (both volume) on metal plate adjoining pickguard, three-way selector on body; side-mounted jack.
- **Hardware:** eight-screw chrome plastic pickguard; six-saddle flat bridge with through-body stringing.
Custom Shop production.

RICK PARFITT SIGNATURE TELECASTER 2003–04

Signature on headstock.
- **Neck:** maple with rosewood fingerboard: truss-rod adjuster at body end; one string-guide; Rick Parfitt signature on headstock.
- **Body:** slab single-cutaway; white only, satin finish.
- **Electronics:** one plain metal-cover pickup (at neck) and one black six-polepiece pickup (angled in cut down bridgeplate); two controls (volume, tone) and three-way selector, all on metal plate adjoining pickguard; side-mounted jack.
- **Hardware:** some of it gold-plated; eight-screw black plastic pickguard; four-saddle wrapover bridge/tailpiece with through-body stringing.

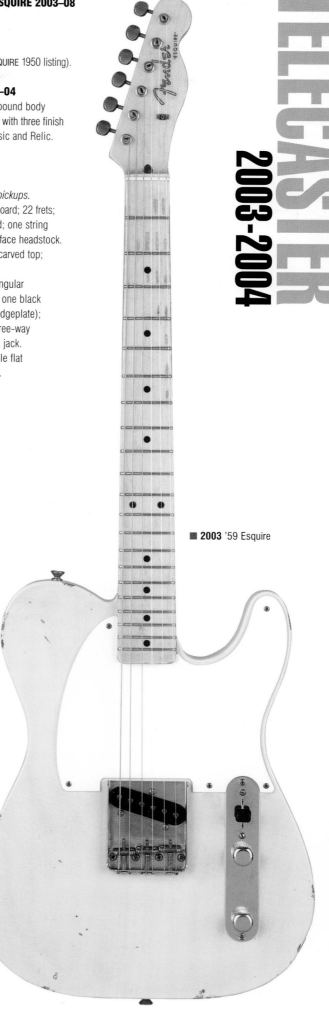

SEYMOUR DUNCAN SIGNATURE ESQUIRE 2003–08
See other Esquire listings.

'59 ESQUIRE 2003–06
Replica of 1959-period original (see ESQUIRE 1950 listing).

'60 TELECASTER CUSTOM 2003–04
Replica of 1960-period original with bound body
(see TELECASTER 1951 listing). Offered with three finish
distress degrees: N.O.S., Closet Classic and Relic.
Custom Shop production.

AERODYNE TELE (MIJ) 2004–06
'Aerodyne Series' on headstock, two pickups.
- **Neck:** maple with rosewood fingerboard; 22 frets;
  truss-rod adjuster at headstock end; one string
  guide; 'Aerodyne Series' on black-face headstock.
- **Body:** single-cutaway bound with carved top;
  black only.
- **Electronics:** one large black rectangular
  six-polepiece pickup (at neck) and one black
  six-polepiece pickup (angled in bridgeplate);
  two controls (volume, tone) and three-way
  selector,all on body; side-mounted jack.
- **Hardware:** no pickguard; six-saddle flat
  bridge with through-body stringing.

■ **2003** '59 Esquire

AMERICAN DELUXE ASH TELECASTER 2004-current

Ash body, 22 frets, volume control with push-switch.
Similar to AMERICAN DELUXE TELECASTER THIRD VERSION
(see later listing this year) except:
- **Neck:** fretted maple only.
- **Body:** unbound ash; sunburst or blonde.
- **Hardware:** eight-screw black plastic pickguard.

AMERICAN DELUXE TELECASTER (third version)
2004–current

Contoured bound body, 22 frets, volume control with
push-switch.
Similar to AMERICAN DELUXE TELECASTER SECOND VERSION
(see 1999 listing) except:
- **Electronics:** one plain metal-cover pickup with visible
  height-adjustment screws (at neck) and one black six-
  polepiece pickup (angled in bridgeplate); two controls
  (volume with push-switch, tone) and three-way selector,
  all on metal plate adjoining pickguard.
- **Hardware:** eight-screw white or tortoiseshell laminated
  plastic pickguard, or gold plastic pickguard.

AMERICAN DELUXE TELECASTER FMT 2004–06

Figured top body, two humbuckers, no pickguard.
- **Neck:** maple with ebony fingerboard; 22 frets;
  truss-rod adjuster at headstock end; one string-guide.
- **Body:** single-cutaway with figured top; sunburst or colors.
- **Electronics:** two black coverless humbuckers; two controls
  (volume with push-switch, tone) and three-way selector,
  all on body; side-mounted jack.
- **Hardware:** no pickguard; six-saddle small bridge
  with through-body stringing.

AMERICAN DELUXE TELECASTER QMT 2004–06

Similar to AMERICAN DELUXE TELECASTER FMT
(see previous listing) but with quilted maple top.
Similar to AMERICAN TELECASTER HS SECOND VERSION
(see next listing) except:
- **Electronics:** two black coverless humbuckers.
- **Hardware:** six-saddle small bridge with
  through-body stringing.

AMERICAN TELECASTER HH
(second version) 2004–06

Two black coverless humbuckers,
black pickguard.

■ **2004** American Deluxe
Ash Telecaster

■ **2005** '72 Telecaster Deluxe

■ **2005** American Deluxe Telecaster

■ **2005** American Deluxe Telecaster QMT

■ **2004** press advertisement

AMERICAN TELECASTER HS (second version) 2004–06
Coverless black humbucker at neck, black pickguard.
Similar to AMERICAN TELECASTER HS FIRST VERSION
(see 2003 listing) except:
• **Electronics:** two controls (volume with push-switch, tone), three-way selector, all on metal plate.
• **Hardware:** eight-screw black plastic pickguard.

ANTIGUA TELECASTER (MIJ) 2004
Replica of 1977-period U.S. original with white/brown shaded body finish and matching pickguard (see TELECASTER 1951 listing).

BLACKOUT TELECASTER HH (MIK) 2004
Glued-in neck, no front markers, two Seymour Duncan humbuckers.
• **Neck:** maple glued-in, with rosewood fingerboard, no front markers; 22 frets; truss-rod adjuster at headstock end; two string-guides.
• **Body:** single-cutaway; black or blue.
• **Electronics:** two Seymour Duncan-logo black coverless humbuckers; two controls (volume, tone) and three-way selector, all on body; side-mounted jack.
• **Hardware:** black-plated; no pickguard; six-saddle small bridge that incorporates through-body stringing.

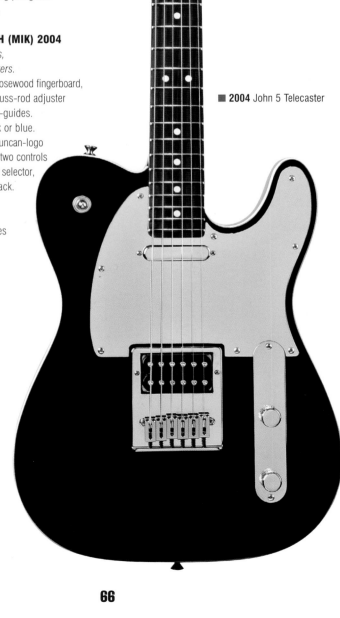

■ **2004** John 5 Telecaster

TELECASTER 2004

JOHN 5 TELECASTER (MIM) 2004–09
Headstock with three tuners each side, humbucker at bridge.
- **Neck:** maple with rosewood fingerboard; 22 frets; truss-rod adjuster at headstock end; no string-guide; black-face, three-tuners-per-side headstock.
- **Body:** slab single-cutaway bound; black only.
- **Electronics:** one plain metal-cover pickup with visible height adjustment screws (at neck) and one black coverless humbucker (in bridgeplate); two controls (volume, tone) on metal plate adjoining pickguard; three-way selector on body; side-mounted jack.
- **Hardware:** eight-screw chrome plastic pickguard; six-saddle flat bridge with through-body stringing.

LITE ASH TELECASTER (MIK) 2004–08
Maple neck with maple fingerboard, black pickguard.
- **Neck:** maple with maple fingerboard; 22 frets; truss-rod adjuster at headstock end; two string-guides.
- **Body:** slab single-cutaway; natural, black or white.
- **Electronics:** one plain metal-cover pickup (at neck) and one Seymour Duncan-logo black six-polepiece pickup (angled in bridgeplate); two controls (volume, tone) and three-way selector, all on metal plate adjoining pickguard; side-mounted jack.
- **Hardware:** eight-screw black plastic pickguard; three-saddle raised-sides bridge/tailpiece with no through-body stringing.

■ **2006** Classic '72 Telecaster Custom

CLASSIC '72 TELECASTER DELUXE (MIJ)
2004–current
Replica of 1972-period original (see 1972 listing).

FLAT HEAD TELECASTER HH 2004–06
Name on headstock, 22 frets, two black plain-top humbuckers, single-cutaway body.
Similar to FLAT HEAD TELECASTER (see 2003 listing) except:
- **Electronics:** two black plain top active humbuckers; one control (volume) and three-way selector, both on body.

Custom Shop production.

CLASSIC 50s ESQUIRE (MIM) 2005–current
Replica of 1950s-period original (see ESQUIRE 1950 listing).

DELUXE BIG BLOCK TELECASTER (MIM)
2005–06
Block markers, black headstock face, chrome pickguard.
- **Neck:** maple with rosewood fingerboard, block markers; truss-rod adjuster at headstock end; one string-guide; black-face headstock.
- **Body:** black only.
- **Electronics:** two plain metal-cover pickups with visible height adjustment screws (at neck and in center) and one black six-polepiece pickup (angled in bridgeplate); two controls (volume, tone) and five-way selector, all on metal plate adjoining pickguard; side-mounted jack.
- **Hardware:** eight-screw chrome plastic pickguard; six-saddle flat bridge with through-body stringing.

■ **2004** Classic 60s Telecaster

TELECASTER 2005

68

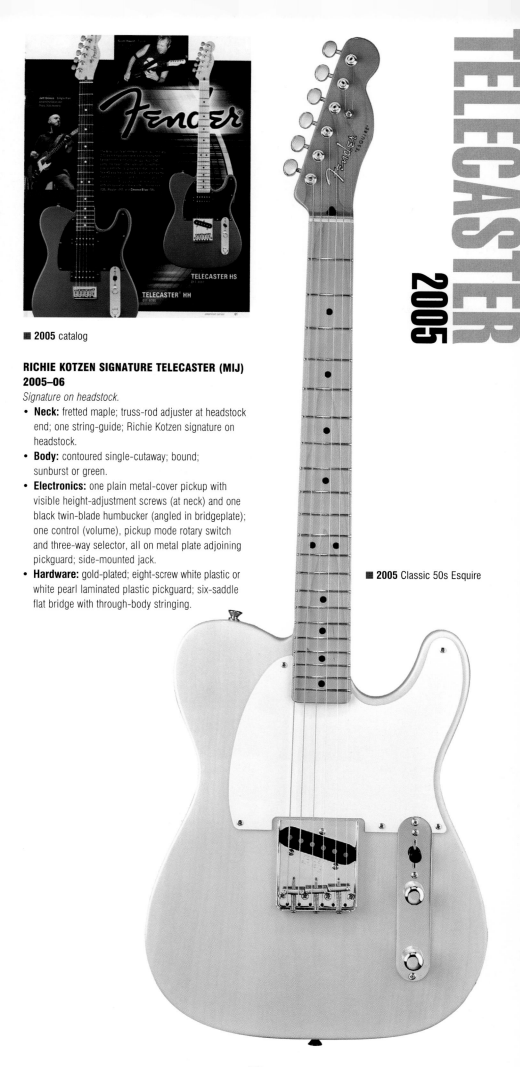

■ **2005** catalog

RICHIE KOTZEN SIGNATURE TELECASTER (MIJ) 2005–06

Signature on headstock.

- **Neck:** fretted maple; truss-rod adjuster at headstock end; one string-guide; Richie Kotzen signature on headstock.
- **Body:** contoured single-cutaway; bound; sunburst or green.
- **Electronics:** one plain metal-cover pickup with visible height-adjustment screws (at neck) and one black twin-blade humbucker (angled in bridgeplate); one control (volume), pickup mode rotary switch and three-way selector, all on metal plate adjoining pickguard; side-mounted jack.
- **Hardware:** gold-plated; eight-screw white plastic or white pearl laminated plastic pickguard; six-saddle flat bridge with through-body stringing.

■ **2005** Classic 50s Esquire

50s TELECASTER WITH BIGSBY (MIJ) 2005–06

Fretted maple neck, 'F' logo Bigsby vibrato tailpiece.
Similar to 50s TELECASTER (see 1951 listing) except:
- **Body:** natural or blonde.
- **Hardware:** six-saddle bridge, 'F' logo Bigsby vibrato tailpiece.

'67 TELECASTER 2005-08

60s TELECASTER WITH BIGSBY (MIJ) 2005–09

Bound body, rosewood fingerboard, 'F' logo Bigsby vibrato tailpiece.
Similar to 60s TELECASTER (see 1951 listing) except:
- **Body:** bound; sunburst or red.
- **Hardware:** six-saddle bridge, 'F' logo Bigsby vibrato tailpiece.

'67 TELECASTER 2005–current

Replica of 1967-period original (see 1951 listing).
Offered with three finish distress degrees: N.O.S.,
Closet Classic, and Relic.
Custom Shop production.

AMERICAN 60th ANNIVERSARY TELECASTER 2006

Commemorative neckplate, maple neck with rosewood fingerboard.
Similar to AMERICAN TELECASTER (see 2000 listing) except:
- **Neck:** maple with rosewood fingerboard only; commemorative headstock logo with jewel inlay; commemorative neckplate.

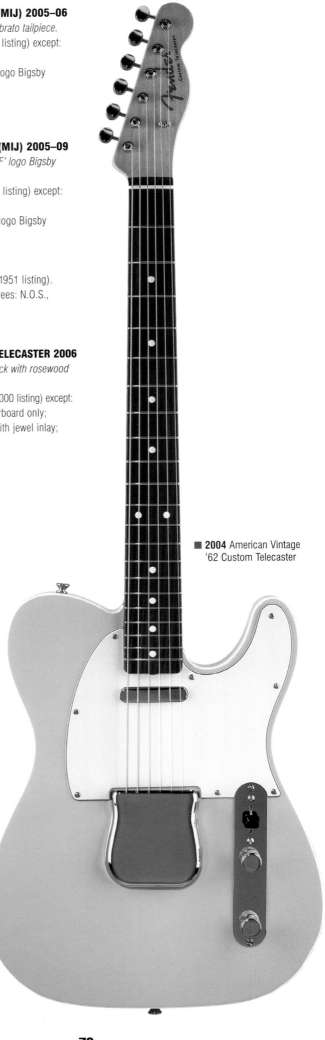

■ **2004** American Vintage '62 Custom Telecaster

TELECASTER 2006

■ **2004** Telesonic

■ **2004** American Vintage '52 Telecaster

■ **2004** American Deluxe Telecaster

CLASSIC PLAYER BAJA TELECASTER (MIM)
2006–current

Similar to CLASSIC 50s TELECASTER (see 1999 listing) except:

- **Neck:** neckplate with 'Custom Shop designed' logo.
- **Body:** blonde or sand.
- **Electronics:** two controls (volume with push-switch, tone) and four-way selector, all on metal plate adjoining pickguard.

■ **2006** Classic Player Baja Telecaster

HIGHWAY ONE TELECASTER (first version)
2002–06

Satin finish, 22 frets, five-screw pickguard.

- **Neck:** fretted maple, or maple with rosewood
  fingerboard; 22 frets; truss-rod adjuster at
  headstock end; one string-guide.
- **Body:** slab single-cutaway; sunburst or colors,
  satin finish.
- **Electronics:** one plain metal-cover pickup
  (at neck) and one black six-polepiece pickup
  (angled in bridgeplate); two controls (volume, tone)
  and three-way selector, all of which are situated
  on the metal plate that adjoins the pickguard;
  side-mounted jack.
- **Hardware:** five-screw white plastic pickguard;
  three-saddle raised-sides bridge with through-body
  stringing.

HIGHWAY ONE TELECASTER (second version)
2006–current

Satin finish, 22 frets, eight-screw pickguard.
Similar to HIGHWAY ONE TELECASTER FIRST VERSION
(see 2002 listing) except:

- **Hardware:** eight-screw white laminate plastic
  pickguard.

TELECASTER 2006

■ **2006** Highway One
Telecaster

JAMES BURTON TELECASTER (second version) 2006–current

Similar to JAMES BURTON TELECASTER FIRST VERSION (see 1990 listing) except:

- **Body:** black with blue or red paisley flame pattern, white.
- **Electronics:** three black plain-top pickups.

KOA TELECASTER (MIK) 2006–08

Rosewood fingerboard, white pearl pickguard.

- **Neck:** maple with rosewood fingerboard; 22 frets; truss-rod adjuster at headstock end; two string-guides.
- **Body:** with koa veneer top; sunburst only.
- **Electronics:** one plain metal-cover pickup (at neck) and one Seymour Duncan-logo black six-polepiece pickup (angled in bridgeplate); two controls (volume, tone) and three-way selector, all on metal plate adjoining pickguard; side-mounted jack.
- **Hardware:** eight-screw white pearl laminated plastic pickguard; three-saddle raised-sides bridge/tailpiece with through-body stringing.

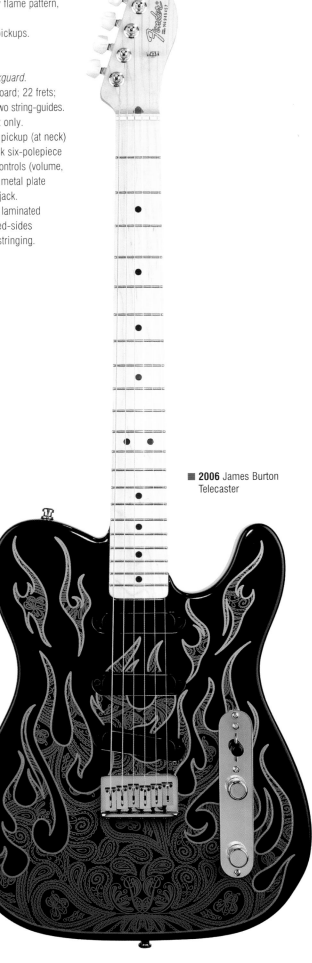

■ **2006** James Burton Telecaster

TELE THINLINE 2006–current

F-hole body, two single-coils, 12-screw white or black pickguard.

- **Neck:** fretted maple; truss-rod adjuster at body end; one string-guide.
- **Body:** semi-solid slab single-cutaway; f-hole; black or blonde, offered with three finish distress degrees: N.O.S., Closet Classic, and Relic.
- **Electronics:** one plain metal-cover pickup (at neck) and one black six-polepiece pickup (angled in bridgeplate); two controls (volume, tone) and three-way selector, all on pickguard; side-mounted jack.
- **Hardware:** 12-screw white or black plastic pickguard; three-saddle raised-sides bridge with through-body stringing.

Custom Shop production.

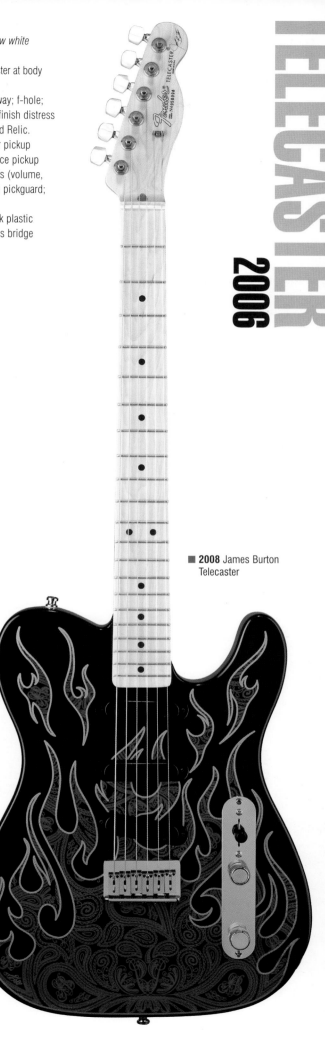

■ **2008** James Burton Telecaster

TELECASTER 2006

G.E. SMITH TELECASTER 2007–current

Differing black position markers, cut down bridge, body-mounted bridge pickup.

- **Neck:** fretted maple, differing-pattern black position markers; truss-rod adjuster at body end; one string-guide, engraved neck plate.
- **Body:** slab single-cutaway body; red or blonde.
- **Electronics:** one plain metal-cover pickup (at neck) and one black six-polepiece pickup (angled at bridge); two controls (volume, tone) and three-way selector, all on metal plate adjoining pickguard; side-mounted jack.
- **Hardware:** five-screw white or black plastic pickguard; three-saddle raised-sides cut-down bridge with through-body stringing.

■ **2007** G.E. Smith Telecaster

TELECASTER 2007

■ **2007** Vintage Hot Rod '52 Tele

■ **2007** Classic Player Tele Deluxe Black Dove

■ **2007** Classic Player Tele Thinline Deluxe

■ **2007** catalog

ROSEWOOD TELECASTER LTD. RELEASE
2007 Replica of 1960s-period original (see TELECASTER
listing in earlier US Regular Telecasters section)
but with commemorative neckplate.
Custom Shop production.

JIM ROOT TELECASTER 2007-current
Signature on back of headstock.
- **Neck:** fretted maple neck, or maple neck with
  ebony fingerboard; 22 frets; truss-rod adjuster at
  headstock end; locking tuners; one string-guide;
  signature on back of headstock.
- **Body:** slab single-cutaway body; satin black
  or satin white.
- **Electronics:** two black plain-top active humbuckers;
  One control (volume) and three-way selector,
  both on body; side-mounted jack socket.
- **Hardware:** eight-screw black or white plastic
  pickguard; six-saddle small bridge with through-
  body stringing; black-plated hardware.

JOE STRUMMER TELECASTER 2007-09
Commemorative neckplate.
Similar to CLASSIC 60S TELECASTER
(see listing in earlier Mexico Replica
Telecasters section), except:
- **Neck:** commemorative
  'Revolution Rock' neckplate.
- **Body:** body sunburst only,
  distressed finish.

■ **2007** Joe Strummer
Telecaster

TELECASTER 2007

■ **2007** press advertisement

■ **2007** Avril Lavigne
Telecaster

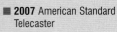

■ **2007** American Standard
Telecaster

TELECASTER 2007

ARTIST SERIES TELECASTERS

Fender was surprisingly slow to grasp the commercial benefits offered by artist-endorsed instruments. While rival U.S. makers were keen to sign up famous-name guitarists as far back as the 20s, it would be a further five decades before Fender first indulged in this marketing-friendly form of autograph hunting. Famous Fender players plus their equally identifiable instruments were prime targets for such attention, and the company's first autographed electric was the Eric Clapton Stratocaster. Introduced in 1988, this was a mass-production model, like Yngwie Malmsteen's signature Strat introduced the same year.

A trio of Telecasters came next, in 1990, bearing the respective autographs of Albert Collins, Danny Gatton, and James Burton. Burton's Tele was another factory-made example, but the other two emanated from Fender's Custom Shop. Established three years previously, this facility initially focused on strictly limited editions but by now was contributing certain artist models on a production basis.

The available choice of artist-endorsed examples increased significantly during the decade, and naturally most were based on Fender's two favorite six-strings. Some deviated more than others from these long-established designs in order to match the varying demands of their high-profile owners. Changes ranged from the minor and mainly cosmetic to comparatively major departures in terms of construction and components.

The Stratocaster served the needs of further famous names, such as Jeff Beck, Robert Cray, Stevie Ray Vaughan, Dick Dale, Buddy Guy, Bonnie Raitt, and Richie Sambora, while even Jimi Hendrix got in on the act – although obviously he was not directly involved. An equally diverse assortment of artists found that the Tele suited them to a T, including Jerry Donahue, Clarence White, Waylon Jennings, Merle Haggard, John Jorgenson, and Will Ray.

The 90s also saw Fender Japan making a contribution to the cause of the famous customer. First from the Far East was Robben Ford, whose model appeared in 1989 and was based on Ford's favorite Japanese-made Master series Esprit from five years earlier. Launched in 1991, the Yngwie Malmsteen Standard Strat set the trend for less-expensive interpretations of U.S.-made signature instruments. Also in this line was the JD Telecaster, introduced the following year, which offered Jerry Donahue's ideas on Tele re-design in a more affordable form.

Fender Japan's roster of artist guitars expanded with Telecasters for Buck Owens and Ventures guitarist Nokie Edwards, while further associations with America's leading American instrumental group came with a Ventures Jazzmaster and Stratocaster. Hank Marvin, Matthias Jabs, Ritchie Blackmore, and Richie Sambora enjoyed their own Stratocasters, while Jerry Donahue, John Jorgenson, and Will Ray were honored with heavily modified Hellecaster models.

Fender's Mexico factory joined in the fun during the 90s and adopted the same economical approach to artist guitars. First to emerge from south of the border were the James Burton Standard Tele and Richie Sambora Standard Strat, soon joined by Strats for UK players Hank Marvin and Chris Rea, while Jimmie Vaughan's Tex-Mex version emphasized the cross-country connections.

Since 2000, Fender has offered many players a chance to update their ideas on design, resulting in suitably revised versions of various U.S. signature six-strings. These partner an ever-increasing number of all-new examples as the company invites yet more artists to play the name game. British and Irish guitarists such as Mark Knopfler, Robin Trower, Rory Gallagher, and David Gilmour have been honored with their own Strats, joining American heroes such as Eric Johnson and John Mayer. The Tele spans five decades with its models for 50s country giant Jimmy Bryant and modern axe man John 5, while the Jazzmaster has finally achieved some much-deserved name-dropping courtesy of Elvis Costello, Lee Ranaldo, and Thurston Moore.

Fender's Mexican lines have seen many additions in more recent years, including Strats for Ritchie Blackmore, Buddy Guy, Robert Cray, Tom Delonge, and Kenny Wayne Shepherd, while players as diverse as Muddy Waters, Joe Strummer, Jim Root, and John 5 are associated with the Tele. Mexico may have taken over the more-affordable market from Fender Japan, but at the time of writing Japan still contributes the J. Mascis Jazzmaster, while Jim Adkins's Tele was the first artist guitar to come from Korea. Add to all these the ever-expanding selection in the Squier lines, and it's obvious that Fender are still very much in favor of linking the stars and their guitars.

AMERICAN STANDARD TELECASTER
second version 2008-current

22 frets, slab single-cutaway body, two single-coils, six-saddle bridge, bent steel bridge saddles.

- **Neck:** fretted maple neck, or maple neck with rosewood fingerboard; 22 frets; truss-rod adjuster at headstock end; staggered height tuners; one string-guide.
- **Body:** slab single-cutaway body; sunburst or colours.
- **Electronics:** one plain metal-cover pickup with visible height-adjustment screws (at neck) and one black six-polepiece pickup (angled in bridgeplate); two controls (volume, tone) and three-way selector, all on metal plate adjoining pickguard; side-mounted jack socket.
- **Hardware:** eight-screw white or black laminated plastic pickguard; six-saddle flat bridge with through-body stringing; bent steel saddles.

■ **2008** American Nashville B-Bender Telecaster

TELECASTER 2008

2008 American Standard
Telecaster

DELUXE BLACKOUT TELECASTER (MIM)
2008-current
Plain metal-cover pickup in neck and centre positions.
Similar to STANDARD TELECASTER (see later listing),
except:
- **Body:** body black only.
- **Electronics:** two plain metal-cover pickups with
  visible height-adjustment screws (at neck and
  in centre) and one black six-polepiece pickup
  (angled in bridgeplate); two controls (volume, tone)
  and five-way selector.
- **Hardware:** eight-screw black laminated plastic
  pickguard.

■ **2008** American Standard
Telecaster (left-hand)

■ **2009** Classic Player Telecaster Deluxe

■ **2009** Blackout Telecaster

■ **2009** Nashville Power Tele catalog

■ **2007** catalog

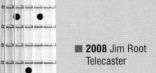

■ **2008** Jim Root Telecaster

TELECASTER 2009

SPALTED MAPLE TELECASTER (MIK)
2008-current

Single-cutaway body with figured carved top,
two black humbuckers, glued-in neck,
bound fingerboard.

- **Neck:** mahogany glued-in neck with bound rosewood fingerboard; 22 frets; truss-rod adjuster at headstock end; two string-guides.
- **Body:** single-cutaway body with figured carved top; natural only.
- **Electronics:** two Seymour Duncan-logo black coverless humbuckers; two controls (volume,tone with pull-switch) and three-way selector, all on body; side-mounted jack socket.
- **Hardware:** six-saddle small bridge with through-body stringing.

■ **2009** 'Natural Wood Beauty' Spalted Maple Telecaster

JIM ADKINS JA-90 TELECASTER (MIK)
2009-current

Signature on back of headstock.

- **Neck:** mahogany glued-in neck with rosewood fingerboard; 22 frets; truss-rod adjuster at headstock end; two string-guides; black- or red-face headstock; Jim Adkins signature on back of headstock.
- **Body:** semisolid slab single-cutaway body with f-hole; black or red.
- **Electronics:** two large rectangular black six-polepiece pickups; four controls (two volume, two tone) and three-way selector, all on body; side-mounted jack socket.
- **Hardware:** four-screw black laminated plastic pickguard; six-saddle bridge, bar tailpiece.

CLASSIC S-1 TELECASTER 2009-current

22 frets, three-saddle bridge, staggered height tuners.

- **Neck:** fretted maple neck; 22 frets; truss-rod adjuster at headstock end; staggered height tuners; one string-guide.
- **Body:** slab single-cutaway body; sunburst or black.
- **Electronics:** one plain metal-cover pickup (at neck) and one black six-polepiece pickup (angled in bridgeplate); two controls (volume, tone with push-switch) and three-way selector, all on metal plate adjoining pickguard; side-mounted jack socket.
- **Hardware:** eight-screw white laminated plastic pickguard; three-saddle raised-sides bridge with through-body stringing. Available with two finish distress degrees: N.O.S. and Relic.

Custom Shop production.

■ **2009** Jim Adkins JA-90 Telecaster

TELECASTER 2009

CUSTOM DELUXE TELECASTER 2009-current
22 frets, six-saddle bridge, staggered height tuners, no string-guide, Custom Shop logo on headstock.
- **Neck:** fretted maple neck, or maple neck with rosewood fingerboard; 22 frets; truss-rod adjuster at headstock end; staggered height tuners; no string-guide.
- **Body:** slab single-cutaway body; sunburst or colors.
- **Electronics:** one plain metal-cover pickup with visible height-adjustment screws (at neck) and one black six-polepiece pickup (angled in bridgeplate); two controls (volume, tone) and three-way selector, all on metal plate adjoining pickguard; side-mounted jack socket.
- **Hardware:** eight-screw white laminated plastic pickguard; six-saddle flat bridge with through-body stringing.

Custom Shop production.

TELECASTER PRO RELIC 2009-current
22 frets, five-screw white pickguard, four-way selector.
- **Neck:** fretted maple neck; 22 frets; truss-rod adjuster at headstock end.
- **Body:** slab single-cutaway body; blonde, black or white, distressed finish.
- **Electronics:** one plain metal-cover pickup (at neck) and one black six-polepiece pickup (angled in bridgeplate); two controls (volume, tone) and four-way selector, all on metal plate adjoining pickguard; side-mounted jack socket.
- **Hardware:** five-screw white plastic pickguard; Three-saddle raised-sides bridge with through-body stringing.

Custom Shop production.

ROAD WORN 50s TELECASTER (MIM) 2009-current
Distressed finish replica of 1950s-period original (see TELECASTER listing in earlier US Regular Telecaster section).

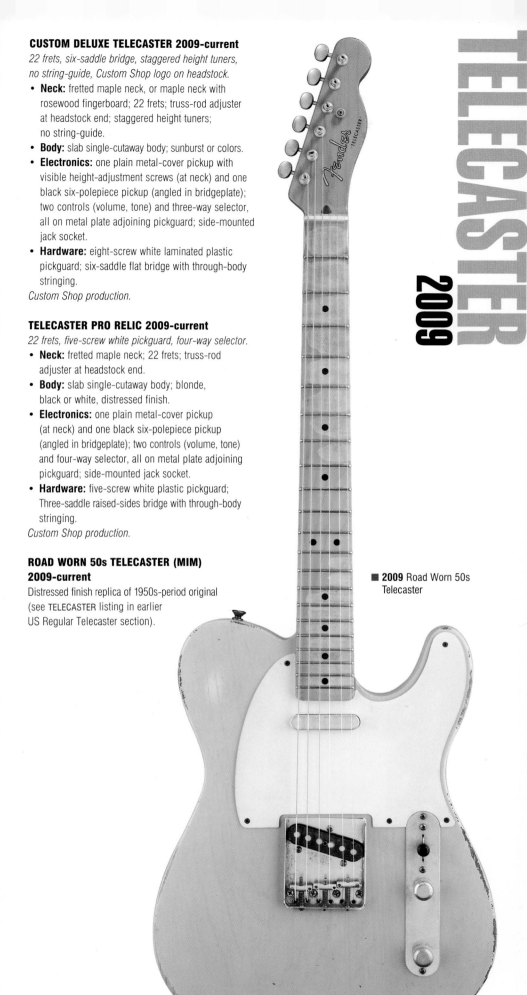

■ **2009** Road Worn 50s Telecaster

AMERICAN SPECIAL TELECASTER 2010-current

22 frets, three-saddle bridge, black pickguard.

- **Neck:** fretted maple neck; 22 frets; truss-rod adjuster at headstock end; one string-guide.
- **Body:** slab single-cutaway body; sunburst or white.
- **Electronics:** one plain metal-cover pickup with visible height-adjustment screws (at neck) and one black six-polepiece pickup (angled in bridgeplate); two controls (volume, tone) and three-way selector, all on metal plate adjoining pickguard; side-mounted jack socket.
- **Hardware:** eight-screw black laminated plastic pickguard; three-saddle raised-sides bridge with through-body stringing.

■ **2010** American Special Tele

TELECASTER 2010

1952 TELECASTER HB RELIC 2010-current

One metal-cover humbucker and one single-coil, two controls.

Similar to 1952-period original (see TELECASTER listing in earlier US Regular Telecasters section), except:
- **Body:** sunburst or blonde, distressed finish.
- **Electronics:** One metal-cover humbucker (at neck) and one black six-polepiece pickup (angled in body).

Custom Shop production.

CLASSIC PLAYER TELECASTER DELUXE BLACK DOVE (MIM) 2010-current

Two rectangular black pickups, four controls and selector on pickguard.

Similar to CLASSIC '72 TELECASTER DELUXE (see listing in earlier Mexico Replica Telecasters section), except:
- **Body:** body black or red.
- **Electronics:** two large rectangular black six-polepiece pickups; four controls (two volume, two tone) and three-way selector, all on pickguard; side-mounted jack socket.
- **Hardware:** 15-screw black laminated plastic pickguard.

CLASSIC PLAYER TELECASTER DELUXE WITH TREMELO (MIM) 2010-current

Two split-polepiece humbuckers, six-pivot vibrato.

Similar to CLASSIC '72 TELECASTER DELUXE (see listing in earlier Mexico Replica Telecasters section), except:
- **Body:** sunburst or black.
- **Hardware:** 15-screw black laminated plastic pickguard; six-pivot bridge/vibrato unit.

CLASSIC PLAYER TELECASTER THINLINE DELUXE (MIM) 2010-current

Four controls on pickguard, selector on body.
- **Neck:** fretted maple neck; 'bullet' truss-rod adjuster at headstock end; one string-guide.
- **Body:** semi-solid slab single-cutaway body with f-hole; sunburst or black.

- **Electronics:** two metal-cover split-polepiece humbuckers; four controls (two volume, two tone) on pickguard; three-way selector on body; side-mounted jack socket.
- **Hardware:** 13-screw white laminated plastic pickguard; six-saddle small bridge with through-body stringing.

DELUXE ACOUSTASONIC TELECASTER (MIM) 2010-current

Single-saddle flat wooden bridge, side-mounted controls.
- **Neck:** maple neck with rosewood fingerboard; truss-rod adjuster at headstock end; one string-guide.
- **Body:** semi-solid slab single-cutaway body; sunburst or white.
- **Electronics:** one plain metal-cover pickup (at neck) and one piezo-pickup in bridge; two controls (volume, tone) and three-way selector, all on metal plate adjoining pickguard; piezo-pickup controls on side-mounted panel; side-mounted jack socket; active circuit.
- **Hardware:** eight-screw tortoiseshell laminated plastic pickguard; single-saddle flat wooden bridge with through-body stringing.

ROAD WORN '72 TELECASTER CUSTOM (MIM) 2010-current

Distressed finish replica of 1970s-period original (see listing in earlier US Revised Telecaster section). *Limited production.*

ROAD WORN '72 TELECASTER DELUXE (MIM) 2010-current

Distressed finish replica of 1970s-period original (see listing in earlier US Revised Telecaster section). *Limited production.*

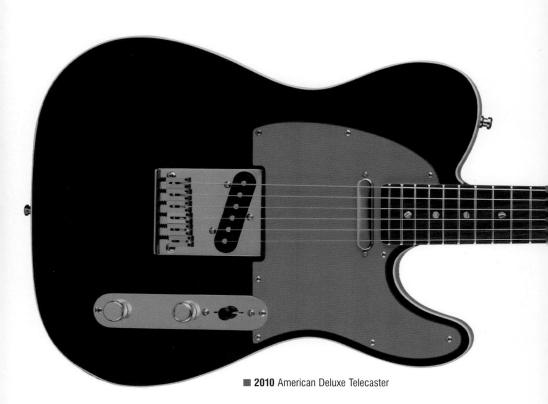

■ **2010** American Deluxe Telecaster

STRATOCASTER: THE FIRST TEN YEARS

As the Telecaster became accepted and established in the still embryonic market for solid electric guitars, Leo Fender and his team were not content to rest and in 1954 they added a second all-new six-string, the Stratocaster. This newcomer was aptly named, because the space-age name perfectly suited its futuristic looks, which put Fender way ahead of the opposition. Fender had a major re-think when the original vibrato unit design suffered at first from performance problems, but with a new design successfully accomplished, the Stratocaster hit the market with features that were advanced for the time, even if today they are very familiar. It is therefore hardly surprising that Fender made comparatively few changes during the model's first five years of manufacture.

The earliest plastic parts had a few minor modifications, while the serial number was re-sited on to the neckplate from the spring-cavity cover plate. This plate initially had round string-access holes, but these became oval in shape from 1955. Up on the headstock, the tuners also moved with the times. The tuner casings were supplied by the Kluson company, and initially they lacked any brand stamp, but from 1957 to 1964 they carried the identifying Kluson Deluxe logo down the center. The headstock's single string-guide switched in 1956 from a round type to a wing-style equivalent that induced less friction.

To make production easier and more economical, Fender altered the body wood from ash to alder midway through 1956, although ash was retained for use with certain translucent color schemes. The Strat's standard two-tone sunburst finish became three-tone during 1958 with the addition of a red blend between the original black and yellow shading. Fender also started to offer in 1958 a selection of solid color finishes, and the choice of these was expanded significantly during the next decade.

A fixed-bridge option was offered from 1955 as an alternative to the original vibrato-equipped guitar. The same year saw a clip-on chromed-metal cover added over the bridge saddles, but this impeded string damping, and most players promptly removed it (and lost it). By 1956, Fender had changed the neck shape from the original somewhat club-like cross-section to a distinctly 'V' profile, but within two years this was superseded by slimmer and more curved proportions.

The first major alteration occurred in 1959, when Fender decided to change from the original maple neck with integral fingerboard to a two-piece construction that had a separate rosewood playing surface. This revision had first appeared the previous year on the Jazzmaster model and would soon be applied across the Fender line. The amendment also affected the way the truss-rod was installed, and the maple neck accordingly no longer needed the contrasting 'skunk stripe' fillet along the back. The construction of the rosewood cap varied over the next three years as Fender continued to devise the ideal combination of the two timbers. Until mid 1962, the fingerboard had a flat base (leading to its later 'slab board' nickname), and it then changed to a curve that matched the top surface radius. After about a year, the amount of rosewood was thinned down to almost veneer-like proportions, and this style remained until the early 80s.

For the first five years of Strat production, the pickguard was made from a single-layer white plastic, although some examples had an anodized aluminum alternative. By mid '59, the standard material had switched to a white/black/white laminated plastic, now using eleven securing screws rather than the previous eight.

When CBS assumed control of the company in 1965, the new owner instigated a few minor modifications of its own, but again the Stratocaster was essentially left alone – further proof that Fender more or less got it right the first time.

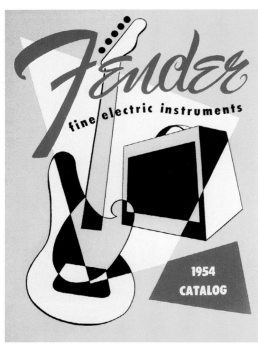

■ **1954** catalog

92

STRATOCASTER (pre-CBS) 1954–65

21 frets, small headstock, one string guide,
four-screw neckplate, three controls.

- **Neck:** fretted maple (maple with rosewood
  fingerboard from 1959); truss-rod adjuster
  at body end; one string-guide.
- **Body:** sunburst or colors.
- **Electronics:** three white six-polepiece pickups
  (bridge pickup angled). Three controls (volume,
  two tone) and three-way selector, all on pickguard;
  jack in body face.
- **Hardware:** eight-screw white plastic or anodized
  metal pickguard (11-screw white or tortoiseshell
  laminated plastic from 1959). Six-saddle small
  bridge with through-body stringing or six-pivot
  bridge/vibrato unit.

Some examples were fitted with gold-plated hardware.
(This gold-plated hardware option coupled with
a blonde-finish body became unofficially known
as the Mary Kaye model.)

■ **1954** Stratocaster

STRATOCASTER 1954

1954 press advertisement

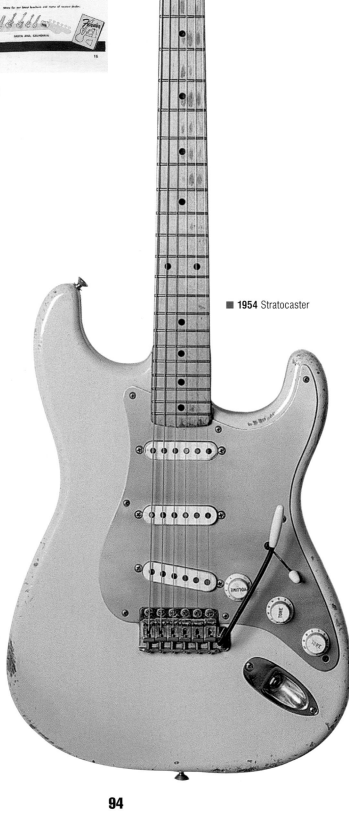

1954 Stratocaster

STRATOCASTER
1954-1957

1956-57 catalog

STRATOCASTER
1954-1957

1957 Stratocaster

STRATOCASTER (pre-CBS) 1958–63
As STRATOCASTER PRE CBS (see 1954 listing).
Now available in custom colors.

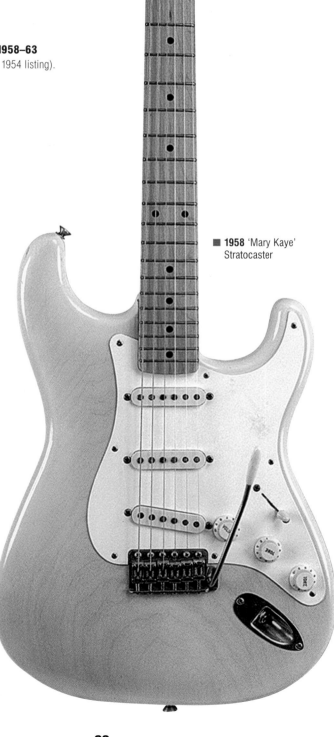

■ **1958** 'Mary Kaye'
Stratocaster

■ **1958** Stratocaster

■ **1958** Stratocaster

■ **1958** Stratocaster

STRATOCASTER (pre-CBS) 1954–65

21 frets, small headstock, one string guide,
four-screw neckplate, three controls.

- **Neck:** fretted maple (maple with rosewood
  fingerboard from 1959); truss-rod adjuster
  at body end; one string-guide.
- **Body:** sunburst or colors.
- **Electronics:** three white six-polepiece pickups
  (bridge pickup angled). Three controls (volume,
  two tone) and three-way selector, all on pickguard;
  jack in body face.
- **Hardware:** eight-screw white plastic or anodized
  metal pickguard (11-screw white or tortoiseshell
  laminated plastic from 1959). Six-saddle small
  bridge with through-body stringing or six-pivot
  bridge/vibrato unit.

Some examples were fitted with gold-plated hardware.
(This gold-plated hardware option coupled with
a blond-finish body became unofficially known as
the Mary Kaye model.)

■ **1959** Stratocaster

STRATOCASTER 1959

■ **1959** Stratocaster

■ **1959** Stratocaster

■ **1959** Stratocaster

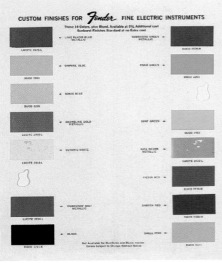

■ **1961** custom color chart

STRATOCASTER (pre-CBS) 1958–63

As STRATOCASTER PRE CBS (see 1954 listing).
Now available in custom colors with official color chart.
*First optional neck widths available from 1962
(A,B,C or D, narrow to wide).*

■ **1961** Stratocaster owned
by Rory Gallagher

STRATOCASTER
1961-1963

■ **1962** Stratocaster

■ **1962** Stratocaster

■ **1963** Stratocaster

101

STRATOCASTER (pre-CBS) 1958–63

As STRATOCASTER PRE CBS (see 1954 listing).
In 1963 the color Shell Pink was dropped as
an option and Candy Apple Red Metallic added
to the official color chart.

■ **1964** Stratocaster owned and
painted by George Harrison

STRATOCASTER
1963-1965

1965-66 catalog

1965 letterhead

1965 Stratocaster

THE CBS YEARS

At the very start of January 1965, Fender was sold to the enormous Columbia Broadcasting System Inc for a sum of $13 million, which was far and away the highest price paid for a musical instrument manufacturer to date. When CBS took over, sales were booming, prospects were rosy, and the financial rewards rapidly became apparent, with Fender's income almost doubling during that initial year. At first, CBS seemed content simply to invest money, but the new regime soon started introducing numerous organizational changes, although during the early period most Fender products were left substantially alone.

It wasn't considered as such at the time, but the sale created an easy delineation for players and collectors, giving birth to the 'pre-CBS' tag that forever after has been the hallmark of some of the most desirable Fender guitars and amplifiers. It so happens, however, that some of the changes recognizable as 'CBS' had actually been launched in the previous year.

In Summer 1964, the Stratocaster was given a more modern-looking Fender logo, first seen on the Jaguar model introduced two years earlier. In contrast, the regular Telecasters retained the thinner, old-style "spaghetti" logo, right into 1967. By the end of 1965, the Strat's headstock was enlarged considerably, becoming the wider design that is so recognizable now as marking out examples from the late 60s and 70s.

The headstock became thicker on most models, but with the Stratocaster this extra depth tended to emphasize the less-streamlined looks of an already increased outline. Appearances aside, the additional mass all round had a practical benefit, as it helped to reduce twisting induced by string tension, something that the Strat's earlier, slimmer style seemed to suffer. The problem was certainly less common on the already sizeable Jazzmaster and Jaguar headstocks, while the Telecaster's different shape put more wood in the middle where it mattered and prevented such stress-related warping.

One obvious alteration made by CBS across the electric instrument catalog concerned the neckplate. From 1965, this carried a stamped backward 'F', providing us with a very visible pointer to the company's change of ownership. The same logo appeared on the angled casings of the tuners that replaced the standard Kluson Deluxe type in 1967. The Tele and Strat generally escaped the switch elsewhere to a bound fingerboard, although rare examples do exist. The two classic six-string models also managed to avoid the accompanying move from position dots to blocks that soon followed on other models.

Since 1959, all Fenders had featured a rosewood fingerboard rather than maple, although the company continued to offer maple on a strictly limited custom-order basis – and now this too had a separate fretboard. In 1967, CBS reinstated maple as an official option, and three years later Fender reverted to the original one-piece maple construction with integral fingerboard.

Amplifiers too changed only gradually. Although the company name under the model name on the front control panel changed from Fender Electric Instrument Co (sometimes just 'Fender Elect Inst Co' where space was tight) to Fender Musical Instruments around the time of the CBS sale, the now-legendary blackface control panel remained until 1968, when a silver control panel was introduced to replace it.

The design and construction of both guitars and amps changed only gradually, too, a fact that has more recently been recognized by players and has helped early CBS-era guitars and amps to become quite collectable.

■ **1966-67** catalog

STRATOCASTER (CBS Sixties) 1965–71

21 frets, enlarged headstock, one string-guide,
four-screw neckplate, three controls.

- **Neck:** maple with rosewood fingerboard
  (maple option 1967–69, replaced by fretted
  maple from 1969); truss-rod adjuster at body end;
  one string-guide; enlarged headstock.
- **Body:** sunburst or colors.
- **Electronics:** three white six-polepiece pickups
  (bridge pickup angled); three controls (volume,
  two tone) and three-way selector, all on pickguard;
  jack in body face.
- **Hardware:** 11-screw white or tortoiseshell
  laminated plastic pickguard (only white from 1967);
  six-saddle small bridge with through-body stringing
  or six-pivot bridge/vibrato unit.

Early examples with STRATOCASTER PRE-CBS small
headstock (see 1954 listing). Some examples with
bound rosewood fingerboard.

STRATOCASTER 1965

■ **1965** Stratocaster

STRATOCASTER 1965-1966

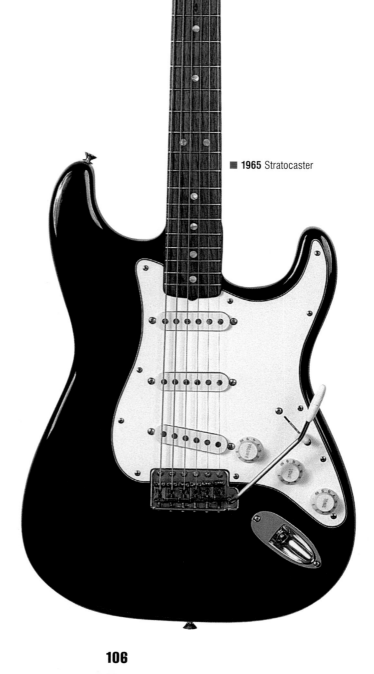

■ **1965** Stratocaster

■ **1965** Stratocaster

■ **1966** Stratocaster

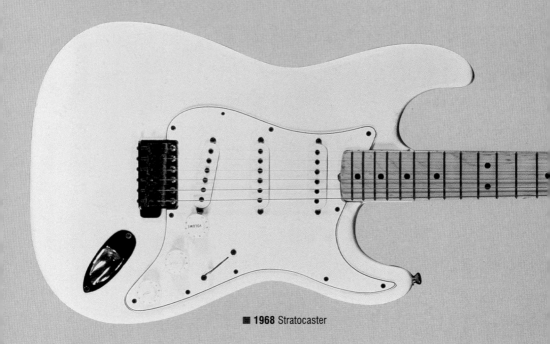

■ **1968** Stratocaster

Think Fender

Price List

FENDER GUITARS, AMPLIFIERS & ACCESSORIES
JANUARY 1970

■ **1971** price list

■ **1971** Stratocaster

STRATOCASTER 1971-1973

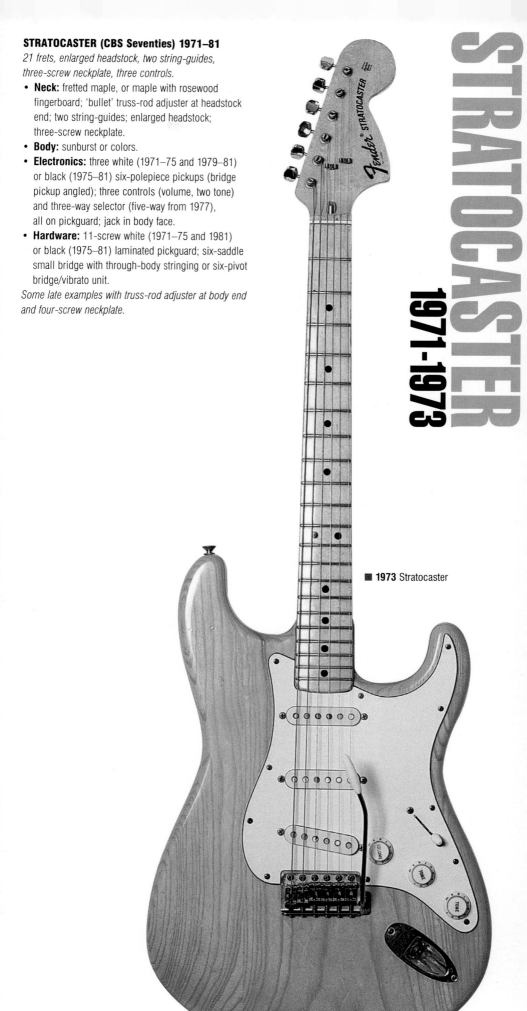

STRATOCASTER (CBS Seventies) 1971–81

*21 frets, enlarged headstock, two string-guides,
three-screw neckplate, three controls.*

- **Neck:** fretted maple, or maple with rosewood
  fingerboard; 'bullet' truss-rod adjuster at headstock
  end; two string-guides; enlarged headstock;
  three-screw neckplate.
- **Body:** sunburst or colors.
- **Electronics:** three white (1971–75 and 1979–81)
  or black (1975–81) six-polepiece pickups (bridge
  pickup angled); three controls (volume, two tone)
  and three-way selector (five-way from 1977),
  all on pickguard; jack in body face.
- **Hardware:** 11-screw white (1971–75 and 1981)
  or black (1975–81) laminated pickguard; six-saddle
  small bridge with through-body stringing or six-pivot
  bridge/vibrato unit.

*Some late examples with truss-rod adjuster at body end
and four-screw neckplate.*

STRATOCASTER 1971-1973

■ **1973** Stratocaster

AND THEN THERE WERE THREE

In mid 1971, the Stratocaster became the subject of further changes to construction and components when the new tilt-neck design was adopted. This also incorporated a three-screw neck attachment to replace the former four-screw fitting, and there was now a truss-rod adjuster in the form of a 'bullet' located on the headstock, just behind the nut.

The 'three-bolt neck' is often derided now as indicative of the gradual downward spiral in the quality of Fender instruments under CBS during the 70s. Nevertheless, the tilt-neck system was devised by Leo Fender. In principle, it's an ingenious idea. The neck is secured by two conventional screws, while the third is a bolt. The bolt combines with a sturdy grub-screw sited in the heel block of the body to allow fine adjustment of the neck angle, without the need to physically remove the neck and insert any spacing shims. Fender offered further convenience with a new headstock-mounted truss-rod adjuster, and this again eliminated the need to loosen the neck, which had previously been necessary to reach the recessed adjustment-nut hidden away at the body end of the neck.

Regardless of these apparently user-friendly improvements, it's generally accepted that, while sales figures went up, the changes placed increasing pressure on mass production and, along with other financial considerations, caused a general downturn in the build quality of the Stratocaster and other Fender models. This was the case in the early 70s and, more particularly, during the latter part of that decade. The loss of one neck screw and the 'bullet' truss-rod have come to symbolize this decline.

CBS didn't intentionally cut down on quality, but the corporation dealt with the problems of ever-growing demand by favoring solutions offered by financial people rather than manufacturing staff. This meant that while Fender's new features may have been sound in principle, the cost-cutting measures caused problems in practice. One seemingly simple and minor manufacturing amendment instigated for economic reasons would cause significant repercussions.

CBS decided that enlarging the snug-fit body holes for the neck-fixing screws could speed up production. The modification was duly made, and while assembly time was indeed reduced as forecast, the neck now moved about in its moorings – no matter how many screws were used. This alone provoked complaints from many players, but CBS either didn't care or didn't consider them important enough to make changes. Consequently, the three-bolt system gained a bad reputation – although Leo Fender's later G&L instruments confirmed it could work very well. The standard Telecaster did not share this flaw of the Strat of the period, but it was employed on a succession of Tele variations introduced during the decade. The revised Thinline Telecaster, Telecaster Custom, and Telecaster Deluxe all enjoyed the system's dubious benefits, as did another new six-string, the semi-acoustic Starcaster.

Other alterations inflicted on the Strat in the early 70s served to take the instrument further away from its pre-CBS roots. The two-part vibrato unit, with its separate screwed-on steel inertia block, was superseded in 1971 by a single-piece die-cast equivalent made of Mazac. This same material was used for the accompanying bridge saddles that replaced the vintage bent-steel saddles. In 1974, the Strat's single-coil pickups were equipped with equal-height polepieces rather than the staggered formation formerly employed.

On top of all this, Fender's use of 'thick skin' polyester paint in place of the thinner nitro-cellulose finishes of the pre- and early-CBS years made the guitars feel different. This was more apparent on instruments with maple fingerboards, where the heavily-applied plastic lacquer threatened to almost obscure the frets, in a way that was certainly not finger-friendly. Even the sound could be affected, especially when the neck heel and body pocket received enough paint to inhibit sonic transfer between these components, dulling tone and reducing inherent sustain.

RHINESTONE STRATOCASTER 1975

Based on STRATOCASTER CBS SEVENTIES (see 1971 listing) but with replacement bonded metal and fibreglass body by British sculptor Jon Douglas, specially ordered by Fender's UK agent in 1975. Front has heavy-relief floral leaf scroll design, inset with rhinestones on some examples. Very small quantity produced. Unauthorized 1990s versions are identifiable by a plaque on back of body.

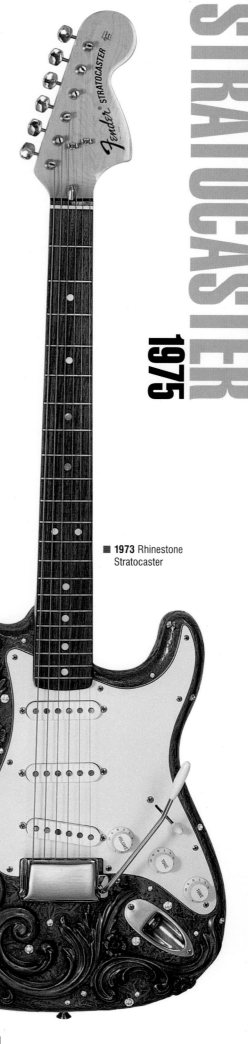

■ **1973** Rhinestone Stratocaster

■ **1977** press advertisement

ANTIGUA STRATOCASTER 1977–79

As STRATOCASTER CBS SEVENTIES
(see 1971 listing)
but with white/brown shaded body finish and
matching-color laminated plastic pickguard.

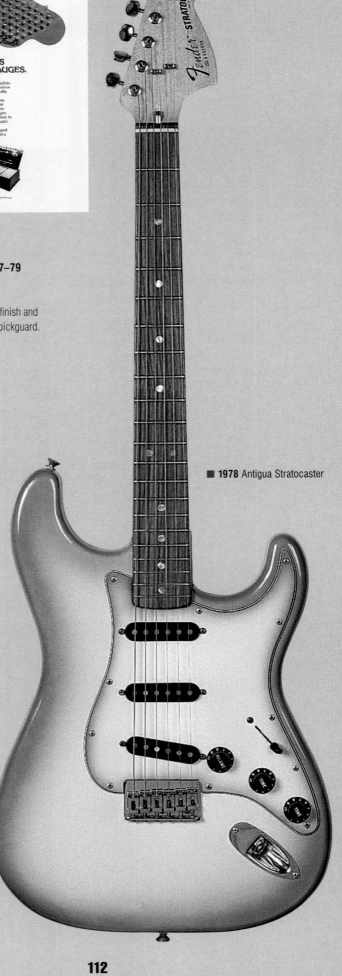

■ **1978** Antigua Stratocaster

STRATOCASTER
1977-1979

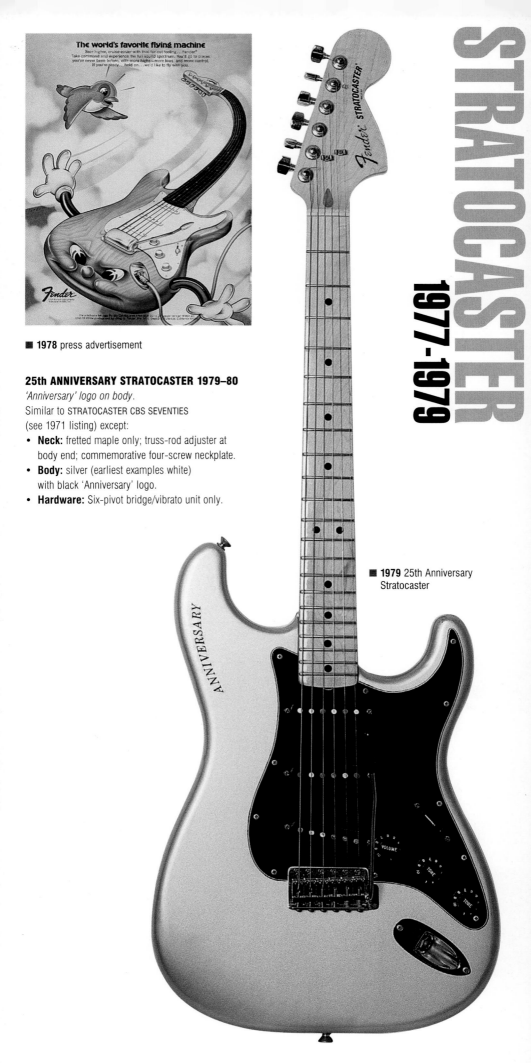

■ **1978** press advertisement

25th ANNIVERSARY STRATOCASTER 1979–80
'Anniversary' logo on body.
Similar to STRATOCASTER CBS SEVENTIES
(see 1971 listing) except:

• **Neck:** fretted maple only; truss-rod adjuster at
  body end; commemorative four-screw neckplate.
• **Body:** silver (earliest examples white)
  with black 'Anniversary' logo.
• **Hardware:** Six-pivot bridge/vibrato unit only.

■ **1979** 25th Anniversary
Stratocaster

■ **1981** catalog

HENDRIX STRATOCASTER 1980

Six-pivot vibrato, large inverted headstock.

- **Neck:** fretted maple; truss-rod adjuster at body
  end; two string-guides; large reverse headstock;
  four-screw neckplate.
- **Body:** with additional front contouring; white only.
- **Electronics:** three white six-polepiece pickups
  (bridge pickup angled); three controls (volume,
  two tone) and five-way selector, all on pickguard;
  jack in body face.
- **Hardware:** 11-screw white laminated plastic
  pickguard; six-pivot bridge/vibrato unit.
Only 25 produced.

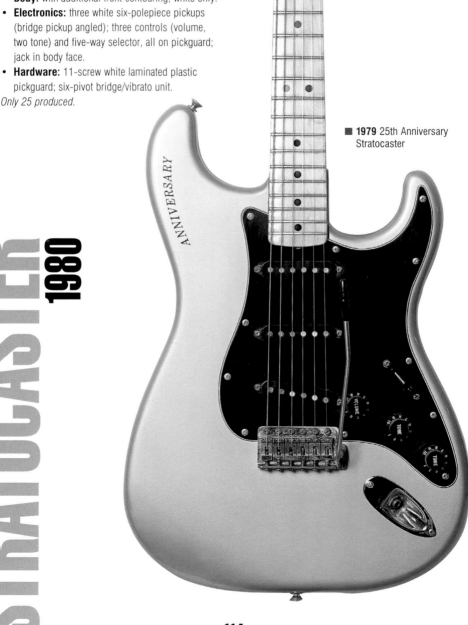

■ **1979** 25th Anniversary
Stratocaster

STRATOCASTER 1980

114

STRAT 1980–83

Six-pivot vibrato, 'Strat' logo on headstock.

- **Neck:** fretted maple, or maple with rosewood fingerboard; truss-rod adjuster at body end; two string-guides; 'Strat' logo on re-styled headstock with face matching body color.
- **Body:** red, blue, or white.
- **Electronics:** three white six-polepiece pickups (bridge pickup angled); three controls (volume, tone, two-way rotary switch) and five-way selector, all situated on the guitar's pickguard; jack in body face.
- **Hardware:** gold-plated brass (early examples have chrome machine heads and polished brass hardware); 11-screw white laminated plastic pickguard; redesigned six-pivot bridge-and-vibrato unit.

■ **1980** Strat

EASTERN PROMISE

During the late 70s and early 80s, well-made but inexpensive Japanese-made copies of Fender guitars were taking an increasingly big bite from the company's sales in the U.S. and elsewhere around the world. Fender was finally forced to acknowledge this threat and, after failing to come up with viable home-grown competition of its own, the company opted for an 'if you can't beat them, join them' approach, making major moves to play the competition at its own game. With this aim in mind, Fender commenced negotiations with two major Japanese distributors, Kanda Shokai and Yamano Music. The resulting Fender Japan company was established in March 1982. This joint East-West venture would last until early 2005.

Various Japanese manufacturers were approached to produce the guitars for this new company, and ironically enough these included some of those responsible for creating Fender's greatest competition with the copy guitars, such as Tokai and Kawai. Fujigen was the final choice. This factory was best known in the West for instruments bearing the Ibanez brand, among many others. Fujigen's products naturally included more than a few Fender copies, but now the factory was given the go-ahead to make official its art of imitation.

The original deal was that these licensed lookalikes were to be manufactured solely for the Japanese market, but Fender's European agents realized these lower-price equivalents would prove effective against the imported opposition from other Japanese makers. In a move not sanctioned by the parent company, vintage-style Fenders made by Fender Japan appeared on the U.K. market in 1982, creating an immediate impact and equally instant confusion, as they carried no clue to their country of origin. These repros also beat Fender U.S. to the punch, as the American firm had intended to introduce its own vintage reissue line in 1982, but production problems caused that launch to be postponed until the following year. This was not received well at Fender in America, but the company could not deny the obvious commercial potential involved, and so it quickly devised a solution in the form of the Squier brand. Initially intended for use on all electrics from Fender Japan, the name was taken from V. C. Squier, a Michigan-based string-making company that Fender had acquired back in 1965. The new logo started as a subtle addition to the headstock, with the Fender name still occupying pride of place, but the order was soon reversed. From 1983, instruments employed the Squier brand in large letters, while a suitably small but all-important suffix, 'by Fender,' was included underneath.

Copies had to be Squiers, but all-new Japanese electrics could carry the Fender name. Introduced in 1984, the Master series comprised the distinctly Gibson-flavored Flame and Esprit semi-solids plus big-bodied archtop-acoustics designed in collaboration with renowned U.S. luthier Jimmy D'Aquisto. Despite their undeniable high quality, these un-Fender-like instruments failed to attract much interest and lasted only a year.

Following Fender's change of ownership in 1985, the new company's marketing policies were significantly changed. Directly following the CBS sale, the entire Fender U.S. catalog was supplied by Far Eastern associates, because American manufacturing had yet to be re-established. Along with models that targeted the modern market, the Japanese-made versions of old favorites were once again available worldwide as proper Fenders, offered as more expensive alternatives to equivalents in the ongoing Squier line.

The great success enjoyed by both brands was subsequently echoed by an ever-expanding choice of Japanese-made examples. These included a comprehensive range of reissues, plus numerous new interpretations of established designs, covering all quality levels and price-points. Many models were reserved for the home Japanese market only, as those made for official export were consistently fewer and often comparatively sporadic.

This continued to be the case until 2005, when Fender Japan became an entirely autonomous entity. From that time, even fewer instruments were officially available elsewhere in the world, and Japanese products made diminishing contributions to the Fender U.S. catalog. Combined with continuing demand, this scarcity has since led to a trade in 'gray imports,' where various independent distributors outside Japan sell the most desirable but otherwise unobtainable instruments from the Fender Japan lines around the world.

1983 press advertisement

GOLD/GOLD STRATOCASTER 1981–83
Six-pivot vibrato, gold body and hardware.
Similar to STRAT (see 1980 listing) except:
- **Neck:** fretted maple only; 'Stratocaster'
  logo on headstock.
- **Body:** gold only; three controls
  (volume, two tone) and five-way selector.
- **Hardware:** gold-plated; normal-type
  six-pivot bridge/vibrato unit.
Some examples with pearl fingerboard
position markers.

1981 Gold/
Gold Stratocaster

INTERNATIONAL COLOR STRATOCASTER 1981
As STRATOCASTER of the period but with special
color finishes, white laminated plastic pickguard,
and black-plated pickguard screws.

■ **1981** International Color
Stratocaster

STRATOCASTER 1981

■ **1981** International Color Stratocaster

■ **1981** International Color Stratocaster

■ **1981** International Color Stratocaster

STRATOCASTER STANDARD (first version) 1981–83

21 frets, small headstock, two string-guides, four-screw neckplate, three controls.

- **Neck:** fretted maple, or maple with rosewood fingerboard; truss-rod adjuster at body end; two string-guides; small headstock.
- **Body:** sunburst or colors.
- **Electronics:** three white six-polepiece pickups (bridge pickup angled); three controls (volume, two tone) and five-way selector, all on pickguard; jack in body face.
- **Hardware:** 11-screw white or black laminated plastic pickguard; six-saddle small bridge with through-body stringing or six-pivot bridge/ vibrato unit.

■ **1981** Stratocaster signed by Hank Marvin

STRATOCASTER 1981-1982

WALNUT STRAT 1981–83

As STRAT (see 1980 listing) but with fretted walnut neck (some with walnut neck and ebony fingerboard), walnut body, black laminated plastic pickguard, and gold-plated hardware.

SQUIER SERIES '57 STRATOCASTER (MIJ) 1982–83

Replica of 1957-period U.S. original (see STRATOCASTER PRE-CBS 1954 listing) with small Squier Series logo on headstock 1982–83. Also version with six-saddle bridge and through-body stringing. Known as 50s STRATOCASTER from 1985 onward. Sold under the Squier brandname (1983–85) and new Fender version introduced in 1985, although Japanese market manufacture continuous since 1982. Also Foto Flame fake figured wood finish option (1992–94).

SQUIER SERIES '62 STRATOCASTER (MIJ) 1982–83

Replica of 1962-period U.S. original (see STRATOCASTER PRE-CBS 1954 listing) with small Squier Series logo on headstock 1982–83. Also version with six-saddle bridge and through-body stringing. Known as 60s STRATOCASTER from 1985 onward. Sold under the Squier brandname (1983–85) and new Fender version introduced in 1985, although Japanese market manufacture continuous since 1982. Also Foto Flame fake figured wood finish option (1992–94).

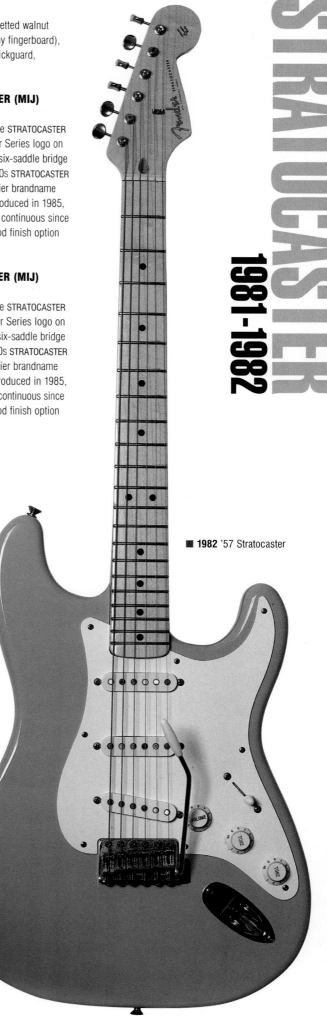

STRATOCASTER 1981-1982

■ **1982** '57 Stratocaster

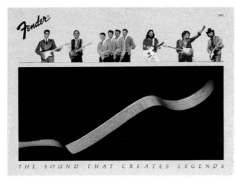

■ **1983** catalog

ELITE STRATOCASTER 1983–84
Single-pivot vibrato, three pushbutton switches.
- **Neck:** fretted maple, or maple with rosewood fingerboard; truss-rod adjuster at headstock end; two string-guides.
- **Body:** sunburst or colors.
- **Electronics:** three white plain-top pickups (bridge pickup angled); three controls (volume, two tone) and three pushbutton selectors, all on pickguard; side-mounted jack; active circuit.
- **Hardware:** 11-screw white laminated plastic pickguard; redesigned six-saddle bridge/tailpiece or single-pivot bridge/vibrato unit.

STRATOCASTER STANDARD (second version) 1983–84
21 frets, small headstock, two string-guides, four-screw neckplate, two controls.
- **Neck:** fretted maple only; truss-rod adjuster at headstock end; two string-guides; small headstock.
- **Body:** sunburst or colors; also in red, yellow, or blue streaked finish, unofficially known as BOWLING BALL OR MARBLE STRATOCASTER (1984).

■ **1983** Elite Stratocaster

STRATOCASTER 1983

1995 press advertisement

1987 American Standard Stratocaster

VINTAGE REISSUES AND THE DECLINE OF CBS

Although the 1970s are usually thought of as the CBS years, Fender remained under the Columbia Broadcasting System's ownership until early 1985, when the company was sold to a group of investors headed by William Schultz, president of Fender Musical Instruments, and including Dan Smith and other Fender managers.

Smith in particular had recognized the decline in quality that had resulted from CBS's failure to invest in Fender from the late 1970s onward. He also perceived that the best way forward for the company might involve, in some measure, a lingering look into the rearview mirror.

While Fender was still a part of CBS, and virtually simultaneous to the move to develop a more affordable Japan-made line for the brand, Smith and the Fender R&D team began studying and measuring vintage models. Toward the end of 1982 they announced the Vintage Reissue Series. The '52 Telecaster, '57 Stratocaster, and '62 Stratocaster went into regular production in 1983 and were very well received.

Purists were swift to point out certain inconsistencies between the reissues and original vintage examples from the respective periods – unlikely neck profiles (back shapes), wrongly spaced 12th-fret position markers, a lack of 'clay' dots and 'green' celluloid pickguard on the '62 model – but overall these new instruments were closer to the guitars that Fender had produced 20 years ago and better than anything that had been available for, well, 20 years.

When Schultz, Smith, and the other managers and investors purchased Fender they didn't have the funds to also purchase the enormous Fullerton factory. So for approximately the first three-quarters of 1985 Fender guitars were made in Japan only, until the new factory in Corona, CA, came online in October 1985. When it did, the newly popular Vintage Reissues were the first guitars to go into production, at which time Fender took the opportunity to improve some of the finer points to make these guitars more vintage-correct.

A newly revitalized, independently owned Fender Musical Instruments Corp went on to introduce the American Standard Stratocaster in late 1986 and the Strat Plus in 1987. Since that time the company has gone from strength to strength with very few major hiccups, regaining both the quality and the reputation that it enjoyed in the first two decades of its existence.

■ **1988** catalog

GOLD ELITE STRATOCASTER 1983–84

As ELITE STRATOCASTER listing this year but with pearl tuner buttons and gold-plated hardware.

- **Electronics:** three white six-polepiece pickups (bridge pickup angled); two controls (volume, tone) and jack, all on pickguard.
- **Hardware:** 12-screw white plastic pickguard; re-designed six-saddle bridge/tailpiece or single-pivot bridge/vibrato unit.

WALNUT ELITE STRATOCASTER 1983–84

As ELITE STRATOCASTER listing this year but with walnut neck and ebony fingerboard, walnut body, pearl tuner buttons, and gold-plated hardware.

'57 STRATOCASTER 1983–85, 86–98

Replica of 1957-period original (see 1954 listing).

'62 STRATOCASTER 1983–85, 86–98

Replica of 1962-period original (see 1954 listing).

BOWLING BALL STRATOCASTER 1984

Also known as Marble Stratocaster.
See STRATOCASTER STANDARD SECOND VERSION 1983 listing.

CONTEMPORARY STRATOCASTER (MIJ) (first type) 1985–87

One black humbucker, normal logo, black neck.

- **Neck:** maple with rosewood fingerboard; 22 frets; truss-rod adjuster at headstock end; string-clamp; black neck.
- **Body:** various colors.
- **Electronics:** one black coverless humbucker (at bridge); one control (volume) on body; side-mounted jack.
- **Hardware:** black-plated; no pickguard; two-pivot bridge/vibrato unit.

CONTEMPORARY STRATOCASTER (MIJ) (second type) 1985–87

Two black humbuckers, black neck.
Similar to CONTEMPORARY STRATOCASTER FIRST TYPE (see previous listing) except:

- **Electronics:** two black coverless humbuckers; two controls (volume, tone) and three-way selector, all on pickguard.
- **Hardware:** 11-screw black plastic pickguard.

CONTEMPORARY STRATOCASTER (MIJ) (third type) 1985–87

Two black single-coils and one black humbucker, black neck.
Similar to CONTEMPORARY STRATOCASTER FIRST TYPE (see earlier listing this year) except:

- **Electronics:** two black six-polepiece pickups and one black coverless humbucker (at bridge); two controls (volume, tone), five-way selector and coil-switch, all on pickguard.
- **Hardware:** 11-screw black plastic pickguard.

CONTEMPORARY STRATOCASTER (MIJ) (fourth type) 1985–87

Lever-type locking nut, two black single-coils and one black coverless humbucker.
Similar to CONTEMPORARY STRATOCASTER FIRST TYPE (see earlier listing this year) except:

- **Neck:** two string-guides; lever-type locking nut; black-face headstock.
- **Electronics:** two black six-polepiece pickups and one black coverless humbucker (at bridge); two controls (volume, tone), five-way selector and coil-switch, all on pickguard.
- **Hardware:** chrome-plated; 11-screw black plastic pickguard.

CONTEMPORARY STRATOCASTER DELUXE (MIJ) (first type) 1985–87

Two black cover humbuckers, normal color neck.
Similar to CONTEMPORARY STRATOCASTER FIRST TYPE (see earlier listing this year) except:

- **Neck:** two string-guides; lever-type locking nut; black-face headstock.
- **Electronics:** two black cover humbuckers; two controls (volume, tone), three-way selector and coil-switch, all on pickguard.
- **Hardware:** chrome-plated; 11-screw black plastic pickguard.

CONTEMPORARY STRATOCASTER DELUXE (MIJ) (second type) 1985–87

Two black single-coils and one black covered humbucker.
Similar to CONTEMPORARY STRATOCASTER FIRST TYPE (see earlier listing this year) except:

- **Neck:** two string-guides; lever-type locking nut; black-face headstock.
- **Electronics:** two black six-polepiece pickups and one black cover humbucker (at bridge); two controls (volume, tone), five-way selector and coil-switch, all on pickguard.
- **Hardware:** chrome-plated; 11-screw black plastic pickguard.

COST CUTTING EXERCISES

Saving money during manufacturing was important at Fender from the earliest days. Most of the changes that Leo and his team devised were made with this aim in mind rather than any particular need to improve quality. Financial survival was always the prime consideration – but build standards did not suffer during the company's first 15 years of electric guitar production.

The same can be said about the initial period under the aegis of CBS: comparatively little changed in the way the instruments were made. The first real indications of accountancy exerting unwelcome influence over Fender's production processes did not occur until the mid 70s. By this time, guitar sales were booming and the pressure was on to increase output with ever-faster methods of manufacturing. Fender began to cut corners in the interests of efficiency, and certain design changes, originally intended as genuine improvements, were unwise or were poorly implemented, causing subsequent problems with performance and numerous complaints.

The company also began to alter body shapes for the worse, with the Telecaster assuming an increasingly clumsy outline, while the Strat's smoothly streamlined contours progressively diminished during the decade, becoming especially poor by the start of the 80s. Shoddy selection of body woods meant that instrument weight often exceeded acceptable proportions, and too much thrift when sourcing components resulted in inferior pickups and other parts.

This downturn in quality was allied to a seeming inability or even unwillingness to rectify matters. The combination certainly contributed to dwindling sales, a situation not helped by ever-increasing competition from the Far East. CBS finally realized something had to be done to stop the process and restore Fender's by-now tarnished reputation. New personnel with the necessary know-how were brought in, including Bill Schultz and Dan Smith, recruited from Yamaha's U.S. musical instrument division and appointed respectively as Fender's president and electric-guitar marketing director.

The situation at the Fender factory was worse than these newcomers imagined and required a radical re-think to put matters right after the series of bad decisions made during the 70s. Some improvements soon became apparent, including a welcome return to earlier design ideas, such as the Stratocaster's small headstock and original four-bolt neck. However, the Stratocaster and the Telecaster were soon on the receiving end of major changes, made with the company's cost-consciousness still very much in evidence.

In 1983, Fender decided that the regular version of both models should be replaced by two alternatives: the budget-conscious Standard equivalent and the upscale Elite. The Elites ventured into novel design territory with the hope of attracting a wider audience that would appreciate such differences. The Standard Telecaster and Stratocaster certainly lived up to their names: both took a simplified approach that resulted in a basic interpretation.

On the Tele, the most obvious departure from the original design was that the strings were anchored along the rear of the bridgeplate rather than going through the body. To keep costs down, the Standard Strat was taken even further from traditional styling, losing the classic recessed jackplate and the second tone control, which was replaced by the relocated output jack. An all-new vibrato unit employed twin tension-springs positioned beneath the pickguard. This revised arrangement saved the expense and time involved in routing the familiar rear body cavity of earlier Strats, but it made setting up more difficult, especially as the system suffered from inherent operational flaws. Unsurprisingly, both models were poorly received, and their lack of popularity played a part in the company's imminent commercial downfall.

■ **1985** Standard Stratocaster
(left-hand)

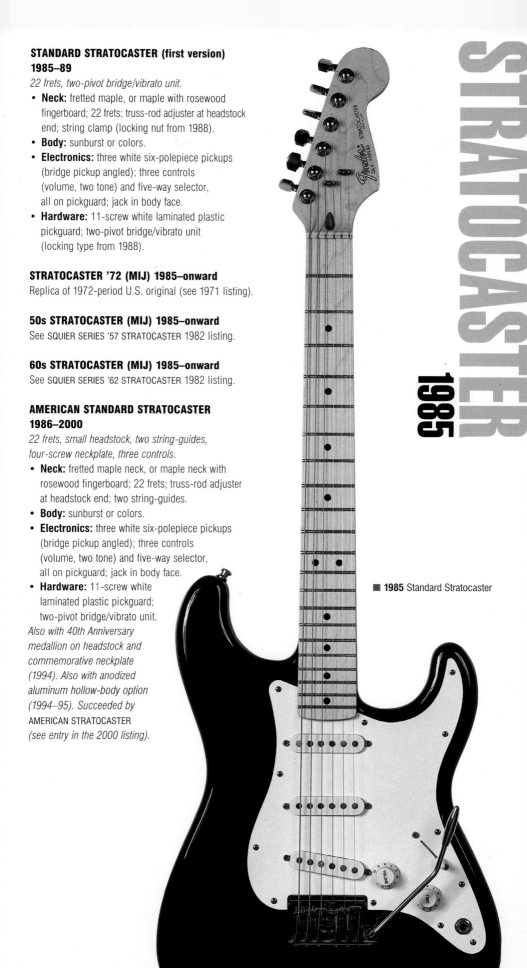

STANDARD STRATOCASTER (first version)
1985–89
22 frets, two-pivot bridge/vibrato unit.
- **Neck:** fretted maple, or maple with rosewood fingerboard; 22 frets; truss-rod adjuster at headstock end; string clamp (locking nut from 1988).
- **Body:** sunburst or colors.
- **Electronics:** three white six-polepiece pickups (bridge pickup angled); three controls (volume, two tone) and five-way selector, all on pickguard; jack in body face.
- **Hardware:** 11-screw white laminated plastic pickguard; two-pivot bridge/vibrato unit (locking type from 1988).

STRATOCASTER '72 (MIJ) 1985–onward
Replica of 1972-period U.S. original (see 1971 listing).

50s STRATOCASTER (MIJ) 1985–onward
See SQUIER SERIES '57 STRATOCASTER 1982 listing.

60s STRATOCASTER (MIJ) 1985–onward
See SQUIER SERIES '62 STRATOCASTER 1982 listing.

AMERICAN STANDARD STRATOCASTER
1986–2000
22 frets, small headstock, two string-guides, four-screw neckplate, three controls.
- **Neck:** fretted maple neck, or maple neck with rosewood fingerboard; 22 frets; truss-rod adjuster at headstock end; two string-guides.
- **Body:** sunburst or colors.
- **Electronics:** three white six-polepiece pickups (bridge pickup angled); three controls (volume, two tone) and five-way selector, all on pickguard; jack in body face.
- **Hardware:** 11-screw white laminated plastic pickguard; two-pivot bridge/vibrato unit.

Also with 40th Anniversary medallion on headstock and commemorative neckplate (1994). Also with anodized aluminum hollow-body option (1994–95). Succeeded by
AMERICAN STRATOCASTER
(see entry in the 2000 listing).

STRATOCASTER 1985

■ **1985** Standard Stratocaster

BLUE FLOWER STRATOCASTER (first version) (MIJ) 1988–93

Blue floral-pattern body finish, large headstock.
Similar to STRATOCASTER '72 (see 1985 listing) except:
- **Neck:** fretted maple only.
- **Body:** blue floral-pattern only.
- **Hardware:** 11-screw blue floral-pattern pickguard.

STRAT PLUS 1987–98

Two-pivot vibrato, no string-guides, three differing white plain-top pickups.
- **Neck:** fretted maple, or maple with rosewood fingerboard; 22 frets; truss-rod adjuster at headstock end; locking tuners; roller nut.
- **Body:** sunburst or colors.
- **Electronics:** three same-type white plain-top Lace Sensor pickups (bridge pickup angled); three controls (volume, two tone) and five-way selector, all on pickguard; jack in body face.
- **Hardware:** 11-screw white or white pearl laminated plastic pickguard; two-pivot bridge/ vibrato unit.

Also with anodized aluminum hollow body option (1994–95).

■ **1989** Blue Flower Stratocaster

STRATOCASTER 1988

■ **1988** catalog

ERIC CLAPTON STRATOCASTER (first version) 1988–2001
Signature on headstock, three white plain-top pickups, active circuit.
- **Neck:** fretted maple; 22 frets; truss-rod adjuster at headstock end; one string-guide; Eric Clapton signature on headstock.
- **Body:** various colors.
- **Electronics:** three white plain-top Lace Sensor pickups (bridge pickup angled); three controls (volume, two tone) and five-way selector, all on pickguard; jack in body face; active circuit.
- **Hardware:** eight-screw white plastic pickguard; six-pivot bridge/vibrato unit.

Earliest examples with 21 frets and/or mini-switch.

HM POWER STRAT (MIJ) (first type) 1988–89
One black humbucker, black-face headstock with large flamboyant 'Strat' logo.
- **Neck:** fretted maple, or maple with rosewood fingerboard; 25-inch scale, 24 frets; truss-rod adjuster at headstock end; locking nut; flamboyant 'Strat' logo on black-face headstock.
- **Body:** smaller; various colors.
- **Electronics:** one black coverless humbucker (at bridge); two controls (volume, tone) and coil-switch, all on body; side-mounted jack.
- **Hardware:** black-plated; no pickguard; two-pivot locking bridge/vibrato unit.

Some examples with 'International' Series logo on headstock.

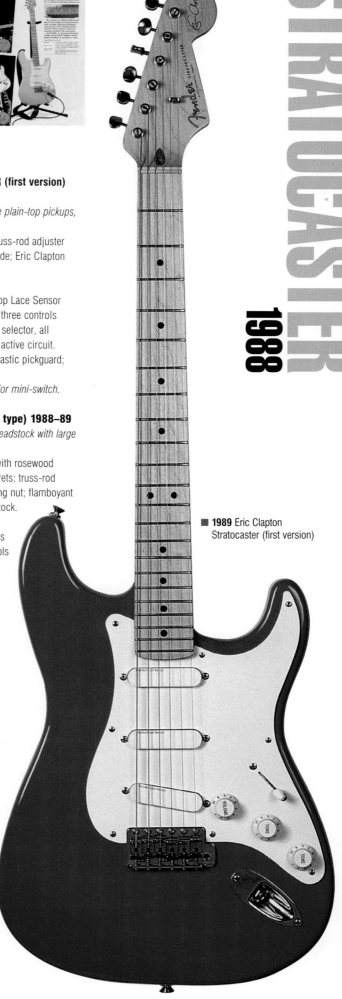

■ **1989** Eric Clapton Stratocaster (first version)

1988 catalog

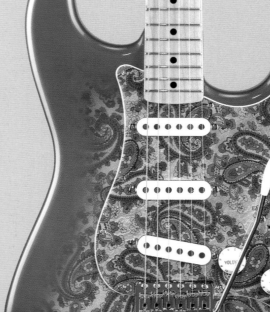

1988 Paisley Strat

STRATOCASTER 1988

PAISLEY STRATOCASTER (MIJ) 1988–onward

Pink paisley-pattern body finish.

Similar to STRATOCASTER '72 (see 1985 listing) except:

- **Neck:** fretted maple only.
- **Body:** pink paisley-pattern only.
- **Hardware:** 11-screw pink paisley-pattern pickguard.

**STANDARD STRATOCASTER (second version)
1988–91**

21 frets, two string-guides.

Similar to 50s STRATOCASTER and 60s STRATOCASTER
(see 1985 listings) except:

- **Neck:** two string-guides.

*Also version with six-saddle bridge and through-body
stringing.*

Previously sold under Squier brandname (1986–88).

Later, production moved to Mexico (see 1991 listing).

■ **1988** 'Mary Kaye'
Stratocaster

STRAT XII 12-string (MIJ) 1988-96

12-string headstock, offset-cutaway body.

- **Neck:** maple with rosewood fingerboard; 24.75-inch scale, 22 frets; truss-rod adjuster at body end; one 'bracket' string-guide; six-tuners-per-side headstock.
- **Body:** sunburst only
- **Electronics:** three white six-polepiece pickups (bridge pickup angled); three controls (volume, two tone) and five-way selector, all on pickguard; jack in body face.
- **Hardware:** 11-screw white laminated plastic pickguard; 12-saddle bridge with through-body stringing.

STRATOCASTER '68 (MIJ) 1988–onward

Replica of 1968-period U.S. original
(see STRATOCASTER CBS SIXTIES 1965 listing).

■ **1988** Strat XII

STRATOCASTER 1988

**YNGWIE MALMSTEEN STRATOCASTER
(first version) 1988–98**

Signature on small headstock, two-pivot vibrato.

- **Neck:** fretted maple, or maple with rosewood
  fingerboard, both with scalloping between frets;
  truss-rod adjuster at body end; one string-guide;
  brass nut; Yngwie Malmsteen signature on
  headstock.
- **Body:** red, white, or blue.
- **Electronics:** three white six-polepiece pickups
  (bridge pickup angled); three controls (volume,
  two tone) and five-way selector, all on pickguard;
  jack socket in body face.
- **Hardware:** 11-screw white laminated plastic
  pickguard; two-pivot bridge/vibrato unit.

STRATOCASTER

1988

■ **1988** Yngwie Malmsteen
Stratocaster

133

OVER THE BORDER

Like so many American manufacturers, Fender sought more affordable production in the late 1980s and early '90s. A short hop over the boarder to a plant in Ensenada, Baja California, Mexico, provided considerable savings on labor costs while still allowing easy control of quality and production from Fender's main U.S. factory in Corona, CA, less than 180 miles north. (The location also allowed for the comforting, if easily misunderstood, 'Made in Ensenada, Baja California' label of origin on the backs of many Mexican-made Fender products.)

Fender amps began rolling out of Mexico in 1989, and the factory produced its first guitars in 1991. Production ramped up from around 175 instruments a day in 1992 to some 600 a day by 1995 (following the rebuilding of the factory after a fire in 1994). By 1998, the Ensenada plant had a workforce approximately 40 per cent larger than that of the Corona plant and was producing nearly twice the number of instruments.

This capacity was put to good use. Mexican production took over the Standard line of Fender guitar models that had come from Japan since the early 1980s, while Japanese Fenders were relegated almost exclusively to domestic sales within Japan.

The most prominent Mexican models would take shape in 1999 as the Classic 50s, 60s, and 70s Stratocaster and Classic 50s Telecaster (and a Classic 60s Telecaster with rosewood fingerboard arrived in 2001).

Alongside these came numerous revised and modified models – such as the Tex-Mex Strat, Traditional Fat Strat, Deluxe Nashville Tele, and Deluxe Powerhouse Strat – and a pair of popular new retro models, the Toronado and Cyclone.

Meanwhile, in 1998 Fender U.S.A. opened a new state-of-the-art factory in Corona. Since the start of production at Corona in 1985, after the curtain fell on CBS's ownership, Fender's production facility had grown to encompass ten buildings spread around Corona, with a total of 115,000 square feet of space. The new 177,000-square-foot factory cost $20 million to build. It centralized production and offered room for expansion. In addition, the new factory included a finishing department with zero toxic emission, a boon to both environmental conservation and statutory compliance, given California's stringent environmental laws.

■ **1999** classic series press advertisement

1989 Double Neck
Stratocaster (Custom Shop)

AMERICAN STANDARD DELUXE STRATOCASTER 1989–90

Two pivot vibrato, two string-guides, three Lace Sensor pickups.
Similar to AMERICAN STANDARD STRATOCASTER (see 1986 listing) except:
• **Electronics:** three white plain top Lace Sensor pickups (bridge pickup angled).

HM STRAT (first type) 1989–90

Two-pivot locking vibrato system, two black single-coils and one black humbucker, black-face headstock.
• **Neck:** fretted maple, or maple with rosewood fingerboard; 25-inch scale, 24 frets; truss-rod adjuster at headstock end; locking nut; large flamboyant 'Strat' logo on black-face headstock.
• **Body:** smaller; various colors.
• **Electronics:** two black six-polepiece pickups and one black coverless humbucker (at bridge); three controls (volume, two tone), five-way selector and coil-switch, all situated on body; side-mounted jack.
• **Hardware:** black-plated; no pickguard; two-pivot locking bridge/vibrato unit.

ROBBEN FORD (MIJ) 1989–94

Name on truss-rod cover.
Similar to ESPRIT ULTRA (see 1984 listing) except:
• **Neck:** 'Robben Ford' on truss-rod cover.
• **Body:** sunburst, natural, or black.
• **Electronics:** two black coverless humbucker pickups.

SHORT-SCALE STRATOCASTER (MIJ) 1989–95

Two controls, 22 frets.
• **Neck:** fretted maple, or maple with rosewood fingerboard; 24-inch scale, 22 frets; truss-rod adjuster at headstock end; one string-guide.
• **Body:** sunburst or colors.
• **Electronics:** three white six-polepiece pickups (bridge pickup angled); two controls (volume, tone) and five-way selector, all on pickguard; jack in body face.
• **Hardware:** eight-screw white laminated plastic pickguard; two-pivot bridge/vibrato unit.

HM STRAT (second type) 1989–90

Two-pivot locking vibrato system, one angled black plain-top pickup and one black humbucker.
Similar to HM STRAT FIRST TYPE (see previous listing) except:
• **Electronics:** one angled black plain-top Lace Sensor and one black coverless humbucker (at bridge); two controls (volume, tone), three-way selector and coil-switch, all on body.
• **Hardware:** black laminated plastic pickguard.

HM STRAT (third type) 1989–90

Two-pivot locking vibrato system, two black humbuckers.
Similar to HM STRAT FIRST TYPE (see earlier listing this year) except:
• **Electronics:** two black two coverless humbuckers; two controls (volume, tone), three-way selector and coil-switch, all on body.

U.S. CONTEMPORARY STRATOCASTER 1989–91

Two-pivot locking vibrato system, two white single-coils and one white humbucker, straight-sided humbucker cut-out in pickguard.
• **Neck:** maple with rosewood fingerboard; 22 frets; truss-rod adjuster at headstock end; locking nut.
• **Body:** sunburst or colors.
• **Electronics:** two white six-polepiece pickups and one white coverless humbucker (at bridge); three controls (volume, two tone) and five-way selector, all on pickguard; jack in body face.
• **Hardware:** 11-screw white laminated plastic pickguard; two-pivot locking bridge/vibrato unit.

STRAT PLUS DELUXE 1989–98

Two-pivot vibrato, no string-guides,
three differing white plain-top pickup.
Similar to STRAT PLUS (see 1987 listing) except:

- **Electronics:** three differing white plain-top
  Lace Sensor pickups (bridge pickup angled).
- **Hardware:** 11-screw white, white pearl,
  or tortoiseshell laminated plastic pickguard;
  two-pivot bridge/vibrato unit.

Also with anodized aluminum hollow body option
(1994–95).

STRATOCASTER 1989

■ **1989** Strat Plus Deluxe

137

HM STRAT ULTRA 1990–92

Two-pivot locking vibrato system, four black plain-top pickups.

Similar to HM STRAT FIRST TYPE (see 1989 listing) except:
- **Neck:** ebony fingerboard with split-triangle markers.
- **Electronics:** four black plain-top Lace Sensor pickups (two at bridge).

HRR STRATOCASTER (MIJ) 1990–94

22 frets, three controls on pickguard with rectangular hole for humbucker, two pivot locking bridge/vibrato system.

- **Neck:** fretted maple, or maple with rosewood fingerboard; 22 frets; truss-rod adjuster at headstock end; single-bar string-guide; locking nut.
- **Body:** sunburst or colors.
- **Electronics:** two white six-polepiece pickups and one coverless humbucker (at bridge); three controls (volume, two tone) and five-way selector, all situated on the guitar's pickguard; jack in body face.
- **Hardware:** 11-screw white plastic or laminated plastic pickguard; two-pivot locking bridge/vibrato unit.

Also known as FLOYD ROSE HRR STRATOCASTER *(1992–94). Foto Flame fake figured wood finish option (1992–94).*

■ **1989** 35th Anniversary Stratocaster

STRAT ULTRA 1990–98

Two-pivot vibrato, no string-guides, four white
plain-top pickups (two at bridge), bolt-on neck.

- **Neck:** maple with ebony fingerboard;
  22 frets;truss-rod adjuster at headstock end;
  locking tuners; roller nut.
- **Body:** sunburst or colors.
- **Electronics:** four white plain-top Lace Sensor
  pickups (two at bridge); three controls (volume,
  two tone), five-way selector and coil-switch,
  all on pickguard; jack in body face.
- **Hardware:** 11-screw white or white pearl laminated
  plastic pickguard; two-pivot bridge/vibrato unit.

Also with anodized aluminum hollow body option
(1994–95).

STRATOCASTER 1990

■ **1989** HLE Stratocaster

HM STRAT (first type) (MIJ) 1991–92
Black-face headstock with 'stencil'-style Strat logo.
- **Neck:** fretted maple, or maple with rosewood fingerboard; 25.1-inch scale, 24 frets; truss-rod adjuster at headstock end; single-bar string-guide; locking nut; 'stencil'-style Strat logo on black-face headstock.
- **Body:** smaller; various colors.
- **Electronics:** two black six-polepiece pickups and one black coverless humbucker (at bridge); two controls (volume, tone) and five-way selector, all on body; side-mounted jack.
- **Hardware:** black-plated; no pickguard; two-pivot locking bridge/vibrato unit.

HM STRAT (second type) (MIJ) 1991–92
Drooped black-face headstock with long 'streamlined' Fender logo.
- **Neck:** fretted maple, or maple with rosewood fingerboard; 25.1-inch scale, 22 frets; truss-rod adjuster at headstock end; single-bar string-guide; locking nut; long 'streamlined' Fender logo on drooped black-face headstock.
- **Body:** smaller; various colors.
- **Electronics:** two black coverless humbuckers and one black six-polepiece pickup (in center); two controls (volume, tone) and five-way selector, all situated on the guitar's pickguard; side-mounted jack.
- **Hardware:** black-plated; eight-screw black laminated plastic pickguard; two-pivot locking bridge/vibrato unit.

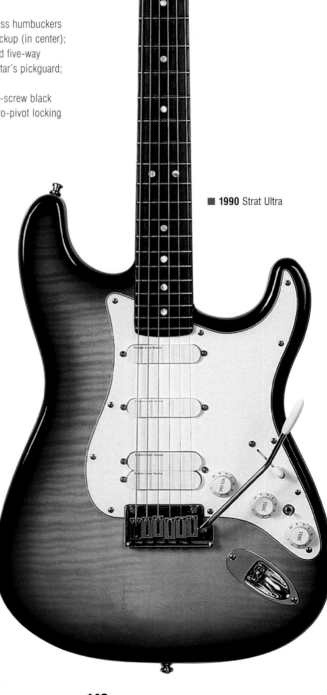

■ **1990** Strat Ultra

STRATOCASTER 1991

STRATOCASTER 1991

1990 catalog

1990 Hank Marvin Stratocaster

When you're cooking, use the best ingredients.
Robert Cray

141

■ **1991** press advertisement

JEFF BECK STRATOCASTER (first version)
1991–2001

Signature on headstock, four white plain-top pickups.

- **Neck:** maple with rosewood fingerboard; 22 frets; truss-rod adjuster at headstock end; locking tuners; roller nut; Jeff Beck signature on headstock.
- **Body:** white, green or purple. Four white plain-top Lace Sensor pickups (two at bridge); three controls (volume, two tone), five-way selector and pushbutton coil-switch, all on pickguard; jack in body face.
- **Hardware:** 11-screw white laminated plastic pickguard; two-pivot bridge/vibrato unit.

■ **1991** Jeff Beck Stratocaster

STRATOCASTER 1991

STANDARD STRATOCASTER (MIM) 1991–current
Modern-style 'thick' Fender headstock logo in silver, three white single-coils, six-pivot vibrato.
- **Neck:** fretted maple, or maple with rosewood fingerboard; truss-rod adjuster at headstock end; one string-guide.
- **Body:** sunburst or colors.
- **Electronics:** three white six-polepiece pickups (bridge pickup angled); three controls (volume, two tone) and five-way selector, all on pickguard; jack in body face.
- **Hardware:** 11-screw white laminated plastic pickguard; six-pivot bridge/vibrato unit.

Modern-style 'thick' Fender headstock logo in black (2010-current).

YNGWIE MALMSTEEN STANDARD STRATOCASTER 1991–94
Signature on headstock.
- **Neck:** scalloped fretted maple; 'bullet' truss-rod adjuster at headstock end; two string-guides; three-screw neckplate.
- **Body:** black, blue, or white.
- **Electronics:** three black six-polepiece pickups (pickup at bridge is angled); three controls (volume, two tones) and five-way selector, all on pickguard; jack in body face.
- **Hardware:** 11-screw white laminated plastic pickguard; six-pivot bridge/vibrato unit.

STRATOCASTER 1991

■ **1991** Standard Stratocaster

143

AMERICAN CLASSIC STRATOCASTER 1992–99

Two-pivot vibrato, one string-guide.
Similar to AMERICAN STANDARD STRATOCASTER
(see 1986 listing) except:
- **Neck:** one string-guide.
- **Hardware:** 11-screw white pearl or tortoiseshell
  laminated plastic pickguard.

Gold-plated hardware option. Custom Shop production.

FLOYD ROSE CLASSIC STRATOCASTER 1992–98

*Two-pivot locking vibrato system, two white single-coils
and one white humbucker, curved-ends humbucker
cut-out in pickguard.*
- **Neck:** fretted maple, or maple with rosewood
  fingerboard; 22 frets; truss-rod adjuster at
  headstock end; single-bar string-guide; locking nut.
- **Body:** sunburst or colors.
- **Electronics:** two white six-polepiece pickups and
  one white coverless humbucker (at bridge); three
  controls (volume, two tone) and five-way selector,
  all on pickguard; jack in body face.
- **Hardware:** 11-screw white laminated plastic
  pickguard; two-pivot locking bridge/vibrato unit.

*Replaced by FLOYD ROSE CLASSIC STRAT HSS
(see 1998 listing).*

ROBERT CRAY STRATOCASTER 1992–current

Signature on headstock.
- **Neck:** maple with rosewood fingerboard;
  truss-rod adjuster at body end; one string-guide;
  Robert Cray signature on headstock.
- **Body:** sunburst, silver, or violet.
- **Electronics:** three white six-polepiece pickups
  (bridge pickup angled); three controls (volume,
  two tone) and five-way selector, all on pickguard;
  jack in body face.
- **Hardware:** 11-screw white
  laminated plastic pickguard;
  six-saddle small bridge with
  through-body stringing.

*Also with gold-plated
hardware (1998–current).
Custom Shop production.*

■ **1992** Alex Gregory
seven-string prototype

STRATOCASTER 1992

SET NECK FLOYD ROSE STRATOCASTER
1992–95

Two-pivot locking vibrato system, two black single-coils and one black humbucker, reverse headstock, glued-in neck.

- **Neck:** maple glued-in with ebony fingerboard; 22 frets; truss-rod adjuster at headstock end; locking nut; black-face reverse headstock.
- **Body:** smaller; sunburst or colors.
- **Electronics:** two black six-polepiece pickups and one black coverless humbucker (at bridge); two controls (volume, tone) and five-way selector, all on body; side-mounted jack.
- **Hardware:** black-plated or gold-plated; no pickguard; two-pivot locking bridge/vibrato unit.

Custom Shop production.

SET NECK STRATOCASTER (first version)
1992–95

Two-pivot vibrato, no string-guides, four white plain-top pickups (two at bridge), glued-in neck.

- **Neck:** maple glued-in with ebony fingerboard; 22 frets; truss-rod adjuster at headstock end; locking tuners; roller nut.
- **Body:** with figured top; sunburst or colors.
- **Electronics:** four white plain-top Lace Sensor pickups (two at bridge); three controls (volume, two tone), five-way selector and coil-switch, all on pickguard; jack in body face.
- **Hardware:** 11-screw white laminated plastic pickguard; two-pivot bridge/vibrato unit.

Custom Shop production. Also Custom Shop limited edition.

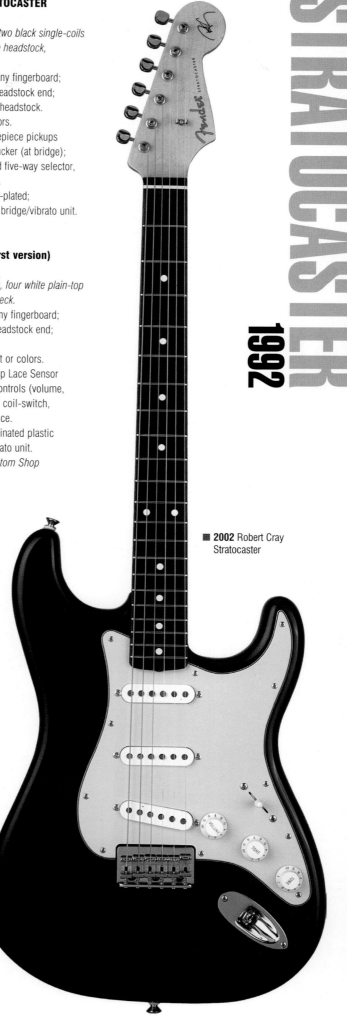

■ **2002** Robert Cray Stratocaster

SQUIER SERIES FLOYD ROSE STANDARD STRATOCASTER (MIJ) 1992–96

Another name for the FLOYD ROSE STANDARD STRATOCASTER (see 1994 listing).

SQUIER SERIES STANDARD STRATOCASTER (MIK) 1992–94

Modern-style 'thick' Fender headstock logo in black, three single-coils.

- **Neck:** fretted maple, or maple with rosewood fingerboard; truss-rod adjuster at headstock end; one string-guide.
- **Body:** black, red, or white.
- **Electronics:** three white six-polepiece pickups (bridge pickup angled); three controls (volume, two tone) and five-way selector, all on pickguard; jack in body face.
- **Hardware:** 11-screw white laminated plastic pickguard; six-pivot bridge/vibrato unit.

Later made in Mexico, with small Squier Series logo on headstock (see 1994 listing), then name changed to TRADITIONAL STRATOCASTER *(see 1996 listing).*

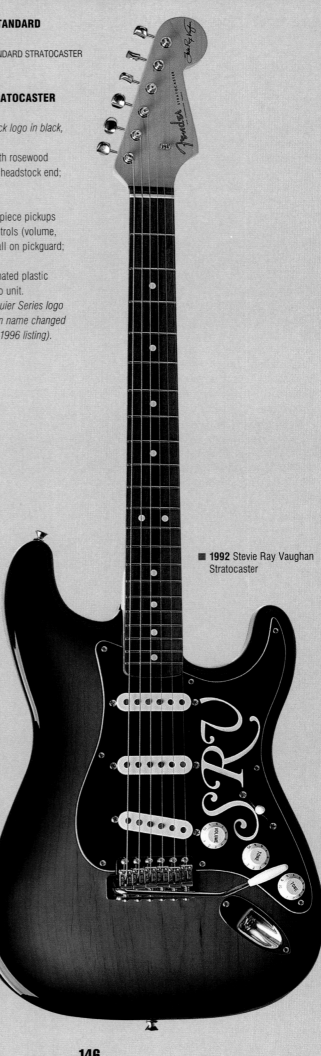

■ **1992** Stevie Ray Vaughan Stratocaster

STRATOCASTER 1992-1994

146

ALUMINUM-BODY STRATOCASTER 1994–95

Anodized aluminum hollow-body option offered on AMERICAN STANDARD STRATOCASTER, STRAT PLUS, STRAT PLUS DELUXE, and STRAT ULTRA (see the relevant entries in the listings for 1986, for 1987, for 1989, and for 1990).

DICK DALE STRATOCASTER 1994–current
Signature on headstock.
- **Neck:** maple with rosewood fingerboard; truss-rod adjuster at body end; two string guides; Dick Dale signature on reverse headstock.
- **Body:** gold only.
- **Electronics:** three white six-polepiece pickups (bridge pickup reverse-angled); one control (volume), three-way selector and two-way switch, all on pickguard; jack in body face.
- **Hardware:** 11-screw white laminated plastic pickguard, metal covers over three 'spare' holes; six-pivot bridge/vibrato unit.

Custom Shop production.

STEVIE RAY VAUGHAN STRATOCASTER 1992–current
Signature on headstock.
- **Neck:** maple with pao ferro fingerboard; truss-rod adjuster at body end; one string-guide; Stevie Ray Vaughan signature on headstock.
- **Body:** sunburst only.
- **Electronics:** three white six-polepiece pickups (bridge pickup angled); three controls (volume, two tone) and five-way selector, all on pickguard; jack in body face.
- **Hardware:** gold-plated; eight-screw black laminated plastic pickguard with 'SRV' engraving; left-handed six-pivot bridge/vibrato unit.

'54 STRATOCASTER 1992–98
Replica of 1954-period original (see 1954 listing). Gold-plated hardware option.
Custom Shop production.

'60 STRATOCASTER (first version) 1992–98
Replica of 1960-period original (see 1954 listing). Gold-plated hardware option.
Custom Shop production.

RICHIE SAMBORA STRATOCASTER (first version) 1993–99
Signature on headstock.
- **Neck:** fretted maple, star position markers; 22 frets; truss-rod adjuster at headstock end; single-bar string-guide; locking nut; Richie Sambora signature on headstock.
- **Body:** sunburst or white.
- **Electronics:** two white six-polepiece pickups and one white coverless humbucker (at bridge); three controls (volume, two tone), five-way selector and push-switch, all on pickguard; jack in body face; active circuit.
- **Hardware:** 11-screw white laminated plastic pickguard; two-pivot locking bridge/vibrato unit.

SPECIAL EDITION 1993 STRATOCASTER 1993
Commemorative neckplate.
Similar to AMERICAN STANDARD STRATOCASTER (see 1986 listing) except:
- **Hardware:** gold-plated; 11-screw white pearl laminated plastic pickguard.

FLOYD ROSE STANDARD STRATOCASTER (MIJ) 1994–96
Two white single-coils and one white humbucker, normal color neck, locking vibrato system.
- **Neck:** maple with rosewood fingerboard; truss-rod adjuster at headstock end; single-bar string-guide; locking nut.
- **Body:** with Foto Flame fake figured wood finish; sunburst, blue, or red.
- **Electronics:** two white six-polepiece pickups and one white coverless humbucker (at bridge); two controls (volume, tone) and five-way selector, all on **pickguard;** jack in body face.
- **Hardware:** 11-screw white laminated plastic pickguard; two-pivot locking bridge/vibrato unit.

Also known as SQUIER SERIES FLOYD ROSE STANDARD STRATOCASTER, with small Squier Series logo on headstock (see 1992 listing).

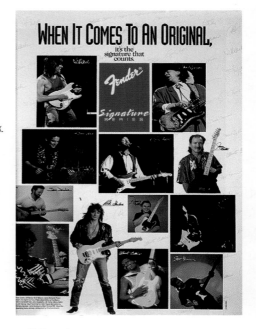

■ **1993** press advertisement

FLOYD ROSE STANDARD STRATOCASTER (MIM)
1994–98
Two-pivot locking vibrato system, two white single-coils and one white humbucker, white pickguard, small headstock, two controls.
Similar to STANDARD STRATOCASTER (see 1991 listing) except:
- **Neck:** single-bar string-guide; locking nut.
- **Body:** black or white.
- **Electronics:** two white six-polepiece pickups and one white coverless humbucker (at bridge); two controls (volume, tone) and five-way selector, all on pickguard.
- **Hardware:** two-pivot locking bridge/vibrato unit.

Also known as SQUIER SERIES FLOYD ROSE STANDARD STRATOCASTER, *with small Squier Series logo on headstock (see later listing this year).*

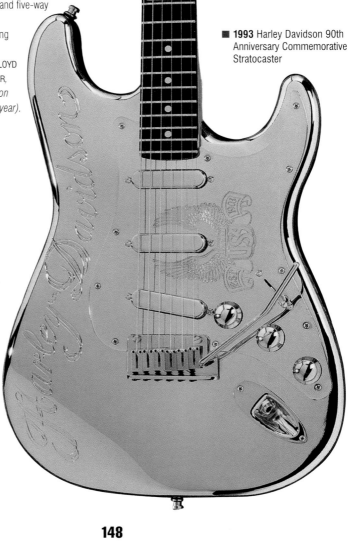

■ **1993** Harley Davidson 90th Anniversary Commemorative Stratocaster

STRATOCASTER 1994

148

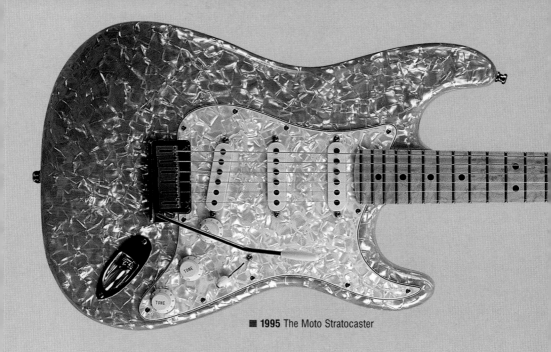

■ **1995** The Moto Stratocaster

■ **1995** 40th Anniversary 1954 Stratocaster

RICHIE SAMBORA STANDARD STRATOCASTER (MIM) 1994–2002

Signature on headstock.
Similar to STANDARD STRATOCASTER
(see 1991 listing) except:

- **Neck:** maple with rosewood fingerboard only; single-bar string-guide; locking nut; Richie Sambora signature on headstock.
- **Body:** various colors.
- **Electronics:** two white six-polepiece pickups and one white coverless humbucker (at bridge); two-pivot locking bridge/vibrato unit.

SPECIAL EDITION 1994 STRATOCASTER 1994

Commemorative neckplate.
Similar to AMERICAN STANDARD STRATOCASTER
(see 1986 listing) except:

- **Body:** black or blonde.
- **Hardware:** 11-screw gray pearl or tortoiseshell laminated plastic pickguard; commemorative neckplate.

SQUIER SERIES STANDARD STRATOCASTER (MIM) 1994–96

Another name for TRADITIONAL STRATOCASTER
(see 1996 listing).

STRAT SPECIAL (MIM) 1994–96

Black pickups and pickguard.
Similar to STANDARD STRATOCASTER
(see 1991 listing) except:

- **Electronics:** two black six-polepiece pickups and one black coverless humbucker (at bridge); two controls (volume, tone), five-way selector and coil-switch, all on pickguard.
- **Hardware:** black-plated; 11-screw black laminated plastic pickguard.

40th ANNIVERSARY 1954 STRATOCASTER 1994

Replica of 1954-period original (see STRATOCASTER PRE-CBS 1954 listing) but with commemorative neckplate.
Numbered factory production run of 1,954.

AMERICAN STANDARD ROLAND GR-READY STRATOCASTER 1995–98

Two-pivot vibrato, two string-guides, extra slim white pickup at bridge.

Similar to AMERICAN STANDARD STRATOCASTER (see 1986 listing) except:

- **Electronics:** additional slim white plain-top Roland synthesizer pickup (at bridge); three controls (volume, tone, synth volume), five-way selector, two pushbuttons and mini-switch, all on pickguard; jack in body face; side-mounted multi-pin synth output.

BONNIE RAITT STRATOCASTER 1995–2001

Signature on headstock.

- **Neck:** narrow, maple, with rosewood fingerboard; 22 frets; truss-rod adjuster at headstock end; one string-guide; Bonnie Raitt signature on large headstock.
- **Body:** sunburst or blueburst.
- **Electronics:** three white six-polepiece pickups (bridge pickup angled); three controls (volume, two tone) and five-way selector, all on pickguard; jack in body face.
- **Hardware:** 11-screw white pearl laminated plastic pickguard; six-pivot bridge/vibrato unit.

Also Custom Shop limited edition.

■ **1995** Bonnie Raitt Stratocaster

STRATOCASTER 1995

The Choice of
Every Generation.

Fender Guitar and
Bass Amplifiers.

Fender
ELECTRONICS

1993 catalog

1995 Foto-Flame
Stratocaster

151

BUDDY GUY STRATOCASTER 1995–09

Signature on headstock.

- **Neck:** fretted maple; 22 frets; truss-rod adjuster at headstock end; one string-guide; Buddy Guy signature on headstock.
- **Body:** sunburst or blonde.
- **Electronics:** three white plain-top Lace Sensor pickups (bridge pickup angled); three controls (volume, tone, boost), five-way selector and mini-switch, all on pickguard; jack in body face; active circuit.
- **Hardware:** eight-screw (11-screw from 2000) white pearl or tortoiseshell laminated plastic pickguard; six-pivot bridge/vibrato unit.

CARVED TOP STRAT 1995–98

Two-pivot vibrato, no string-guides, two single-coils and one humbucker, figured carved-top body.

- **Neck:** fretted maple, or maple with rosewood fingerboard; 22 frets; truss-rod adjuster at headstock end; locking tuners; roller nut.
- **Body:** with figured carved top; sunburst or colors.
- **Electronics:** two cream six-polepiece pickups and one black/cream coverless humbucker (at bridge); two controls (volume, tone) and five-way selector, all on body; side-mounted jack.
- **Hardware:** no pickguard; two-pivot bridge/vibrato unit.

Known as CARVED TOP STRAT HSS (1998).
Custom Shop production.

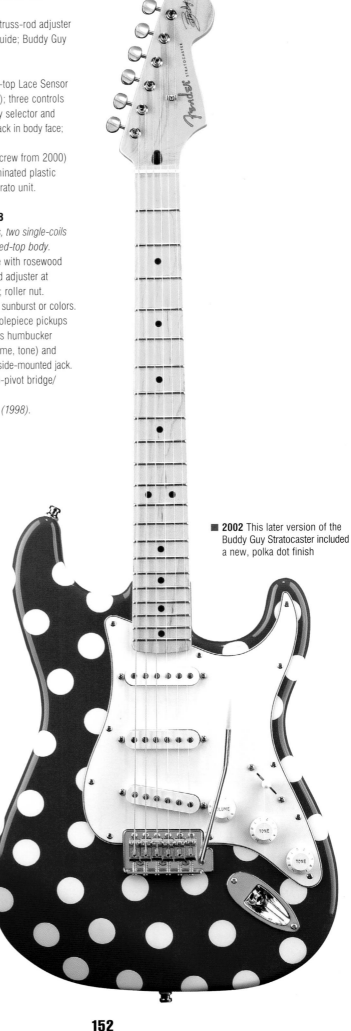

■ **2002** This later version of the Buddy Guy Stratocaster included a new, polka dot finish

CONTEMPORARY STRAT 1995–98

Two-pivot vibrato, no string-guides, two white single-coils and one white humbucker, smaller body with slimmer horns.

- **Neck:** fretted maple, or maple with rosewood fingerboard; 22 frets; truss-rod adjuster at headstock end; locking tuners; roller nut.
- **Body:** smaller, with slimmer horns; sunburst or colors.
- **Electronics:** two white six-polepiece pickups and one white coverless humbucker (at bridge).
- **Hardware:** 11-screw white pearl laminated plastic pickguard; two-pivot bridge/vibrato unit.

Custom Shop production.

SET NECK STRATOCASTER (second version) 1995–98

Two-pivot vibrato, no string-guides, two white single-coils and one white humbucker, glued-in neck.
Similar to SET NECK STRATOCASTER FIRST VERSION (see 1992 listing) except:

- **Neck:** rosewood fingerboard.
- **Body:** sunburst or natural.
- **Electronics:** two white six-polepiece pickups and one white coverless humbucker (at bridge).

Custom Shop production.

CONTEMPORARY STRAT FMT 1995–98

Similar to CONTEMPORARY STRAT (see previous listing) but with figured-top body and two-pivot locking bridge/vibrato unit.
Custom Shop production.

'54 STRATOCASTER FMT 1995–98

Replica of 1954-period original (see STRATOCASTER PRE-CBS 1954 listing) but with figured body top. Gold-plated hardware option.
Custom Shop production.

'60 STRATOCASTER FMT 1995–98

Replica of 1960-period original (see STRATOCASTER PRE-CBS 1954 listing) but with figured body top. Gold-plated hardware option.
Custom Shop production.

■ **1996** '54 Stratocaster FMT

■ **1996** Lone Star Strat

153

CUSTOM AGED

Fender's strength continued to grow alongside the breadth of its catalog in the 1990s, but a studied look back over the shoulder continued to offer a reliable means of success in model development. Namely, more players than ever seemed to want guitars that not only were made like they were in the old days but also looked like they were made 40 or 50 years ago.

After building a handful of aged or 'distressed' instruments for name artists, often as replicas of much-played favorite guitars that had become too valuable to take on tour, the Fender Custom Shop formally introduced its Relic series in 1995. These guitars included intentional dings, scuffs, and scratches and 'arm rubs' in the finish, along with artificially aged and tarnished hardware.

The line proved extremely popular, and in fact the Mary Kaye Stratocaster (a blonde-finish version of the 1956 Stratocaster with gold-plated hardware) proved the Custom Shop's best seller of the late 1990s. Between the official launch of the Relics in 1995 and May of 1999, the ageing of bodies, necks, and parts that would be assembled at the Custom Shop was outsourced to Vince Cunetto, who established a shop and workforce in Bolivar, Missouri, for this purpose.

Cunetto's own aged custom-made Fender replicas had impressed his friend Jay Black, a Custom Shop Master Builder, who in turn showed the work to Custom Shop Manager John Page. Page was equally impressed and hired the craftsman to provide the look that would define the Relic series. An occasional request for a 'slightly less aged' guitar led Cunetto to develop the less-distressed models, dubbed Closet Classics in 1998 for their 'gently played but cared for' look.

Later in '98 Fender formally expanded the distressed line into the Time Machine series, which included the relatively well-aged Relics, the gently aged Closet Classics, and the entirely un-distressed N.O.S. guitars. The

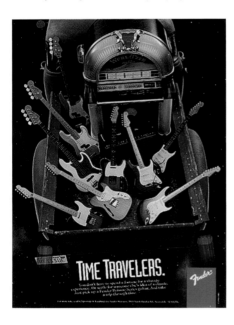

■ **1994** press advertisement

N.O.S models were intended to look as if an original vintage model had been zapped into the future by a time machine. (N.O.S. means 'new old stock,' a term commonly used for amplifier tubes manufactured many years ago but which have remained unused on the shelf and therefore in 'new' condition.)

In 1999, Fender moved the ageing of all Time Machine models in-house, although the majority of Closet Classic guitars were already being produced in the Custom Shop itself during 1998, as of course were the non-aged N.O.S. guitars. In the intervening years, the Relics of 1995-'99, known in collector's parlance as 'Cunetto-era' instruments, have become collector's items, just a notch down on the desirability ladder from refinished original vintage guitars, themselves a notch below entirely original examples. It's worth noting that Cunetto never 'made' guitars for Fender but simply finished and aged bodies, necks, and parts that were sent to him by Fender.

STRATOCASTER 1995-1996

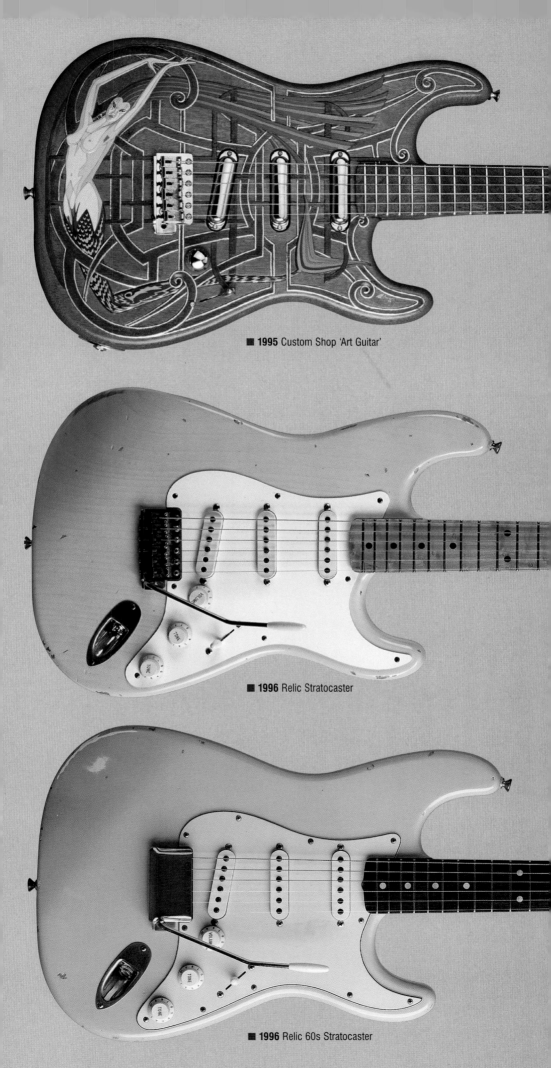

■ **1995** Custom Shop 'Art Guitar'

■ **1996** Relic Stratocaster

■ **1996** Relic 60s Stratocaster

155

HANK MARVIN STRATOCASTER (MIJ) 1996–97

Signature on headstock.
Similar to Japan-made 50s STRATOCASTER
(see 1985 listing) except:
- **Neck:** Hank Marvin signature on headstock.
- **Body:** red only.

LONE STAR STRAT 1996–2000

Two-pivot vibrato, two string-guides,
two white single-coils and one white humbucker.
Similar to AMERICAN STANDARD STRATOCASTER
(see 1986 listing) except:
- **Electronics:** two white six-polepiece pickups
  and one Seymour Duncan-logo white coverless
  humbucker (at bridge).
- **Hardware:** 11-screw white pearl or tortoiseshell
  laminated plastic pickguard.

RELIC 50s STRATOCASTER 1996–98

Distressed-finish replica of 1950s-period original
(see STRATOCASTER PRE-CBS 1954 listing).
Gold-plated hardware option.
Custom Shop production.

RELIC 60s STRATOCASTER 1996–98

Distressed-finish replica of early 1960s-period
original (see STRATOCASTER PRE-CBS 1954 listing).
Gold-plated hardware option.
Custom Shop production.

■ **1996** ’60 Stratocaster

STRATOCASTER 1996

RICHIE SAMBORA PAISLEY STRATOCASTER (MIJ) 1996

Signature on headstock, black paisley-pattern body finish.

- **Neck:** fretted maple, star markers; 22 frets; truss-rod adjuster at headstock end; pearl tuner buttons; single-bar string-guide; locking nut; Richie Sambora signature on headstock.
- **Body:** black paisley-pattern only.
- **Electronics:** two black six-polepiece pickups and one black coverless humbucker (at bridge); three controls (volume, two tone) and five-way selector, all on pickguard; jack in body face.
- **Hardware:** 11-screw black paisley laminated plastic pickguard; two-pivot locking bridge/vibrato unit.

TEX-MEX STRAT (MIM) 1996–97

Vintage-style 'thin' Fender headstock logo in gold, three white single-coils.
Similar to STANDARD STRATOCASTER (see 1991 listing) except:
- **Neck:** Headstock with vintage-style Fender headstock logo in gold.

Fitted with different specification but visually similar pickups.

THE VENTURES STRATOCASTER (MIJ) 1996

The 'Ventures' logo on headstock, three white plain-top pickups.

- **Neck:** maple with bound rosewood fingerboard, block markers; 22 frets; truss-rod adjuster at body end; one string-guide; 'The Ventures' logo on black-face headstock.
- **Body:** black only.
- **Electronics:** three white plain-top Lace Sensor pickups (pickup at bridge is angled); three controls (volume, tone, boost) and five-way selector, all on pickguard; jack in body face; active circuit.
- **Hardware:** gold-plated; 11-screw white pearl laminated plastic pickguard; six-pivot bridge/vibrato unit.

Optional Ventures logo for body.

■ **1996** '62 Stratocaster

TRADITIONAL FAT STRAT (MIM) 1996–98

Modern-style 'thick' Fender headstock logo in black, two white single-coils and one white humbucker.
Similar to TRADITIONAL STRATOCASTER (see next listing) except:
- **Electronics:** two white six-polepiece pickups and one white coverless humbucker (at bridge).

TRADITIONAL STRATOCASTER (MIM) 1996–98

Modern-style 'thick' Fender headstock logo in black, three white single-coils.
- **Neck:** fretted maple, or maple neck with rosewood fingerboard; truss-rod adjuster at headstock end; one string-guide.
- **Body:** black, red, or white.
- **Electronics:** three white six-polepiece pickups (bridge pickup angled); three controls (volume, two tone) and five-way selector, all on pickguard; jack in body face.
- **Hardware:** 11-screw white laminated plastic pickguard; six-pivot bridge/vibrato unit.

Previously known as SQUIER SERIES STANDARD STRATOCASTER, *with small Squier Series logo on headstock (see 1994 listing).*

50th ANNIVERSARY STRATOCASTER 1996

Commemorative neckplate.
Similar to AMERICAN STANDARD STRATOCASTER (see 1986 listing) except:
- **Neck:** maple with rosewood fingerboard only; commemorative neckplate.
- **Body:** sunburst only.
- **Hardware:** gold-plated.

Numbered factory production run of 2,500.
Also Custom Shop limited editions.

'58 STRATOCASTER 1996–98

Replica of 1958-period original (see STRATOCASTER PRE-CBS 1954 listing). Gold-plated hardware option.
Custom Shop production.

'69 STRATOCASTER (first version) 1996–98

Replica of 1969-period original (see STRATOCASTER CBS SIXTIES entry in the 1965 listing).
Custom Shop production.

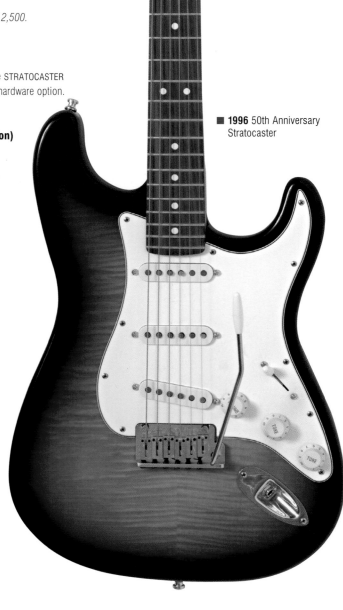

■ **1996** 50th Anniversary Stratocaster

STRATOCASTER
1996-1997

BIG APPLE STRAT 1997–2000

Two-pivot vibrato, two string-guides,
two white humbuckers.

Similar to AMERICAN STANDARD STRATOCASTER
(see 1986 listing) except:

- **Electronics:** two white coverless humbuckers.
- **Hardware:** 11-screw white pearl or tortoiseshell
  laminated plastic pickguard.

CALIFORNIA FAT STRAT 1997–98

Six-pivot vibrato, 'California Series' on headstock,
two white singles-coils and one white humbucker.

- **Neck:** fretted maple, or maple neck with rosewood
  fingerboard; truss-rod adjuster at headstock end;
  one string-guide; California Series on headstock.
- **Body:** sunburst or colors.
- **Electronics:** two white six-polepiece pickups
  and one white coverless humbucker (at bridge);
  three controls (volume, two tone) and five-way
  selector, all on pickguard; jack in body face.
- **Hardware:** 11-screw white laminated plastic
  pickguard; six-pivot bridge/vibrato unit.

CALIFORNIA STRAT 1997–current

Six-pivot vibrato, 'California Series' on headstock,
three white single-coils.

Similar to CALIFORNIA FAT STRAT
(see earlier listing this year) except:

- **Electronics:** three white six-polepiece pickups
  (bridge pickup angled).

■ **1997** Big Apple Strat

COLLECTORS EDITION STRATOCASTER 1997

Six-pivot vibrato, '1997' inlay at 12th fret position.
- **Neck:** maple with rosewood fingerboard; truss-rod adjuster at body end; one string-guide; oval-shape '1997' inlay at 12th fret.
- **Body:** sunburst only.
- **Electronics:** three white six-polepiece pickups (bridge pickup angled); three controls (volume, two tone) and five-way selector, all on pickguard; jack in body face.
- **Hardware:** gold-plated; 11-screw tortoiseshell laminated plastic pickguard; six-pivot bridge/ vibrato unit.

Numbered factory production run of 1,997.

DELUXE POWERHOUSE STRAT (MIM) 1997–07

White pearl pickguard, active circuit.
Similar to STANDARD STRATOCASTER (see 1991 listing) except:
- **Body:** various colors.
- **Electronics:** three controls (volume, tone, boost) and five-way selector, all on pickguard; active circuit.
- **Hardware:** 11-screw white pearloid plastic pickguard.

DELUXE SUPER STRAT (MIM) 1997–2004

Gold-plated hardware, push-switch.
Similar to STANDARD STRATOCASTER (see 1991 listing) except:
- **Electronics:** three controls (volume, two tone), five-way selector and push-switch, all on pickguard.
- **Hardware:** gold-plated; 11-screw tortoiseshell laminated plastic pickguard.

HANK MARVIN STRATOCASTER (MIM) 1997

Signature on body.
Similar to TRADITIONAL STRATOCASTER (see 1996 listing) except:
- **Neck:** fretted maple only; Hank Marvin signature on body.
- **Body:** red only.
Limited edition of 300.

STRATOCASTER 1997

■ **1997** Jimi Hendrix Monterey Strat

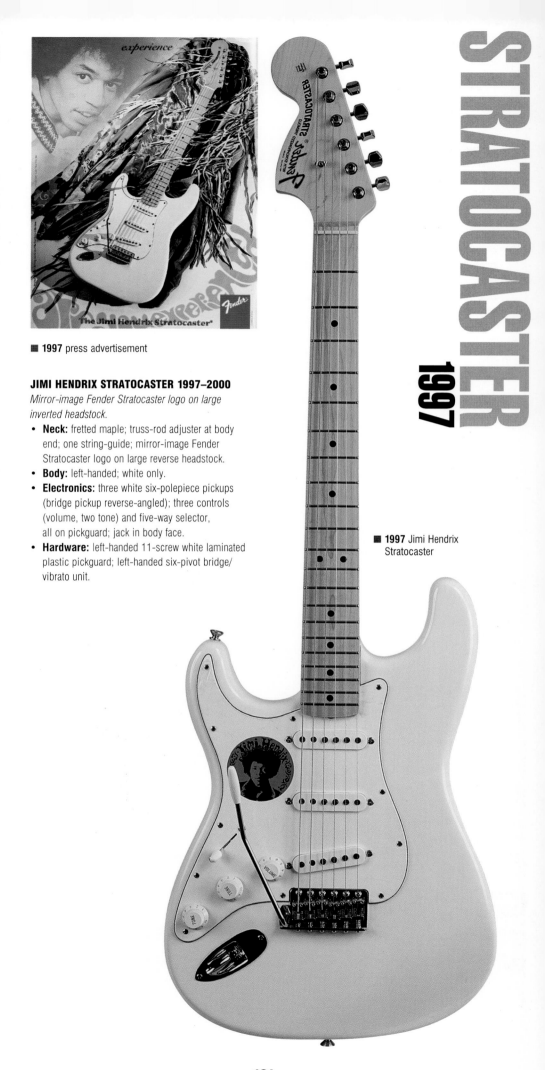

■ **1997** press advertisement

JIMI HENDRIX STRATOCASTER 1997–2000
Mirror-image Fender Stratocaster logo on large inverted headstock.

- **Neck:** fretted maple; truss-rod adjuster at body end; one string-guide; mirror-image Fender Stratocaster logo on large reverse headstock.
- **Body:** left-handed; white only.
- **Electronics:** three white six-polepiece pickups (bridge pickup reverse-angled); three controls (volume, two tone) and five-way selector, all on pickguard; jack in body face.
- **Hardware:** left-handed 11-screw white laminated plastic pickguard; left-handed six-pivot bridge/vibrato unit.

■ **1997** Jimi Hendrix Stratocaster

JERRY DONAHUE HELLECASTERS STRATOCASTER (MIJ) 1997–98

Signature on headstock, 'Hellecasters' inlay at 12th fret.

- **Neck:** fretted maple; truss-rod adjuster at headstock end; one string-guide; roller nut; 'Hellecasters' inlay at 12th fret; Jerry Donahue signature on headstock.
- **Body:** blue only.
- **Electronics:** three white six-polepiece pickups (bridge pickup angled); three controls (volume, tone, two-way rotary switch) and five-way selector, all on pickguard; jack in body face.
- **Hardware:** 11-screw blue sparkle laminated plastic pickguard; six-pivot bridge/vibrato unit.

JOHN JORGENSON HELLECASTER (MIJ) 1997–98

Signature and model name on headstock, three split pickups.

- **Neck:** maple with rosewood fingerboard, gold sparkle dot markers; 22 frets; truss-rod adjuster at headstock end; locking tuners; 'Hellecasters' inlay at 12th fret; John Jorgenson signature on large Stratocaster reverse headstock.
- **Body:** black sparkle only.
- **Electronics:** three black plain-top split pickups (bridge pickup angled); three controls (volume, two tone) and five-way selector, all on pickguard; jack in body face.
- **Hardware:** gold-plated; 11-screw gold sparkle laminated plastic pickguard; two-pivot bridge/ vibrato unit.

■ **1997** John Jorgenson Hellecaster

STRATOCASTER 1997-1998

ROADHOUSE STRAT 1997–2000

Two-pivot vibrato, two string-guides, three white single-coils, white pearl or tortoiseshell pickguard.
Similar to AMERICAN STANDARD STRATOCASTER (see 1986 listing) except:
- **Electronics:** visually similar pickups but different specification.
- **Hardware:** 11-screw white pearl or tortoiseshell laminated plastic pickguard.

TEX-MEX STRAT SPECIAL (MIM) 1997

Vintage-style 'thin' Fender headstock logo in gold, two white single-coils and one white humbucker.
Similar to STANDARD STRATOCASTER (see 1991 listing) except:
- **Electronics:** two white six-polepiece pickups and one white coverless humbucker (at bridge).

JIMMIE VAUGHAN TEX-MEX STRATOCASTER (MIM) 1997–current

Signature on back of headstock.
Similar to STANDARD STRATOCASTER (see 1991 listing) except:
- **Neck:** fretted maple only; Jimmie Vaughan signature on back of headstock.
- **Electronics:** modified control operation.
- **Hardware:** 11-screw white plastic pickguard.

AMERICAN DELUXE FAT STRAT 1998–2003

Two Noiseless logo white pickups and one white humbucker, staggered height locking tuners, two-pivot vibrato.
Similar to AMERICAN DELUXE STRATOCASTER FIRST VERSION (see later listing this year) except:
- **Neck:** no string-guide; roller nut.
- **Electronics:** two Noiseless logo white six-polepiece pickups and one white coverless humbucker (at bridge).

AMERICAN DELUXE FAT STRAT/LOCKING TREM 1998–2003

Two Noiseless logo white pickups and one white humbucker, staggered height locking tuners, two-pivot locking vibrato.
Similar to AMERICAN DELUXE STRATOCASTER FIRST VERSION (see next listing) except:
- **Neck:** no string-guide; roller nut.
- **Electronics:** two Noiseless logo white six-polepiece pickups and one white coverless humbucker (at bridge).
- **Hardware:** two-pivot locking bridge/vibrato unit.

AMERICAN DELUXE STRATOCASTER (first version) 1998–2003

Three Noiseless logo white pickups, staggered height locking tuners, two-pivot vibrato.
- **Neck:** fretted maple, or maple with rosewood fingerboard; 22 frets; truss-rod adjuster at headstock end; staggered height locking tuners; one string-guide.
- **Body:** sunburst or colors.
- **Electronics:** three Noiseless logo white six-polepiece pickups (bridge pickup angled); three controls (volume, two tone) and five-way selector, all on pickguard; jack in body face.
- **Hardware:** 11-screw white laminated plastic pickguard; two-pivot bridge/vibrato unit.

AMERICAN STANDARD STRATOCASTER HARD-TAIL 1998–2000

22 frets, small headstock, two string-guides, four-screw neckplate, three controls, six-saddle bridge with through-body stringing.
Similar to AMERICAN STANDARD STRATOCASTER (see 1986 listing) except:
- **Hardware:** six-saddle bridge with through-body stringing.

■ 1997 Jimmie Vaughan Tex-Mex Strat

AMERICAN VINTAGE '57 STRATOCASTER
1998–current
Replica of 1957-period original
(see STRATOCASTER PRE-CBS 1954 listing).

AMERICAN VINTAGE '62 STRATOCASTER
1998–current
Replica of 1962-period original
(see STRATOCASTER PRE-CBS 1954 listing).

BIG APPLE STRAT HARD-TAIL 1998–2000
Two string-guides, two white humbuckers,
six-saddle bridge with through-body stringing.
Similar to BIG APPLE STRAT (see 1997 listing) except:
- **Hardware:** six-saddle small bridge with through-body stringing.
- **Neck:** maple with rosewood fingerboard; truss-rod adjuster at body end; one string- guide; red, silver and blue sparkle striped headstock face; Buck Owens signature on headstock.
- **Body:** slab single-cutaway, bound; red, silver, and blue sparkle striped front.
- **Electronics:** one plain metal-cover pickup (at neck) and one black six-polepiece pickup (angled in bridgeplate); two controls (volume, tone) and three-way selector, all on metal plate adjoining pickguard; side-mounted jack.
- **Hardware:** gold-plated; eight-screw gold pickguard; three-saddle raised-sides bridge with through-body stringing.

■ **1998** American Vintage '62 Stratocaster (left-hand)

■ **1998** American Vintage '57 Stratocaster

■ **1998** Big Apple Stratocaster

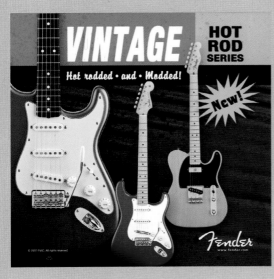
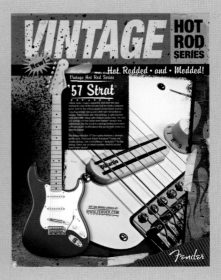

■ **2007** press advertisements

CARVED TOP STRAT HH 1998

Carved top, two metal-cover humbuckers.
Similar to CARVED TOP STRAT (see 1995 listing) except:
• **Electronics:** two metal-cover humbuckers.

CARVED TOP STRAT HSS 1998

Another name for CARVED TOP STRAT (see 1995 listing).

CLASSIC PLAYER STRAT 1998–2005

*Custom Shop headstock logo, two-pivot vibrato,
no string-guides, three Noiseless logo white pickups.*
• **Neck:** fretted maple, or maple with rosewood
  fingerboard; 22 frets; truss-rod adjuster at headstock
  end; staggered height locking tuners.
• **Body:** sunburst or colors.
• **Electronics:** three Noiseless logo white six-
  polepiece pickups (bridge pickup angled); three
  controls (volume, two tone) and five-way selector,
  all on pickguard; jack in body face.
• **Hardware:** eight-screw white laminated plastic
  or anodized metal pickguard; two-pivot bridge/
  vibrato unit.
Custom Shop production.

■ **1997** Carved Top Strat

STRATOCASTER 1998

DELUXE DOUBLE FAT STRAT FLOYD ROSE (MIM) 1998–2004

Two-pivot locking vibrato system, two black humbuckers, black pickguard, large headstock.
Similar to DELUXE FAT STRAT (see 1999 listing) except:
- **Neck:** single-bar string-guide; locking nut.
- **Electronics:** two black coverless humbuckers.
- **Hardware:** two-pivot locking bridge/vibrato unit.
Known as DELUXE DOUBLE FAT STRAT HH WITH LOCKING TREMOLO *(see 2002 listing).*
Known as DELUXE STRAT HH WITH LOCKING TREMOLO *(see 2004 listing).*

DELUXE FAT STRAT HSS FLOYD ROSE (MIM) 1998–2005

Two-pivot locking vibrato system, two black single-coils and one black humbucker, black pickguard, large headstock.
Similar to DELUXE FAT STRAT (see 1999 listing) except:
- **Neck:** single-bar string-guide; locking nut.
- **Hardware:** two-pivot locking bridge/vibrato unit.
Known as DELUXE FAT STRAT HSS WITH LOCKING TREMOLO *(see 2002 listing).*
Known as DELUXE STRAT HSS WITH LOCKING TREMOLO *(see 2004 listing).*

FLOYD ROSE CLASSIC STRAT HH 1998–2002

Two-pivot locking vibrato system, two white humbuckers, three-screw fixing for each humbucker.
Similar to FLOYD ROSE CLASSIC STRAT HSS (see next listing) except:
- **Electronics:** two white coverless humbucker pickups.
Known as STRAT SPECIAL WITH LOCKING TREMOLO HH *(see 2002 listing).*

FLOYD ROSE CLASSIC STRAT HSS 1998–2002

Two-pivot locking vibrato system, two white single-coils and one white humbucker, three-screw fixing for humbucker.
Similar to FLOYD ROSE CLASSIC STRATOCASTER (see 1992 listing) except:
- **Hardware:** three-screw fixing for humbucker pickup; no curved-ends humbucker cut-out in pickguard.
Known as STRAT SPECIAL WITH LOCKING TREMOLO HSS *(see 2002 listing).*

MATTHIAS JABS STRATOCASTER (MIJ) 1998

Ringed planet position markers.
- **Neck:** maple with rosewood fingerboard, 'ringed planet' position markers; 22 frets; truss-rod adjuster at headstock end; locking tuners; scroll inlay at 12th fret.
- **Body:** red only.
- **Electronics:** two white six-polepiece pickups and one white coverless humbucker (at bridge); three controls (two volume, tone) and five-way selector, all on pickguard; jack in body face.
- **Hardware:** 11-screw white plastic pickguard; six-pivot bridge/vibrato unit.

N.O.S. STRAT 1998

Replica of 1965-period original (see STRATOCASTER CBS SIXTIES 1965 listing). *Custom Shop production.*

■ **1997** flyer

RELIC FLOYD ROSE STRATOCASTER 1998

Two-pivot locking vibrato system, two white single-coils and one black humbucker, large headstock.
- **Neck:** fretted maple, or maple with rosewood fingerboard; truss-rod adjuster at body end; single-bar string-guide; locking nut; large headstock.
- **Body:** black or white, distressed finish.
- **Electronics:** two white six-polepiece pickups and one black coverless humbucker (at bridge); three controls (volume, two tone) and five-way selector, all on pickguard; jack in body face.
- **Hardware:** 11-screw white laminated plastic pickguard; two-pivot locking bridge/vibrato unit.
Custom Shop production.

STANDARD ROLAND READY STRAT (MIM) 1998–current

Six-pivot vibrato, one string-guide, extra slim white pickup at bridge.
Similar to STANDARD STRATOCASTER (see 1991 listing) except:
- **Neck:** maple with rosewood fingerboard only.
- **Electronics:** additional slim white plain-top Roland synthesizer pickup (at bridge); three controls (volume, tone, synth volume), five-way selector, two push-buttons and mini-switch, all on pickguard; jack in body face; side-mounted multi-pin synth output.

■ **1998** press advertisement

YNGWIE MALMSTEEN STRATOCASTER
(second version) 1998–2006
Signature on large headstock, six-pivot vibrato.
Similar to YNGWIE MALMSTEEN STRATOCASTER FIRST
VERSION (see 1988 listing) except:
- **Neck:** Yngwie Malmsteen signature on large
  headstock.
- **Electronics:** three controls (volume, two tone)
  and three-way selector, all on pickguard.
- **Hardware:** six-pivot bridge/vibrato unit.

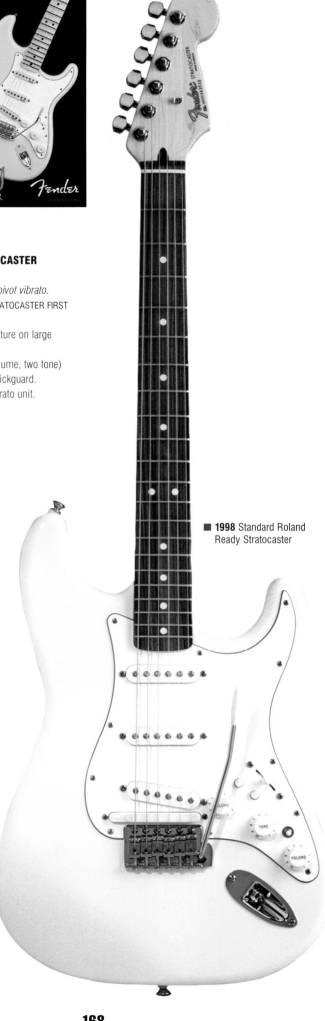

■ **1998** Standard Roland
Ready Stratocaster

■ **1999** Classic 50s Stratocaster

■ **1999** Classic 60s Stratocaster

CHRIS REA CLASSIC STRATOCASTER (MIM) 1998

Signature on headstock.
Similar to CLASSIC 60S STRATOCASTER (see below) but:
- **Neck:** Chris Rea signature on headstock.
- **Body:** red only.

VOODOO STRATOCASTER 1998–2000

Large inverted headstock, reverse-angled bridge pickup, Jimi Hendrix image engraved neckplate.
- **Neck:** maple with maple or rosewood fingerboard; truss-rod adjuster at body end; one string-guide; Jimi Hendrix image engraved neckplate; large reverse headstock.
- **Body:** sunburst, black, or white.

- **Electronics:** three white six-polepiece pickups (bridge pickup reverse-angled); three controls (volume, two tone) and five-way selector, all on pickguard; jack in body face.
- **Hardware:** 11-screw white laminated plastic pickguard; six-pivot bridge/vibrato unit.

CLASSIC 50s STRATOCASTER (MIM) 1999–current

Replica of 1950s-period original (see STRATOCASTER PRE CBS 1954 listing).

CLASSIC 60s STRATOCASTER (MIM) 1999–current

Replica of 1960s-period original (see STRATOCASTER PRE CBS 1954 listing).

CLASSIC 70s STRATOCASTER (MIM) 1999–current
Replica of 1970s-period original
(see STRATOCASTER CBS SEVENTIES 1971 listing).

CUSTOM CLASSIC STRAT 1999–08
22 frets, Custom Shop headstock logo,
two-pivot vibrato, three white single-coils.
Similar to AMERICAN STANDARD STRATOCASTER
(see 1986 listing) except:
• **Neck:** Custom Shop logo on headstock.
Custom Shop production.

DELUXE DOUBLE FAT STRAT (MIM) 1999–2004
Six-pivot vibrato, two black humbuckers,
black pickguard, large headstock.
Similar to DELUXE FAT STRAT (see next listing) except:
• **Electronics:** two black coverless humbuckers.
Known as DELUXE DOUBLE FAT STRAT HH *(see 2002 listing).*
Known as DELUXE STRAT HH *(see 2004 listing).*

DELUXE FAT STRAT (MIM) 1999–2006
Six-pivot vibrato, two black single-coils and one
black humbucker, black pickguard, large headstock.
• **Neck:** maple with rosewood fingerboard;
  truss-rod adjuster at headstock end;
  one string-guide; large headstock.
• **Body:** black or white.
• **Electronics:** two black six-polepiece pickups
  and one black coverless humbucker (at bridge);
  three controls (volume, two tone) and five-way
  selector, all on pickguard; jack in body face.
• **Hardware:** 11-screw black laminated plastic
  pickguard; six-pivot bridge/vibrato unit.
Known as DELUXE FAT STRAT HSS *(see 2002 listing).*
Known as DELUXE STRAT HSS *(see 2004 listing).*

■ **1999** Classic 70s
Stratocaster

STRATOCASTER 1999

170

RICHIE SAMBORA STRATOCASTER
(second version) 1999–2002

Star position markers, three Noiseless logo white pickups.

- **Neck:** fretted maple, star position markers; 22 frets; truss-rod adjuster at headstock end.
- **Body:** sunburst, red, or white.
- **Electronics:** three Noiseless logo white six-polepiece pickups (bridge pickup angled); three controls (volume, two tone), five-way selector and push-switch, all on pickguard; jack in body face; active circuit.
- **Hardware:** 11-screw white laminated plastic pickguard; six-pivot bridge/vibrato unit.

RITCHIE BLACKMORE STRATOCASTER
1999–2005

Signature on headstock, two white plain-top pickups.

- **Neck:** maple glued-in, with rosewood fingerboard, with scalloping between frets; 22 frets; 'bullet' truss-rod adjuster at headstock end; locking tuners; Ritchie Blackmore signature on large headstock.
- **Body:** white only.
- **Electronics:** two white plain-top Lace Sensor pickups (bridge pickup angled); three controls (volume, two tone) and five-way selector, all on pickguard; jack in body face.
- **Hardware:** 11-screw white laminated plastic or anodized metal pickguard; two-pivot bridge/ vibrato unit.

Roland GK-2 synth pickup system option.
Custom Shop production.

STRATOCASTER 1999

■ **1999** Ritchie Blackmore Stratocaster

171

STANDARD FAT STRAT (MIM) 1999–current

Modern-style 'thick' Fender headstock logo in silver,
two single-coils and one humbucker, six-pivot vibrato.
Similar to STANDARD STRATOCASTER
(see 1991 listing) except:
- **Electronics:** two white six-polepiece pickups
  and one white coverless humbucker (at bridge).
Known as STANDARD STRATOCASTER HSS
(see 2004 listing).

STANDARD FAT STRAT FLOYD ROSE (MIM) 1999–current

Two-pivot locking vibrato system, two white
single-coils and one white humbucker,
white pickguard, small headstock, three controls.
Similar to STANDARD STRATOCASTER
(see 1991 listing) except:
- **Neck:** maple with rosewood fingerboard only;
  single-bar string-guide; locking nut.
- **Electronics:** two white six-polepiece pickups
  and one white coverless humbucker (at bridge);
  two-pivot locking bridge/vibrato unit.
Known as STANDARD FAT STRAT WITH LOCKING TREMOLO
(see 2002 listing).
Known as STANDARD STRATOCASTER HSS WITH LOCKING
TREMOLO (see 2004 listing).

'56 STRATOCASTER 1999–current

Replica of 1956-period original (see STRATOCASTER
PRE-CBS 1954 listing). Available with three finish distress
degrees: N.O.S., Closet Classic, and Relic. Gold-plated
hardware option. *Custom Shop production.*

'60 STRATOCASTER (second version) 1999–2009

Revised replica of 1960-period original
(see STRATOCASTER PRE-CBS 1954 listing).
Available with three finish distress degrees: N.O.S.,
Closet Classic, and Relic. Gold-plated hardware option.
Custom Shop production.

'69 STRATOCASTER (second version) 1999–2009

Revised replica of 1969-period original
(see STRATOCASTER CBS SIXTIES 1965 listing).
Available with three finish distress degrees: N.O.S.,
Closet Classic, and Relic. *Custom Shop production.*

AMERICAN DOUBLE FAT STRAT 2000–03

White pearl or tortoiseshell pickguard,
two Seymour Duncan-logo white humbuckers.
Similar to AMERICAN STRATOCASTER
(see 2000 listing) except:
- **Electronics:** two Seymour Duncan-logo
  white coverless humbuckers.
- **Hardware:** 11-screw white pearl or
  tortoiseshell laminated plastic pickguard.

AMERICAN DOUBLE FAT STRAT HARD-TAIL 2000–03

One string-guide, white pearl or tortoiseshell pickguard,
two Seymour Duncan-logo white humbuckers,
six-saddle bridge with through-body stringing.
Similar to AMERICAN STRATOCASTER
(see 2000 listing) except:
- **Electronics:** two Seymour Duncan-logo white
  coverless humbuckers.

- **Hardware:** 11-screw white pearl or tortoiseshell
  laminated plastic pickguard; six-saddle small bridge
  with through-body stringing.

AMERICAN FAT STRAT TEXAS SPECIAL 2000–03

White pearl or tortoiseshell pickguard, two white single-
coils and one Seymour Duncan-logo white humbucker.
Similar to AMERICAN STRATOCASTER (see 2000 listing)
except:
- **Electronics:** two white six-polepiece pickups
  and one Seymour Duncan-logo white coverless
  humbucker (at bridge).
- **Hardware:** 11-screw white pearl or tortoiseshell
  laminated plastic pickguard.

AMERICAN STRAT TEXAS SPECIAL 2000–03

White pearl or tortoiseshell pickguard,
three white single-coils.
Similar to AMERICAN STRATOCASTER
(see 2000 listing) except:
- **Hardware:** 11-screw white pearl or
  tortoiseshell laminated plastic pickguard.
Fitted with different-specification but visually
similar pickups.

AMERICAN STRATOCASTER 2000–07

22 frets, small headstock, one string-guide,
four-screw neckplate, three controls.
- **Neck:** fretted maple, or maple with rosewood
  fingerboard; 22 frets; truss-rod adjuster at headstock
  end; staggered height tuners; one string-guide.
- **Body:** sunburst or colors.
- **Electronics:** three white six-polepiece pickups
  (bridge pickup angled); three controls (volume,
  two tone) and five-way selector, all on pickguard;
  jack in body face.
- **Hardware:** 11-screw white laminated plastic
  pickguard; two-pivot bridge/vibrato unit.

AMERICAN STRATOCASTER HARD-TAIL 2000–06

22 frets, small headstock, one string-guide,
four-screw neckplate, three controls, six-saddle
bridge with through-body stringing.
Similar to AMERICAN STRATOCASTER
(see previous listing) except:
- **Hardware:** six-saddle small bridge with
  through-body stringing.

HANK MARVIN CLASSIC STRATOCASTER (MIM) 2000

Signature on headstock.
Similar to CLASSIC 50S STRATOCASTER
(see 1999 listing) except:
- **Neck:** Hank Marvin signature on headstock.
- **Body:** red only.
- **Hardware:** six-pivot bridge/vibrato unit
  with special design vibrato arm.

SUB-SONIC STRATOCASTER HH baritone 2000–01

Sub-Sonic on headstock, long-scale neck,
white pearl pickguard, two white humbuckers.
Similar to SUB-SONIC STRATOCASTER HSS BARITONE
FIRST VERSION (see next listing) except:
- **Electronics:** two white coverless humbuckers.
Custom Shop production.

SUB-SONIC STRATOCASTER HSS baritone (first version) 2000–01

'Sub-Sonic' on headstock, long-scale neck, white pearl pickguard, two Noiseless logo white single-coils and one white humbucker.

- **Neck:** fretted maple, or maple with rosewood fingerboard; 27-inch scale, 22 frets; truss-rod adjuster at body end; one string-guide; 'Sub-Sonic' on headstock.
- **Body:** sunburst or colors.
- **Electronics:** two Noiseless logo white six-polepiece pickups and one white coverless humbucker (at bridge); three controls (volume, two tone) and five-way selector, all on pickguard; jack in body face.
- **Hardware:** 11-screw white pearl laminated plastic pickguard; six-saddle small bridge with through-body stringing.

Custom Shop production.

ERIC CLAPTON STRATOCASTER (second version) 2001–current

Signature on headstock, three Noiseless logo white pickups, active circuit.

Similar to ERIC CLAPTON STRATOCASTER FIRST VERSION (see 1988 listing) except:

- **Electronics:** three Noiseless logo white six-polepiece pickups.

IRON MAIDEN SIGNATURE STRATOCASTER (MIJ) 2001–02

Iron Maiden on headstock.

- **Neck:** fretted maple only; 22 frets; truss-rod adjuster at headstock end; single-bar string-guide; locking nut; Iron Maiden on headstock.
- **Body:** black only.

- **Electronics:** two black twin-blade humbuckers and one small black 12-polepiece humbucker (angled at bridge); three controls (volume, two tone) and five-way selector, all on pickguard; jack in body face.
- **Hardware:** 11-screw mirror plastic pickguard; two-pivot locking bridge/vibrato unit.

JEFF BECK STRATOCASTER (second version) 2001–current

Signature on headstock, three Noiseless logo white pickups.

Similar to JEFF BECK STRATOCASTER FIRST VERSION (see 1991 listing) except:

- **Body:** green or white.
- **Electronics:** three Noiseless logo white six-polepiece pickups (bridge pickup angled); three controls (volume, two tone), five-way selector and push-switch, all on pickguard; jack in body face.

SUB-SONIC STRATOCASTER HSS baritone (second version) 2001

'Sub-Sonic' on headstock, long-scale neck, white pickguard, two white single-coils and one white humbucker.

- **Neck:** fretted maple, or maple with rosewood fingerboard; 27-inch scale, 22 frets; truss-rod adjuster at body end; one string-guide.
- **Body:** sunburst or colors.
- **Electronics:** two white six-polepiece pickups and one white coverless humbucker (at bridge); three controls (volume, two tone) and five-way selector, all on pickguard; jack in body face.
- **Hardware:** 11-screw white laminated plastic pickguard; six-saddle small bridge with through-body stringing.

■ 2001 Jeff Beck Stratocaster

BUDDY GUY POLKA DOT STRAT (MIM)
2002–current

Signature on headstock, black/white polka dot body finish.
Similar to STANDARD STRATOCASTER
(see 1991 listing) except:

- **Neck:** Buddy Guy signature on headstock.
- **Body:** black/white polka dot finish only.
- **Electronics:** three black six-polepiece pickups.
- **Hardware:** eight-screw black laminated
  plastic pickguard.

■ **2002** Buddy Guy
Polka Dot Stratocaster

STRATOCASTER
2001-2003

174

DELUXE DOUBLE FAT STRAT HH (MIM) 2002–03
Another name for DELUXE DOUBLE FAT STRAT
(see 1999 listing).

DELUXE DOUBLE FAT STRAT HH WITH LOCKING TREMOLO (MIM) 2002–03
Another name for DELUXE DOUBLE FAT STRAT FLOYD ROSE
(see 1998 listing).

DELUXE FAT STRAT HSS (MIM) 2002–03
Another name for DELUXE FAT STRAT HSS
(see 1999 listing).

TOM DELONGE STRATOCASTER (MIM) 2001–03
One white humbucker, one control.
- **Neck:** maple with rosewood fingerboard; truss-rod adjuster at headstock end; one string-guide; large headstock; Tom Delonge engraved neckplate.
- **Body:** various colors.
- **Electronics:** one white coverless humbucker (at bridge); one control (volume) on pickguard; jack in body face.
- **Hardware:** 11-screw white or white pearl laminated plastic pickguard; six-saddle small bridge with through-body stringing.

DELUXE FAT STRAT HSS WITH LOCKING TREMOLO (MIM) 2002–03
Another name for DELUXE FAT STRAT HSS FLOYD ROSE
(see 1998 listing).

HIGHWAY ONE STRATOCASTER (first version) 2002–06
Satin body finish, white pickguard, three white single-coils, small headstock.
- **Neck:** fretted maple, or maple with rosewood fingerboard; 22 frets; truss-rod adjuster at headstock end; two string-guides.
- **Body:** various colors, satin finish.
- **Electronics:** three white six-polepiece pickups (bridge pickup angled); three controls (volume, two tone) and five-way selector, all on pickguard; jack in body face.
- **Hardware:** 11-screw white laminated plastic pickguard; six-pivot bridge/vibrato unit.

STANDARD FAT STRAT WITH LOCKING TREMOLO (MIM) 2002–03
Another name for STANDARD FAT STRAT FLOYD ROSE
(see 1999 listing).

STRAT SPECIAL WITH LOCKING TREMOLO HH 2002
Another name for FLOYD ROSE CLASSIC STRAT HH
(see 1998 listing).

STRAT SPECIAL WITH LOCKING TREMOLO HSS 2002
Another name for FLOYD ROSE CLASSIC STRAT HSS
(see 1998 listing).

'68 REVERSE STRAT SPECIAL 2002
Large inverted headstock, reverse-angled bridge pickup.
- **Neck:** maple with maple fingerboard; truss-rod adjuster at body end; one string-guide; large reverse headstock.
- **Body:** sunburst, black, or white.
- **Electronics:** three white six-polepiece pickups (bridge pickup reverse-angled); three controls (volume, two tone) and five-way selector, all on pickguard; jack in body face.
- **Hardware:** 11-screw white laminated plastic pickguard; six-pivot bridge/vibrato unit.

AMERICAN STRATOCASTER HH 2003–06
One string-guide, black pickguard, two black humbuckers.
Similar to AMERICAN STRATOCASTER (see 2000 listing) except:
- **Electronics:** two black coverless humbuckers; three controls (volume with push switch, two tone) and five-way selector, all on pickguard.
- **Hardware:** 11-screw black laminated plastic pickguard.

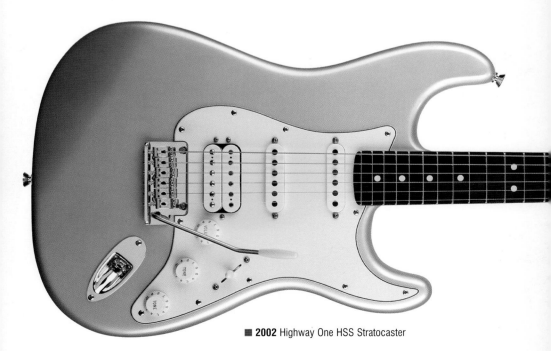

■ **2002** Highway One HSS Stratocaster

AMERICAN STRATOCASTER HH HARD-TAIL 2003–05

One string-guide, black pickguard, two black humbuckers, six-saddle bridge with through-body stringing.
Similar to AMERICAN STRATOCASTER
(see 2000 listing) except:
- **Electronics:** two black coverless humbuckers; three controls (volume with push switch, two tone) and five-way selector, all on pickguard.
- **Hardware:** 11-screw black laminated plastic pickguard; six-saddle small bridge with through-body stringing.

AMERICAN STRATOCASTER HSS 2003–07

One string-guide, black pickguard, two black single-coils and one black humbucker.
Similar to AMERICAN STRATOCASTER
(see 2000 listing) except:
- **Electronics:** two black six-polepiece pickups and one black coverless humbucker (at bridge); three controls (volume with push switch, two tone) and five-way selector, all on pickguard.
- **Hardware:** 11-screw black laminated plastic pickguard.

BLUE FLOWER STRATOCASTER
(second version) (MIJ) 2003

Blue floral-pattern body finish, small headstock.
Similar to BLUE FLOWER STRATOCASTER FIRST VERSION
(see 1988 listing) except:
- **Neck:** small headstock; truss-rod adjuster at body end.

HIGHWAY ONE STRATOCASTER HSS
(first version) 2003–06

Satin body finish, large headstock, white pickguard, two white single-coils and one black humbucker.
Similar to HIGHWAY ONE STRATOCASTER
FIRST VERSION (see 2002 listing) except:
- **Neck:** maple with rosewood fingerboard only; large headstock.
- **Electronics:** two white six-polepiece pickups and one black coverless humbucker (at bridge).

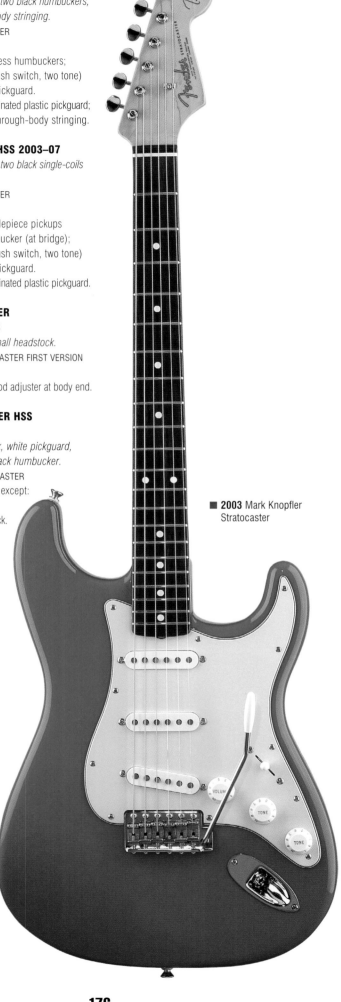

■ **2003** Mark Knopfler Stratocaster

MARK KNOPFLER STRATOCASTER 2003–current

Signature on headstock.

- **Neck:** maple with rosewood fingerboard; truss-rod adjuster at body end; one string-guide; Mark Knopfler signature on headstock.
- **Body:** red only.
- **Electronics:** three white six-polepiece pickups (bridge pickup angled); three controls (volume, two tone) and five-way selector, all on pickguard; jack in body face.
- **Hardware:** 11-screw white laminated plastic pickguard; six-pivot bridge/vibrato unit.

ROBERT CRAY STRATOCASTER (MIM) 2003–current

Signature on headstock.

Similar to CLASSIC 60S STRATOCASTER (see 1999 listing) except:

- **Neck:** Robert Cray signature on headstock.
- **Body:** sunburst, silver, or violet.
- **Hardware:** six-saddle small bridge with through-body stringing.

SPLATTER STRATOCASTER (MIM) 2003

Colored splatter finish on body and pickguard.

Similar to STANDARD STRATOCASTER (see 1991 listing) except:

- **Body:** various colors, splatter finish.
- **Hardware:** 11-screw plastic pickguard in splatter finish matching body color.

STANDARD SATIN STRATOCASTER (MIM) 2003–06

Satin body finish, small headstock, white black pickguard, three black single-coils.

Similar to STANDARD STRATOCASTER (see 1991 listing) except:

- **Body:** various colors, satin finish.
- **Electronics:** three black six-polepiece pickups.
- **Hardware:** 11-screw black laminated plastic pickguard.

■ **2004** American Deluxe Ash Stratocaster

'65 STRATOCASTER 2003–06
Replica of 1965-period original (see STRATOCASTER CBS SIXTIES 1965 listing). Available with three finish distress degrees: N.O.S., Closet Classic and Relic. *Custom Shop production.*

AERODYNE STRATOCASTER (first version) (MIJ) 2004
'Aerodyne Series' on headstock, three black single-coils, black pickguard.

- **Neck:** maple with rosewood fingerboard; 22 frets; truss-rod adjuster at headstock end; one string-guide; 'Aerodyne Series' on black-face headstock.
- **Body:** bound with carved top; black only.
- **Electronics:** three black six-polepiece pickups (bridge pickup angled); three controls (volume, two tone) and five-way selector, all on pickguard; jack in body face.
- **Hardware:** 11-screw black laminated plastic pickguard; six-pivot bridge/vibrato unit.

■ **2004** American Deluxe Stratocaster (second version)

STRATOCASTER 2003-2004

178

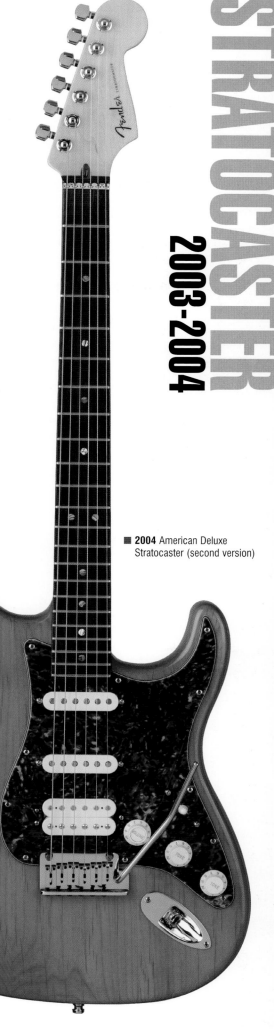

AMERICAN DELUXE ASH STRATOCASTER
2004–current

Three white single coils, staggered height locking tuners, two-pivot vibrato, ash body.

Similar to AMERICAN DELUXE STRATOCASTER SECOND VERSION (see later listing this year) except:
- **Body:** ash body.
- **Hardware:** 11-screw white or black laminated plastic pickguard.

AMERICAN DELUXE STRATOCASTER
(second version) 2004–current

Three white or black single coils, staggered height locking tuners, two-pivot vibrato.

Similar to AMERICAN DELUXE STRATOCASTER FIRST VERSION (see 1998 listing) except:
- **Electronics:** three white or black six-polepiece pickups (bridge pickup angled); three controls (volume with push-switch, two tone) and five-way selector, all on pickguard.
- **Hardware:** 11-screw white, tortoiseshell or black pearl laminated plastic pickguard, or gold plastic pickguard.

AMERICAN DELUXE STRATOCASTER FMT HSS
2004–current

Figured-top body, no pickguard, two black single coils and one black humbucker.
- **Neck:** maple with ebony fingerboard; 22 frets; truss-rod adjuster at headstock end; staggered height locking tuners; roller nut.
- **Body:** figured top; sunburst or colors.
- **Electronics:** two black six-polepiece pickups and one black coverless humbucker (at bridge); two controls (volume with push-switch, tone) and five-way selector, all on body; jack in body face.
- **Hardware:** no pickguard; two-pivot bridge/vibrato unit.

■ **2004** American Deluxe Stratocaster (second version)

AMERICAN DELUXE STRATOCASTER HSS 2004–current

Two white or black single coils and one white or black humbucker, staggered height locking tuners, two-pivot vibrato.
Similar to AMERICAN DELUXE STRATOCASTER SECOND VERSION (see earlier listing this year) except:
- **Neck:** no string-guide; roller nut.
- **Electronics:** two white or black six-polepiece pickups and one white or black coverless humbucker (at bridge).

AMERICAN DELUXE STRATOCASTER HSS LT 2004–06

Two white or black single coils and one white or black humbucker, staggered height locking tuners, two-pivot locking vibrato.
Similar to AMERICAN DELUXE STRATOCASTER SECOND VERSION (see earlier listing this year) except:
- **Neck:** no string-guide; roller nut.
- **Electronics:** two white or black six-polepiece pickups and one white or black coverless humbucker (at bridge).
- **Hardware:** two-pivot locking bridge/vibrato unit

AMERICAN DELUXE STRATOCASTER QMT HSS 2004–09

Similar to AMERICAN DELUXE STRATOCASTER FMT HSS (see earlier listing this year) except figured-top body.

AMERICAN DELUXE STRATOCASTER 'V' NECK 2004–current

Three white single coils, staggered height locking tuners, two-pivot vibrato, fretted maple neck with 'V' profile (a.k.a. 'boat neck').
Similar to AMERICAN DELUXE STRATOCASTER SECOND VERSION (see earlier listing this year) except:
- **Neck:** fretted maple only, 1950s-style 'V'-shaping.
- **Hardware:** 11-screw white, gold, or copper plastic pickguard.

AMERICAN DELUXE 50th ANNIVERSARY STRATOCASTER 2004

Commemorative neckplate, staggered-height locking tuners, gold-plated hardware.
Similar to AMERICAN DELUXE STRATOCASTER SECOND VERSION (see earlier listing this year) except:
- **Neck:** fretted maple only; commemorative neckplate.
- **Body:** sunburst only.
- **Hardware:** gold-plated; 11-screw white plastic pickguard.

■ **2004** American Deluxe Stratocaster 'V' Neck

STRATOCASTER 2004

■ **2004** American Deluxe Stratocaster QMT

■ **2004** American Deluxe 50th Anniversary Stratocaster

■ **2004** Deluxe Player's Strat

AMERICAN 50th ANNIVERSARY STRATOCASTER 2004

Commemorative neckplate, locking tuners'
Similar to AMERICAN STRATOCASTER (see 2000 listing) except:
- **Neck:** fretted maple only; commemorative neckplate.

ANTIGUA STRATOCASTER (MIJ) 2004

Replica of 1977-period U.S. original with white/brown shaded body finish and matching pickguard (see STRATOCASTER CBS SEVENTIES 1971 listing).

DELUXE PLAYER'S STRAT (MIM) 2004–current

Gold-plated hardware, push-switch, three Noiseless logo white pickups.
Similar to STANDARD STRATOCASTER (see 1991 listing) except:
- **Electronics:** three Noiseless logo white six-polepiece pickups; three controls (volume, two tone), five-way switch and push-switch, all on pickguard.
- **Hardware:** gold-plated; 11-screw tortoiseshell pickguard.

DELUXE STRAT HH (MIM) 2004

Another name for DELUXE FAT STRAT (see 1999 listing).

DELUXE STRAT HH WITH LOCKING TREMOLO (MIM) 2004

Another name for DELUXE DOUBLE FAT STRAT FLOYD ROSE (see 1998 listing).

DELUXE STRAT HSS (MIM) 2004–06

Another name for DELUXE FAT STRAT (see 1999 listing).

DELUXE STRAT HSS WITH LOCKING TREMOLO (MIM) 2004–05

Another name for DELUXE FAT STRAT HSS FLOYD ROSE (see 1998 listing).

ERIC CLAPTON STRATOCASTER (third version) 2004–current

Signature on headstock rear, three Noiseless logo white pickups, 'Custom Shop headstock' logo.
Similar to ERIC CLAPTON STRATOCASTER FIRST VERSION (see 1988 listing) except:
- **Neck:** Eric Clapton signature and 'Custom Shop' logo on back of headstock.
- **Electronics:** three Noiseless logo white six-polepiece pickups; no active circuit.
Custom Shop production.

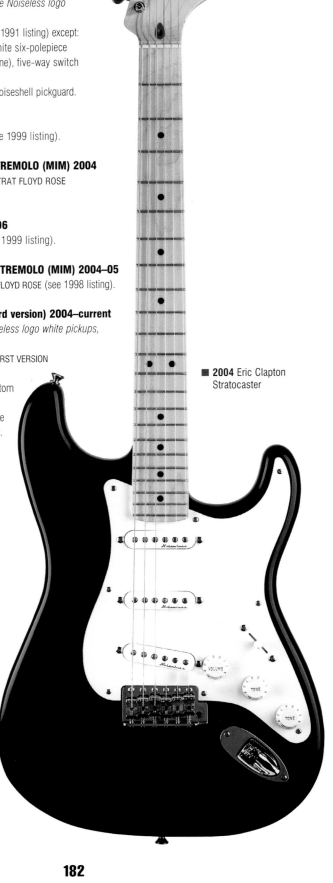

■ **2004** Eric Clapton Stratocaster

STRATOCASTER 2004

■ **2004** Standard Stratocaster HSS

■ **2004** Standard Stratocaster HSS
with Locking Tremolo

JEFF BECK SIGNATURE STRATOCASTER
2004–current
Signature on headstock rear, 'Custom Shop' logo on headstock.
Similar to JEFF BECK STRATOCASTER SECOND VERSION (see 2001 listing) except:
- **Neck:** Jeff Beck signature and 'Custom Shop' logo on back of headstock.

Custom Shop production.

LITE ASH STRATOCASTER (MIK) 2004–08
Maple neck with maple fingerboard, three Seymour Duncan-logo black single-coils, black pickguard.
- **Neck:** maple with maple fingerboard; 22 frets; truss-rod adjuster at headstock end; two string-guides.
- **Body:** natural, black, or white.
- **Electronics:** three Seymour Duncan-logo black six-polepiece pickups (bridge pickup angled); three controls (volume, two tone) and five-way selector, all on pickguard; jack in body face.

- **Hardware:** 11-screw black plastic pickguard; two-pivot bridge/vibrato unit.

RORY GALLAGHER STRATOCASTER
2004–current
Ultra-distressed finish, one mismatching tuner.
- **Neck:** maple with rosewood fingerboard; truss-rod adjuster at body end; one mismatching tuner; two string-guides.
- **Body:** sunburst, ultra-distressed finish.
- **Electronics:** three white six-polepiece pickups (bridge pickup angled); three controls (volume, two tone) and five-way selector, all on pickguard; jack in body face.
- **Hardware:** 11-screw white laminated plastic pickguard; six-pivot bridge/vibrato unit.

Custom Shop production.

183

STANDARD STRATOCASTER HH (MIM) 2004–06
Two-pivot vibrato, two black humbuckers, black pickguard, small headstock.
Similar to STANDARD STRATOCASTER
(see 1991 listing) except:
- **Neck:** maple with rosewood fingerboard only.
- **Electronics:** two black coverless humbuckers.
- **Hardware:** 11-screw black laminated plastic pickguard.

STANDARD STRATOCASTER HSS (MIM) 2004–current
Another name for STANDARD FAT STRAT (see 1999 listing).

STANDARD STRATOCASTER HSS WITH LOCKING TREMOLO (MIM) 2004–current
Another name for STANDARD FAT STRAT FLOYD ROSE (see 1999 listing).

50th ANNIVERSARY GOLDEN STRATOCASTER (MIM) 2004
Gold-finish body.
Similar to CLASSIC 50S STRATOCASTER (see 1999 listing) except:
- **Body:** gold only.

'66 STRATOCASTER 2004–08
Replica of 1966-period original (see STRATOCASTER CBS SIXTIES 1965 listing). Available with three finish distress degrees: N.O.S., Closet Classic, and Relic.
Custom Shop production.

AERODYNE STRATOCASTER second version (MIJ) 2005–06
Aerodyne Series on headstock, three black single coils, no pickguard.
Similar to AERODYNE STRATOCASTER
FIRST VERSION (see 2004 listing) except:
- **Electronics:** three controls (volume, two tone) and five-way selector, all on body; side-mounted jack.
- **Hardware:** no pickguard.

■ **2005** Eric Johnson Stratocaster

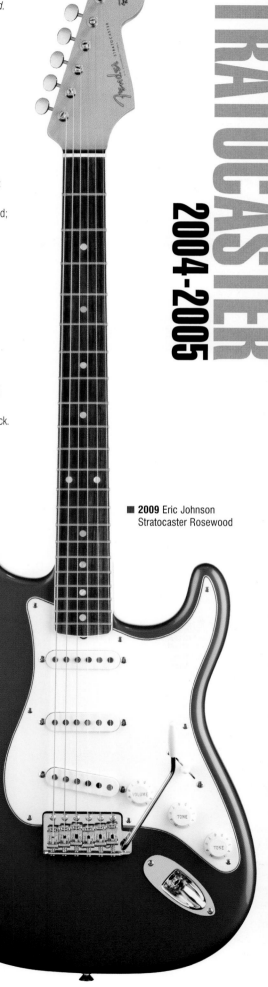

DELUXE BIG BLOCK STRATOCASTER (MIM) 2005–06.

Block markers, black headstock face, chrome pickguard.

- **Neck:** maple with rosewood fingerboard, block markers; truss-rod adjuster at headstock end; one string-guide; black-face headstock.
- **Body:** black only.
- **Electronics:** two black six-polepiece pickups and one black coverless humbucker (at bridge); two controls (volume, tone) and five-way selector, all on pickguard; jack in body face.
- **Hardware:** 11-screw chrome plastic pickguard; six-pivot bridge/vibrato unit.

ERIC JOHNSON STRATOCASTER 2005–current

Engraved neckplate, fretted maple neck

- **Neck:** fretted maple; truss-rod adjuster at body end; staggered height tuners; engraved neckplate.
- **Body:** sunburst or colors.
- **Electronics:** three white six-polepiece pickups (bridge pickup angled); three controls (volume, two tone) and five-way selector, all on pickguard; jack in body face.
- **Hardware:** eight-screw white plastic pickguard; six-pivot bridge/vibrato unit.

JOHN MAYER STRATOCASTER 2005–current

Signature on back of headstock.

- **Neck:** maple with rosewood fingerboard; truss-rod adjuster at body end; one string-guide (further up headstock); John Mayer signature on back of headstock.
- **Body:** sunburst, gold with stripes, or white.
- **Electronics:** three white six-polepiece pickups (bridge pickup angled); three controls (volume, two tone) and five-way selector, all on pickguard; jack in body face.
- **Hardware:** 11-screw white or tortoiseshell laminated plastic pickguard; six-pivot bridge/ vibrato unit.

■ **2009** Eric Johnson Stratocaster Rosewood

ROBIN TROWER STRATOCASTER 2005–current

Signature on back of large headstock.

- **Neck:** fretted maple only; bullet truss-rod adjuster at headstock end; one string-guide; Robin Trower signature on back of large headstock.
- **Body:** various colors.
- **Electronics:** three white six-polepiece pickups (bridge pickup angled); three controls (volume, two tone) and five-way selector, all on pickguard; jack in body face.
- **Hardware:** 11-screw white laminated plastic pickguard; six-pivot bridge/vibrato unit.

Custom Shop production.

STANDARD STRATOCASTER FMT (MIM) 2005–06

Figured-top body, no pickguard, three black single coil pickups.

- **Neck:** maple with rosewood fingerboard; truss-rod adjuster at headstock end; one string guide.
- **Body:** with figured top; cherry sunburst or tobacco sunburst.
- **Electronics:** three black six-polepiece pickups (bridge pickup angled); two controls (volume, tone) and five-way selector, all on body; side-mounted jack.
- **Hardware:** no pickguard; six-pivot bridge/ vibrato unit.

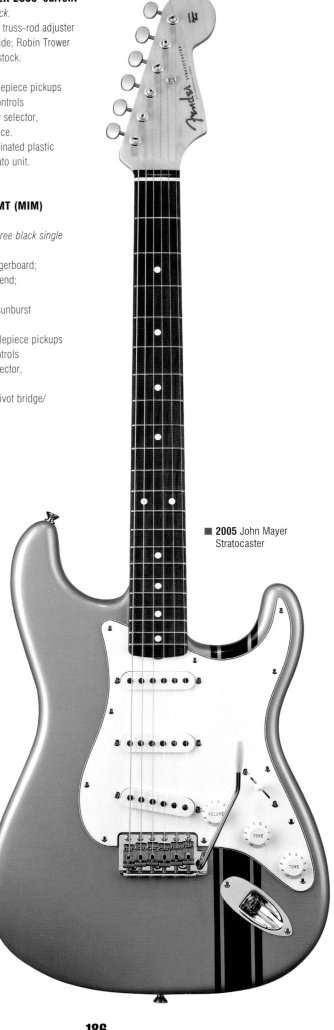

■ **2005** John Mayer Stratocaster

STRATOCASTER 2006

TIE-DYE STRAT HS (MIK) 2005

Multi-colored body front, matching headstock face.
- **Neck:** maple with rosewood fingerboard, no front markers; 22 frets; truss-rod adjuster at headstock end; two string-guides; multi-color headstock face.
- **Body:** black, multi-color front, two color combinations only.
- **Electronics:** one black six-polepiece pickup (at neck) and one black coverless humbucker (at bridge); two controls (volume, tone) and three-way selector, all on body; side-mounted jack.
- **Hardware:** black-plated; no pickguard; two-pivot bridge/vibrato unit.

AERODYNE CLASSIC STRATOCASTER (MIJ) 2006–09

'Aerodyne Series' on headstock, figured carved body top.
Similar to AERODYNE STRATOCASTER FIRST VERSION (see 2004 listing) except:
- **Neck:** 'Aerodyne Series' on matching color headstock face.
- **Body:** bound; figured carved top; various colors.
- **Electronics:** three white six-polepiece pickups (bridge pickup angled).
- **Hardware:** 11-screw white laminated plastic pickguard.

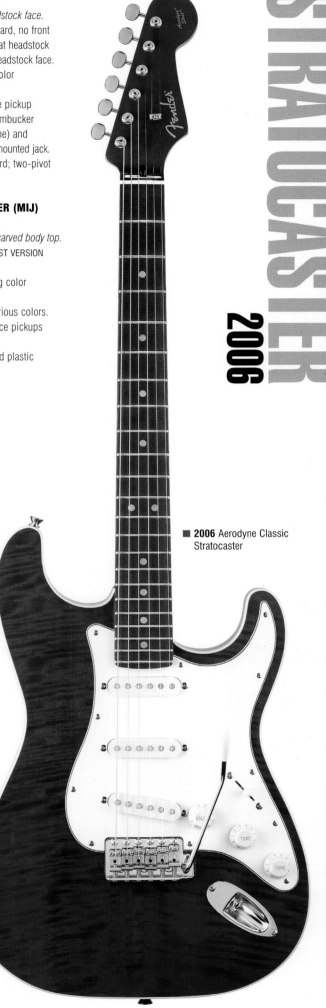

■ **2006** Aerodyne Classic Stratocaster

AMERICAN VINTAGE 70s STRATOCASTER 2006–current

Replica of 1970s-period original
(see STRATOCASTER CBS SEVENTIES 1971 listing).

AMERICAN 60th ANNIVERSARY STRATOCASTER 2006

Commemorative neckplate, maple neck with rosewood fingerboard.
Similar to AMERICAN STRATOCASTER (see 2000 listing) except:
- **Neck:** maple with rosewood fingerboard only; commemorative headstock logo with jewel inlay; commemorative neckplate.

CLASSIC PLAYER 50s STRATOCASTER (MIM) 2006–current

Maple fingerboard, locking tuners, two-pivot vibrato.
Similar to CLASSIC 50S STRATOCASTER (see 1999 listing) except:
- **Neck:** locking tuners; neckplate with 'Custom Shop designed' logo.
- **Body:** sunburst or gold.
- **Hardware:** two-pivot bridge/vibrato unit.

CLASSIC PLAYER 60s STRATOCASTER (MIM) 2006–current

Rosewood fingerboard, locking tuners, two-pivot vibrato.
Similar to CLASSIC 60S STRATOCASTER (see 1999 listing) except:
- **Neck:** locking tuners; neckplate with 'Custom Shop designed' logo.
- **Body:** sunburst or blue.
- **Hardware:** two-pivot bridge/vibrato unit.

DELUXE POWER STRATOCASTER (MIM) 2006–current

Fishman Powerbridge vibrato, two volume controls, one tone control.
Similar to STANDARD STRATOCASTER
(see 1991 listing) except:
- **Electronics:** two white six-polepiece pickups and one white coverless humbucker (at bridge); three controls (volume, tone, piezo volume) and five-way switch, all on pickguard.
- **Hardware:** 11-screw tortoiseshell pickguard; six-pivot Fishman Powerbridge vibrato with six piezo pickup bridge saddles.

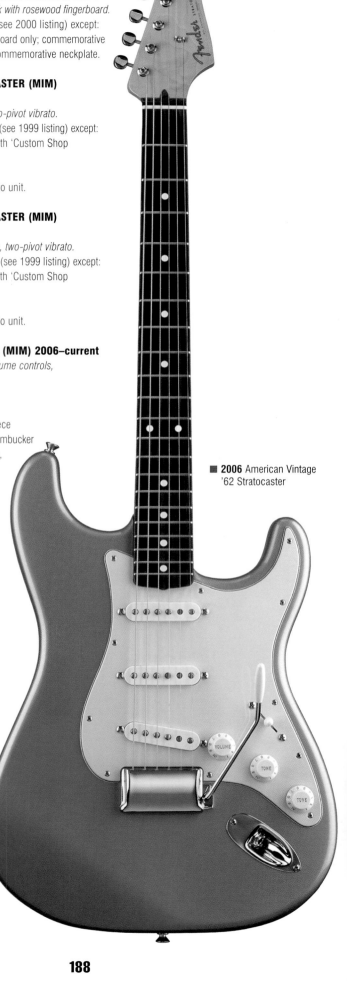

■ **2006** American Vintage '62 Stratocaster

STRATOCASTER 2006

188

■ **2006** Classic Player 50s Stratocaster

■ **2006** Classic Player 60s Stratocaster

■ **2006** Deluxe Power Stratocaster

HIGHWAY ONE STRATOCASTER
(second version) 2006–current

*Satin body finish, white pickguard, three white
single-coils, large headstock.*
Similar to HIGHWAY ONE STRATOCASTER FIRST VERSION
(see 2002 listing) except:
- **Neck:** large headstock.

HIGHWAY ONE STRATOCASTER HSS
(second version) 2006–current

*Satin body finish, large headstock, white pickguard,
two black single-coils and one black humbucker.*
Similar to HIGHWAY ONE STRATOCASTER HSS FIRST VERSION
(see 2003 listing) except:
- **Electronics:** two black six-polepiece pickups
  and one black coverless humbucker (at bridge);
  black plastic knobs.

KOA STRATOCASTER (MIK) 2006–08

Rosewood fingerboard, white pearl pickguard.
- **Neck:** maple with rosewood fingerboard; 22 frets;
  truss-rod adjuster at headstock end; two string-guides.
- **Body:** with Koa veneer top; sunburst only.
- **Electronics:** three white six polepiece pickups
  (bridge pickup angled); three controls (volume,
  two tone) and five-way selector, all on pickguard;
  jack in body face.
- **Hardware:** 11-screw white pearl laminated plastic
  pickguard; two-pivot bridge/vibrato unit.

■ **2006** Highway One
Stratocaster second
version (left-hand)

STRATOCASTER 2006

■ **2004** press advertisement

STRATOCASTER

2006

■ **2006** Highway One
Stratocaster HSS
second version

STANDARD 60th ANNIVERSARY STRATOCASTER (MIM) 2006

Commemorative neckplate, fretted maple neck.
Similar to STANDARD STRATOCASTER
(see 1991 listing) except:
- **Neck:** fretted maple only; commemorative neckplate.
- **Body:** silver grey only.

STRAT PRO 2006–08

Large headstock, roller nut, two-pivot vibrato.
- **Neck:** fretted maple, or maple with rosewood fingerboard; 22 frets (from 2007); truss-rod adjuster at body end; roller nut; large headstock.
- **Body:** black or white, distressed finish.
- **Electronics:** three white six-polepiece pickups (bridge pickup angled); three controls (volume, two tone) and five-way selector, all on pickguard; jack in body face.
- **Hardware:** 11-screw white laminated plastic pickguard; two-pivot bridge/vibrato unit.

Custom Shop production.

1962 STRATOCASTER HEAVY RELIC 2007

Replica of 1962-period original (see STRATOCASTER PRE-CBS listing in earlier US Regular Stratocasters section). Heavy finish distress.
Custom Shop production.

■ **2007** Rory Gallagher Stratocaster

STRATOCASTER 2007

VIRTUAL TONE

The advent of viable 'virtual' instruments, made possible by continuing advances in digital technology, spurred Fender to release the VG Stratocaster in 2007. This guitar was capable of hopping from standard Strat to acoustic guitar to humbucker-loaded rock machine at the flick of a couple of switches.

Unlike models from some rival makers, which displayed no traditional pickups at all and relied entirely on a digital pickup linked to internal emulation circuitry to simulate guitar sounds, Fender packaged the VG Stratocaster within an otherwise standard American Series Stratocaster, wedded to onboard Roland VG technology. Rather than overcomplicating matters and packing in all the potential that digital sound emulation can provide, Fender made a conscious decision to keep the instrument simple and functional, so that players can easily make changes on the fly in live performance without the danger of slipping into an undesired soundscape.

In addition to its three traditional magnetic single-coil pickups, the single master Volume and Tone controls, and five-way pickup selector, the VG Stratocaster carries a slim Roland GK pickup near the bridge, a rotary Mode control to select either Normal (non-digital mode), Stratocaster, Telecaster, Humbucking, or Acoustic sounds, and a rotary Tuning control to select Normal, Dropped D, Open G, D Modal, Baritone, or 12-string sounds. In all, between the Mode control and five-way pickup selector, the VG Stratocaster offers 37 pickup sounds.

Of course, Fender is no newcomer to digital technology. Fender's Cyber series of digital emulation amps was launched in 2001 with the original Cyber-Twin, which was joined for a time by the smaller Cyber-Deluxe, now discontinued. Fender's modeling flagship evolved into the Cyber-Twin SE (Second Edition), a 2x65-watt stereo combo with two 12-inch Celestion speakers, two 12AX7 preamp tubes, and digital amp emulation circuitry. It offered 69 preset sounds, 36 'Your Amp Collection' sounds (with the tones of classic Fender amps alongside the sounds of amps from other makers), and a bevy of digital effects.

Out of the virtual and back into the actual realm, Fender's genuine all-tube amp offerings of 2006 and 2007 included a handful of 'new' models inspired by another lingering glance backward: the Princeton Recording-Amp is a reproduction of the 'blackface' mid-60s Princeton Reverb with added rack-style compressor, overdrive, and power attenuator; the '57 Deluxe Amp is a faithful replica (many players would say long overdue) of the popular 5E3 model tweed Deluxe circa 1957 (the '57 Amp is the same in a custom piano-lacquered maple cabinet); and the Champion 600 is a partial reproduction of the like named model launched almost 60 years before, but with a hotrod preamp stage.

The Super-Sonic of 2006 is a blend of looking both backward and forward: it's a channel-switching tube amp with two different voices in its Vintage channel, inspired by the blackface '65 Vibrolux and blackface '66 Bassman, and contemporary rock sounds in its high-gain Burn channel. The 60-watt amplifier is offered either as a 1x12 combo with Celestion Vintage 60 speaker or as an amp head and separate speaker cabinet.

■ **2006** catalog

■ **2007** press advertisement

AMERICAN VG STRATOCASTER 2007–09
Extra slim white pickup at bridge,
two large and two small controls.
Similar to AMERICAN STRATOCASTER
(see 2000 listing) except:
• **Electronics:** extra slim white plain-top Roland
synthesizer pickup (at bridge); four controls
(two large: volume, tone; two small: Roland
Mode, Tuning), five-way selector and LED,
all on pickguard; jack in body face;
side-mounted multi-pin synth output.

■ **2007** American VG
Stratocaster

STRATOCASTER 2007

VINTAGE HOT ROD '57 STRAT 2007–current

Two white six-polepiece pickups and one white twin-blade pickup.

- **Neck:** fretted maple; truss-rod adjuster at body end; one string guide.
- **Body:** sunburst, black, or red.
- **Electronics:** two white six-polepiece pickups and one white twin-blade pickup (angled at bridge); three controls (volume, two tone) and five-way selector, all on pickguard; jack in body face.
- **Hardware:** eight-screw white plastic pickguard; six-pivot bridge/vibrato unit.

'60s CLOSET CLASSIC COMPETITION STRIPE STRATOCASTER 2007

Three Noiseless logo white pickups, staggered height locking tuners, two-pivot vibrato, roller nut. Distressed finish replica of 1960-period original (see STRATOCASTER PRE-CBS listing in earlier US Regular Stratocasters section). Stripes on body. *Custom Shop production.*

■ **2007** Vintage Hot Rod '57 Stratocaster

■ **2007** Vintage Hot Rod
'62 Stratocaster

STRATOCASTER 2008

VINTAGE HOT ROD '62 STRAT 2007–current
Circuitry modifications.
- **Neck:** maple with rosewood fingerboard; truss-rod adjuster at body end; one string guide.
- **Body:** sunburst, white, or green.
- **Electronics:** three white six-polepiece pickups (bridge pickup angled); three controls (volume, two tone) and five-way selector, all on pickguard; jack in body face.
- **Hardware:** 11-screw white laminated plastic pickguard; six-pivot bridge/vibrato unit.

Circuitry modifications as standard.

YNGWIE MALMSTEEN STRATOCASTER (third version) 2007–current
Signature on large headstock, six-pivot vibrato, 'bullet' truss-rod adjuster at headstock end.
Similar to YNGWIE MALMSTEEN STRATOCASTER SECOND VERSION (see 1998 listing) except:
- **Neck:** 'bullet' truss-rod adjuster at headstock end.

YNGWIE MALMSTEEN STRATOCASTER (second version) 1998–2006
Signature on large headstock, six-pivot vibrato.
Similar to YNGWIE MALMSTEEN STRATOCASTER FIRST VERSION (see 1988 listing) except:
- **Neck:** Yngwie Malmsteen signature on large headstock.
- **Electronics:** three controls (volume, two tone) and three-way selector, all on pickguard.
- **Hardware:** six-pivot bridge/vibrato unit.

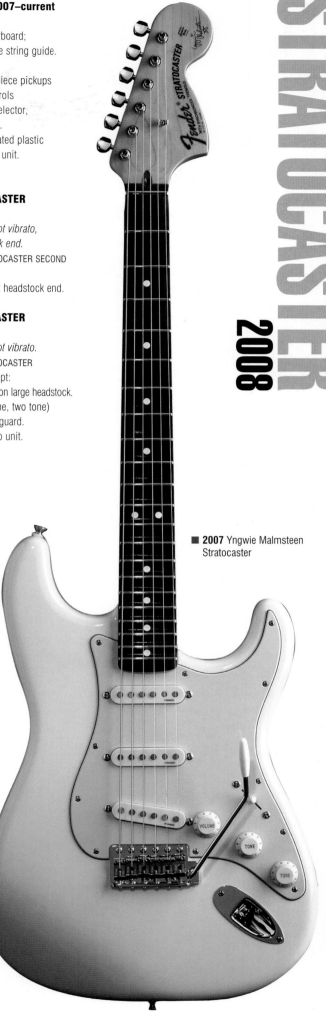

■ **2007** Yngwie Malmsteen Stratocaster

AMERICAN STANDARD STRATOCASTER
second version 2008-current

22 frets, small headstock, one string-guide, four-screw neckplate, three controls, bent steel bridge saddles.

- **Neck:** fretted maple neck, or maple neck with rosewood fingerboard; 22 frets; truss-rod adjuster at headstock end; one string-guide.
- **Body:** body sunburst or colours.
- **Electronics:** three white six-polepiece pickups (bridge pickup angled); three controls (volume, two tone) and five-way selector, all on pickguard; jack socket in body face.
- **Hardware:** 11-screw off-white laminated plastic pickguard; two-pivot bridge/vibrato unit; bent steel saddles.

■ **2008** American Standard (left-hand)

STRATOCASTER 2008

AMERICAN STANDARD STRATOCASTER HSS
2008-current
Two white single-coils and one white humbucker,
staggered height tuners, two-pivot vibrato,
bent steel bridge saddles, one string-guide.
Similar to AMERICAN STANDARD STRATOCASTER
second version (see listing in earlier US Regular
Stratocasters section), except:
- **Electronics:** two white six-polepiece pickups
  and one white coverless humbucker (at bridge).

1957 COMMEMORATIVE STRATOCASTER 2007
Replica of 1957-period original (see STRATOCASTER
PRE-CBS listing in earlier US Regular Stratocasters
section) but with commemorative neckplate.
Blonde finish, gold-plated hardware.

1962 STRATOCASTER HEAVY RELIC 2007
Replica of 1962-period original (see STRATOCASTER
PRE-CBS listing in earlier US Regular Stratocasters
section). Heavy finish distress.
Custom Shop production.

DAVID GILMOUR STRATOCASTER NOS
2008-current
Black body, black pickguard, mini-switch, short vibrato arm.
- **Neck:** fretted maple neck; truss-rod adjuster at body
  end; one string-guide.
- **Body:** black only.
- **Electronics:** three white six-polepiece pickups
  (bridge pickup angled); three controls (volume,
  two tone), five-way selector and mini-switch,
  all on pickguard; jack socket in body face.
- **Hardware:** 11-screw black plastic pickguard;
  six-pivot bridge/vibrato unit, short vibrato arm.
Also DAVID GILMOUR STRATOCASTER RELIC
with distressed finish (2008-current).
Custom Shop production.

■ **2008** George Fullerton 50th Anniversary

■ **2008** American Standard Stratocaster HSS

199

DELUXE ROADHOUSE STRATOCASTER
2008-current

Modern-style 'thick' Fender headstock logo in silver, six-pivot vibrato, tortoiseshell pickguard.
Similar to STANDARD STRATOCASTER (see later listing), except:

- **Neck:** fretted maple neck only.
- **Body:** body sunburst, black or white.
- **Electronics:** visually similar pickups but different specification.
- **Hardware:** 11-screw tortoiseshell laminated plastic pickguard.

DELUXE LONE STAR STRATOCASTER
2008-current

Two white single-coils and one Seymour Duncan-logo white humbucker, tortoisehell pickguard, six-pivot vibrato.
Similar to STANDARD STRATOCASTER (see later listing), except:

- **Neck:** maple neck with rosewood fingerboard only.
- **Body:** body sunburst, black or white.
- **Electronics:** two white six-polepiece pickups and one Seymour Duncan-logo white coverless humbucker (at bridge).
- **Hardware:** 11-screw tortoiseshell laminated plastic pickguard.

DELUXE FAT STRAT second version (MIM)
2008-09

Six-pivot vibrato, two black single-coils and one black humbucker, white pickguard, large headstock.
Similar to DELUXE FAT STRAT first version (see listing), except:

- **Hardware:** 11-screw white laminated plastic pickguard.

■ **2008** Deluxe Lone Star Stratocaster

CLASSIC HBS-1 STRATOCASTER 2009-current

22 frets, six-pivot vibrato, two white single-coils and one black humbucker.

- **Neck:** fretted maple neck; truss-rod adjuster at headstock end; one string-guide.
- **Body:** sunburst or black.
- **Electronics:** two white six-polepiece pickups and one Seymour Duncan logo black coverless humbucker (at bridge); three controls (volume, two tone - one with push-switch) and five-way selector, all on pickguard; jack socket in body face.
- **Hardware:** 11-screw white laminated plastic pickguard; six-pivot bridge/vibrato unit.

Available with two finish distress degrees: N.O.S. and Relic.

Custom Shop production.

BILLY CORGAN STRATOCASTER 2009-current

Signature on back of headstock.

- **Neck:** fretted maple neck; 22 frets; truss-rod adjuster at headstock end; two string-guides; Billy Corgan signature on back of large headstock.
- **Body:** body satin black or satin white.
- **Electronics:** three black twin-blade pickups (bridge pickup angled); three controls (volume, two tone) and five-way selector, all on pickguard; jack socket in body face.
- **Hardware:** 11-screw black or white laminated plastic pickguard; six-saddle small bridge with through-body stringing.

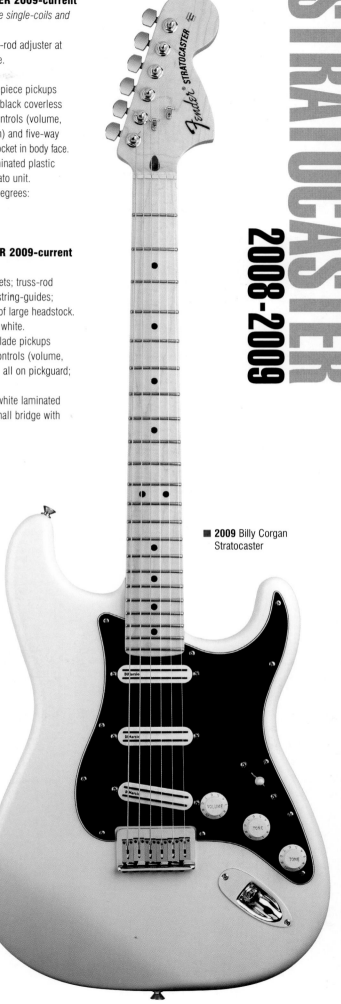

■ **2009** Billy Corgan Stratocaster

RITCHIE BLACKMORE STRATOCASTER (MIM)
2009-current

Signature on headstock.
Similar to CLASSIC 70S STRATOCASTER (see listing in earlier Mexico Replica Stratocasters section), except:
- **Neck:** maple neck with scalloped rosewood fingerboard only; Ritchie Blackmore signature on large headstock.
- **Body:** white only.
- **Electronics:** two black six-polepiece pickups (bridge pickup angled); center pickup missing, cover only installed; three controls (volume, two tone) and three-way selector, all on pickguard; jack socket in body face.

CUSTOM DELUXE STRATOCASTER (MIM)
2009-current

22 frets, two-pivot vibrato, staggered height locking tuners, Custom Shop logo on headstock.
- **Neck:** fretted maple neck, or maple neck with rosewood fingerboard; 22 frets; truss-rod adjuster at headstock end; staggered height locking tuners.
- **Body:** sunburst or colors.
- **Electronics:** three white six-polepiece pickups (bridge pickup angled); three controls (volume, two tone) and five-way selector, all on pickguard; jack socket in body face.
- **Hardware:** 11-screw white laminated plastic pickguard; two-pivot bridge/vibrato unit.

Custom Shop production.

DAVE MURRAY STRATOCASTER 2009-current

Signature on back of headstock.
- **Neck:** fretted maple neck; truss-rod adjuster at body end; one string-guide; Dave Murray signature on back of headstock.
- **Body:** body black only.
- **Electronics:** two white coverless humbuckers (with chrome-plated surrounds) and one white six-polepiece pickup in centre; three controls (volume, two tone) and three-way selector, all on pickguard; jack socket in body face.
- **Hardware:** eight-screw white plastic pickguard; six-pivot bridge/vibrato unit.

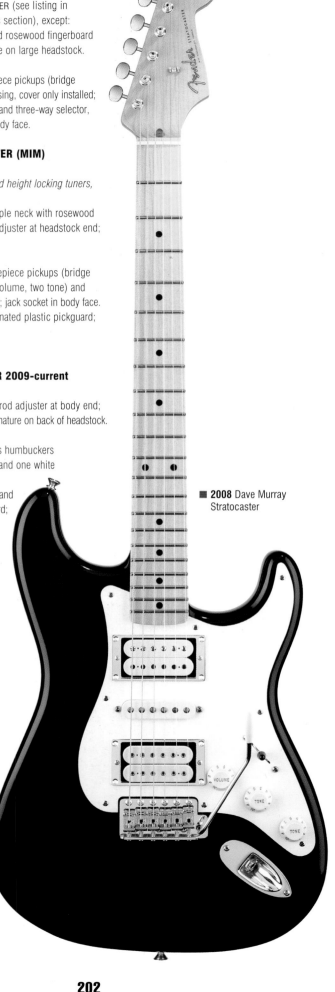

■ **2008** Dave Murray Stratocaster

■ **2008** Roadhouse Stratocaster

■ **2009** American Vintage '62 Stratocaster

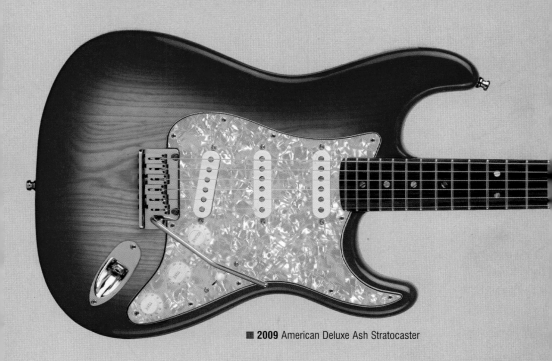

■ **2009** American Deluxe Ash Stratocaster

ERIC JOHNSON STRATOCASTER ROSEWOOD
2009-current
Engraved neckplate, maple neck with rosewood fingerboard.
Similar to ERIC JOHNSON STRATOCASTER MAPLE
(see previous listing), except:
- **Neck:** maple neck with rosewood fingerboard.
- **Body:** colors only.
- **Hardware:** 8-screw white laminated plastic pickguard.

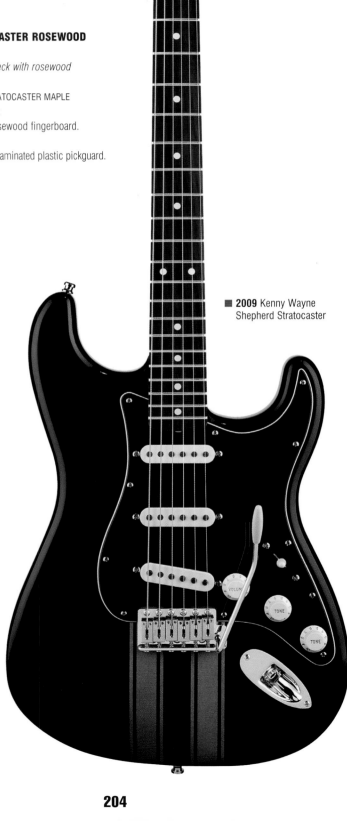

■ **2009** Kenny Wayne Shepherd Stratocaster

STRATOCASTER 2010

ROAD WORN 50s STRATOCASTER 2009-current

Distressed finish replica of 1950s-period original
(see STRATOCASTER PRE-CBS listing in earlier US
Regular Stratocasters section).

ROAD WORN 60s STRATOCASTER 2009-current

Distressed finish replica of 1960s-period original
(see STRATOCASTER PRE-CBS listing in earlier US
Regular Stratocasters section).

KENNY WAYNE SHEPHERD STRATOCASTER
2010-current

Signature on back of headstock.
Similar to CLASSIC 60S STRATOCASTER (see listing in
earlier Mexico Replica Stratocasters section), except:
- **Neck:** Kenny Wayne Shepherd signature on back
  of headstock.
- **Body:** body sunburst, black with silver stripes
  or white with black cross.
- **Hardware:** 11-screw black or white laminated
  plastic pickguard.

STRATOCASTER 2010

■ **2009** Road Worn 50s
Stratocaster

2009 press advertisement

2009 Road Worn
60s Stratocaster

JIM ROOT STRATOCASTER 2010-current
Signature on back of headstock.

- **Neck:** fretted maple neck, or maple neck with ebony fingerboard, no front position markers; 22 frets; truss-rod adjuster at headstock end; locking tuners; one string-guide; signature on back of large headstock.
- **Body:** hard-edge body; satin black or satin white.
- **Electronics:** two black plain-top active humbuckers; one control (volume) and three-way selector, all on pickguard; jack socket in body face.
- **Hardware:** 11-screw black laminated plastic pickguard; Six-saddle small bridge with through-body stringing; black-plated hardware.

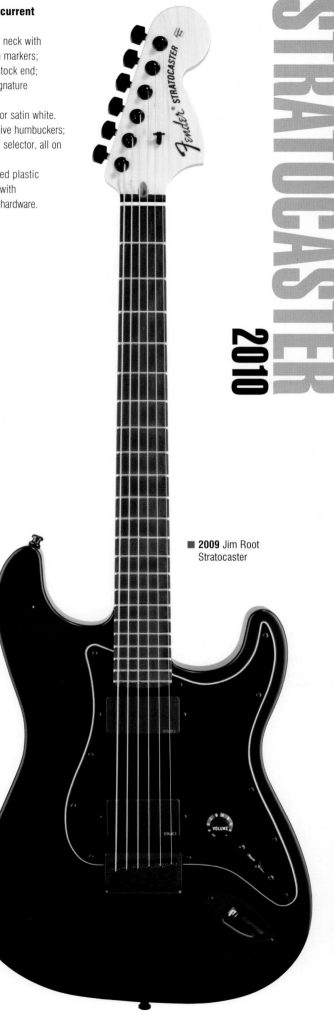

■ **2009** Jim Root Stratocaster

STRATOCASTER 2010

207

AMERICAN SPECIAL STRATOCASTER
2010-current
22 frets, large headstock, two string-guides.
- **Neck:** fretted maple neck; 22 frets; truss-rod adjuster at headstock end; two string-guides; large headstock.
- **Body:** sunburst or red.
- **Electronics:** three white six-polepiece pickups (bridge pickup angled); three controls (volume, two tone) and five-way selector, all on pickguard; jack socket in body face.
- **Hardware:** 11-screw white laminated plastic pickguard; six-pivot bridge/vibrato unit.

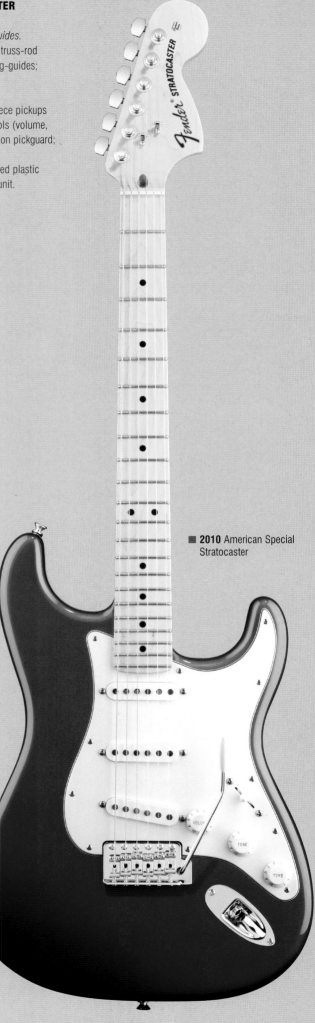

■ **2010** American Special Stratocaster

STRATOCASTER 2010

AMERICAN SPECIAL STRATOCASTER HSS
2010-current

Two black single-coils and one black humbucker, 22 frets, large headstock, two string-guides.
Similar to AMERICAN SPECIAL STRATOCASTER (see previous listing), except:

• **Neck:** maple neck with rosewood fingerboard.
• **Body:** body sunburst or black.
• **Electronics:** two black six-polepiece pickups and one black coverless humbucker (at bridge).
• **Hardware:** 11-screw black laminated plastic pickguard.

■ **2010** American Special
Stratocaster HSS

1963 STRATOCASTER 2010-current

Replica of 1963-period original (see STRATOCASTER PRE-CBS listing in earlier US Regular Stratocasters section). Available with two finish distress degrees: N.O.S. and Relic.
Custom Shop production.

1965 STRATOCASTER 2010-current

Replica of 1965-period original (see STRATOCASTER CBS SIXTIES listing in earlier US Regular Stratocasters section). Available with two finish distress degrees: N.O.S. and Relic.
Custom Shop production.

STRATOCASTER PRO RELIC 2010

Three Noiseless logo white pickups, staggered height locking tuners, two-pivot vibrato, roller nut.

- **Neck:** fretted maple neck, or maple neck with rosewood fingerboard; 22 frets; truss-rod adjuster at headstock end; staggered height locking tuners; roller nut.
- **Body:** Sunburst or red, distressed finish.
- **Electronics:** three Noiseless logo white six-polepiece pickups (bridge pickup angled); three controls (volume, two tone) and five-way selector, all on pickguard; jack socket in body face.
- **Hardware:** 11-screw white laminated plastic pickguard; two-pivot bridge/vibrato unit.

Custom Shop production.

1959 STRATOCASTER HEAVY RELIC 2010-current

Replica of 1959-period original (see STRATOCASTER PRE-CBS listing in earlier US Regular Stratocasters section). Heavy finish distress.
Custom Shop production.

■ **2010** American Special Stratocaster

STRATOCASTER 2010

■ **2010** catalog

■ **2010** American Special
Stratocaster HSS

■ **1957** press advertisement

DUO-SONIC (first version) 1956–64
Model name on headstock, neck pickup angled,
bridge pickup straight.

- **Neck:** fretted maple (maple neck with rosewood
  fingerboard from 1959); 22.5-inch scale, 21 frets;
  truss-rod adjuster at body end; plastic tuner buttons;
  one string-guide.
- **Body:** slab; originally beige only but
  was later offered in sunburst or colors.
- **Electronics:** two plain-top pickups
  (neck pickup angled); two controls
  (volume, tone), three-way selector
  and jack, all on pickguard.
- **Hardware:** eight-screw anodized
  metal pickguard (12-screw white
  or tortoiseshell laminated plastic
  from 1960); three-saddle
  bridge/tailpiece.

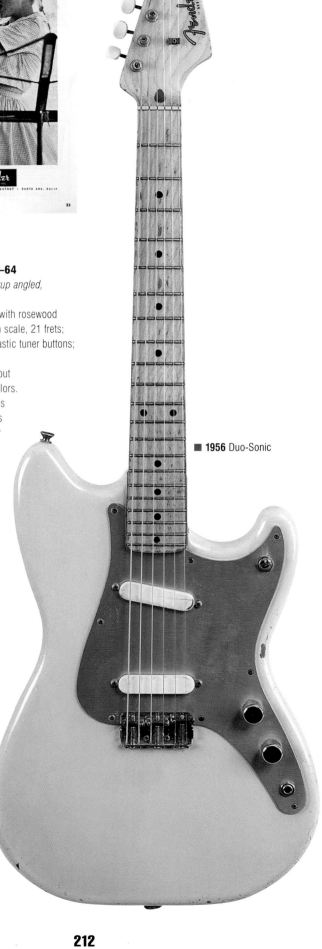

■ **1956** Duo-Sonic

MUSICMASTER
1956-1969

MUSICMASTER (first version) 1956–64

Model name on headstock, one angled pickup at neck.

- **Neck:** fretted maple neck (maple neck with rosewood fingerboard from 1959); 22.5-inch scale, 21 frets; truss-rod adjuster at body end; plastic tuner buttons; one string-guide.
- **Body:** slab body; originally beige only, later sunburst or colors.
- **Electronics:** one plain-top pickup (angled at neck); two controls (volume, tone) and jack, all on pickguard.
- **Hardware:** eight-screw anodized pickguard (12-screw white or tortoiseshell laminated plastic from 1960); three-saddle bridge/tailpiece.

DUO-SONIC (second version) 1964–69

Model name on enlarged headstock, both pickups angled, two slide switches.

- **Neck:** maple with rosewood fingerboard; 22.5-inch scale and 21 frets (or 24-inch scale and 22 frets; see next listing); enlarged headstock.
- **Body:** contoured offset-waist; red, white, or blue.
- **Electronics:** two white or black plain-top pickups (both angled). Two controls (volume, tone) and jack, all on metal plate adjoining pickguard; two selector slide-switches on pickguard.
- **Hardware:** 12-screw white pearl or tortoiseshell laminated plastic re-styled pickguard; enlarged three-saddle bridge/tailpiece.

Early examples with slab body.

DUO-SONIC II 1964–69

Variant of the Duo-Sonic (second version; see previous listing) with 24-inch scale and 22 frets.

MUSICMASTER (second version) 1964–75

Model name on headstock, one angled pickup, controls on metal plate, enlarged headstock.

- **Neck:** maple with rosewood fingerboard (fretted maple option from 1970); 22.5-inch scale and 21 frets (or 24-inch scale and 22 frets; see next listing); enlarged headstock.

- **Body:** contoured offset-waist; red, white, or blue.
- **Electronics:** one white or black plain-top pickup (angled at neck); two controls (volume, tone) and jack, all on metal plate adjoining pickguard.
- **Hardware:** 12-screw white pearl or tortoiseshell laminated plastic re-styled pickguard; enlarged three-saddle bridge/tailpiece.

Early examples with slab body. Version with 24-inch scale and 22 frets known as MUSICMASTER II *(1964–69) then just* MUSICMASTER *(1969–75).*

MUSICMASTER II 1964–69

Variant of the Musicmaster (second version; see previous listing) with 24-inch scale and 22 frets, known as MUSICMASTER II (1964–69) then simply MUSICMASTER (1969–75).

MUSICMASTER (third version) 1975–80

Model name on headstock, one angled pickup at neck, controls on black pickguard.

Similar to MUSICMASTER SECOND VERSION (see 1964 listing) except:

- **Neck:** 24-inch scale, 22 frets only.
- **Body:** black or white.
- **Electronics:** one black plain-top pickup (angled at neck); two controls (volume, tone) on pickguard.
- **Hardware:** 15-screw black laminated plastic pickguard.

DUO-SONIC (MIM) 1993–97

Model name on headstock, 20-fret neck, two angled pickups.

- **Neck:** fretted maple; 22.7-inch scale, 20 frets; truss-rod adjuster at body end; one string-guide.
- **Body:** slab offset-cutaway; black, red, or white.
- **Electronics:** two white six-polepiece pickups (both angled); two controls (volume, tone), three-way selector and jack, all on pickguard.
- **Hardware:** 12-screw white plastic pickguard; three-saddle bridge/tailpiece.

Based on U.S. original (see DUO-SONIC FIRST VERSION *1956 listing).*

■ **1957** Musicmaster

JAZZMASTER 1958–80

Model name on headstock, two large rectangular pickups.

- **Neck:** maple with rosewood fingerboard (bound from 1965), dot markers (blocks from 1966); truss-rod adjuster at body end; one string-guide.
- **Body:** contoured offset-waist; sunburst or colors.
- **Electronics:** two large rectangular white (black from 1977) six-polepiece pickups; two controls (volume, tone), two rollers (volume, tone), three-way selector, slide-switch, jack, all on pickguard.
- **Hardware:** nine-screw anodized metal pickguard (13-screw white or tortoiseshell laminated plastic from 1959; black laminated plastic from 1976); six-saddle bridge, vibrato tailpiece.

Prototype examples with smaller headstock and/or fretted maple neck.
Some examples with gold-plated hardware.

■ **1959** Jazzmaster

JAZZMASTER
1959-1960

■ **1959** Jazzmaster

■ **1960** Jazzmaster

■ **1960** Jazzmaster

A JAZZ GUITAR FOR THE SURF SCENE

In 1958, Fender introduced a new and quite different model that was intended to be its top-of-the-line electric guitar. The Jazzmaster was advertised as 'America's finest electric guitar;' it had a distinctive offset waist and dual-cutaway body, two entirely new pickups, a new wiring and switching circuit designed to offer two different preset sounds, and a new 'floating' vibrato system that was intended to have a smoother action and sound than that of the Stratocaster.

The Jazzmaster still had the Strat and Tele's 25.5-inch scale length and a similar neck, although with slightly different lines to the headstock. But it also carried another new element that seemed radical for Fender at the time: a rosewood fingerboard. From mid 1959 the Stratocaster, Telecaster, and Esquire would also receive rosewood fingerboards, and this component would partly typify the look of Fender guitars into the mid 60s.

Fenders were first fitted with what has become known as a 'slab board' fingerboard, which is to say a plank of rosewood milled flat on the underside and glued to a flat maple neck, radiused on the top side only. From mid 1962 a curved veneer of rosewood was fitted (sometimes referred to as the 'round-lam' fingerboard), and this became the standard thereafter.

The Jazzmaster failed to attract the players it was named for and in fact has rarely been seen for long in the hands of any reputable jazz artist. It did, however, make a pretty big splash with a lot of players on the surf and instrumental scenes that were big in the late 1950s and early 60s, and a decade and a half later became popular with a lot of punk and new wave players.

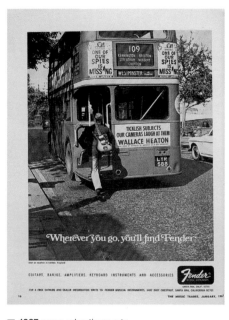

■ **1967** press advertisements

JAZZMASTER 1962-1966

■ **1962** Jazzmaster

■ **1963** Jazzmaster

■ **1966** Jazzmaster

JAZZMASTER (MIJ) 1986–onward
Replica of early 1960s-period U.S. original
(see 1958 listing). Gold-plated hardware option (1994).
Foto Flame fake figured wood finish option (1994–96).

AMERICAN VINTAGE '62 JAZZMASTER
1999–current
Replica of 1962-period original (see 1958 listing).

J. MASCIS JAZZMASTER (MIJ) 2007-current
Signature on back of headstock.
- **Neck:** maple neck with rosewood fingerboard;
  truss-rod adjuster at body end; one string-guide;
  purple sparkle-face headstock. J. Mascis signature
  on back of headstock.
- **Body:** contoured offset-waist body; purple
  sparkle only.
- **Electronics:** two large rectangular white six-
  polepiece pickups; two controls (volume, tone),
  two rollers (volume, tone), three-way selector,
  slide switch and jack socket, all on pickguard.
- **Hardware:** 13-screw gold anodised metal
  pickguard; six-saddle slimmer bridge,
  vibrato tailpiece.

■ **2004** American Vintage
'62 Jazzmaster

JAZZMASTER
1986-2007

JAZZMASTER
1986-2007

1999 press advertisement

2006 J. Mascis Jazzmaster

CLASSIC PLAYER JAZZMASTER SPECIAL (MIM)
2008-current
Six-saddle slimmer bridge, re-positioned vibrato.
Similar to AMERICAN VINTAGE '62 JAZZMASTER
(see listing in earlier Other US-made Models section),
except:
- **Body:** body sunburst or black.
- **Hardware:** 13-screw tortoiseshell laminated
  plastic pickguard; six-saddle slimmer bridge,
  re-positioned vibrato tailpiece.

ELVIS COSTELLO JAZZMASTER 2008-09
Signature on back of headstock.
Similar to AMERICAN VINTAGE '62 JAZZMASTER
(see earlier listing), except:
- **Neck:** Elvis Costello signature on back of headstock.
- **Body:** brown only.
- **Hardware:** 13-screw tortoiseshell laminated
  plastic pickguard.

■ **2008** Classic Player
Jazzmaster Special

JAZZMASTER 2008

2000 press advertisement

2008 Classic Player
Jazzmaster Special

LEE RANALDO JAZZMASTER 2009-current

Black metal pickguard, two split polepiece pickups,
one control.

Similar to AMERICAN VINTAGE '62 JAZZMASTER
(see earlier listing), except:
- **Neck:** black-face headstock.
- **Body:** body blue only.
- **Electronics:** two metal-cover split-polepiece
  humbuckers; One control (volume), three-way
  selector and jack socket, all on pickguard.
- **Hardware:** 13-screw black anodised metal pickguard.

THURSTON MOORE JAZZMASTER 2009-current

Black metal pickguard and control plate,
two large rectangular pickups, one control.
Similar to AMERICAN VINTAGE '62 JAZZMASTER
(see earlier listing), except:
- **Neck:** black-face headstock.
- **Body:** green only.
- **Electronics:** one control (volume), three-way
  selector and jack socket, all on black anodised
  metal plate adjoining pickguard.
- **Hardware:** 10-screw black anodised metal
  pickguard; six-saddle slimmer bridge,
  vibrato tailpiece.

■ **2008** Elvis Costello
Jazzmaster

JAZZMASTER 2009

■ **2008** Limited Edition
American Vintange '58 Jazzmaster

■ **2009** Lee Ranaldo Jazzmaster

■ **2009** Thurston Moore Jazzmaster

A SURF GUITAR FOR THE SURF SCENE

If the Jazzmaster was an accidental hero of the surf-music crowd, the Jaguar, introduced in 1962, seemed to be aimed at these players. The Jaguar hit the scene with even more complex switching options than the Jazzmaster. It used the separate upper control plate that allowed the player to set up a preset rhythm sound for the neck pickup, as did the Jazzmaster, but also carried three somewhat enigmatic slider switches on a separate plate on the pickguard. They are in fact just an on-off switch for each pickup and a two-way tone switch.

The Jag also used the so-called 'Synchronized Tremolo' that first appeared on the Jazzmaster but added a muting pad designed specifically for the popular muted-picking sound used in a lot of surf instrumental recordings. (Any player worth their salt was always able to produce this sound by muting the strings with the edge of the palm, so a lot of people removed this clunky item from their Jaguars.)

Unlike the Jazzmaster, the Jaguar had a shorter 24-inch scale length. It also carried two new-design pickups, which were wound to be brighter than the Jazzmaster's. Each had unique steel 'claws' at the sides – actually U-shaped channels that the pickups sat in – and these helped to focus the magnetic field toward the coil and make the pickup a little fatter and more powerful sounding than such a bright pickup would have been without them.

The Jaguar too failed to live up to its billing as Fender's top-of-the-line electric guitar, and after a brief flurry of interest the Telecaster and Stratocaster continued to outsell it. But it did strike a chord with the surf and instrumental stylists at which it was originally aimed and, like the Jazzmaster, became popular with punk and new wave players in the late 1970s – perhaps because even pre-CBS examples remained far more affordable than Strats and Teles on the used market.

Two years after introducing the Jaguar, Fender revealed another, somewhat simpler 24-inch-scale model, the Mustang (also available for a time with a 22.5-inch scale). Its body edges were only slightly contoured and it had simple switching and a basic vibrato system, aiming the Mustang very much as a student or mid-level electric. As such it was a distinct success. It has even slipped into the hands of a number of professionals over the years, and good vintage examples have recently attained a certain collectable status, especially the sporty 'Competition Stripe' models, although prices hover far below those of the major pre- and early-CBS Fender models.

■ **1962** press advertisements

JAGUAR 1962–75

Model name on headstock, three metal control plates.

- **Neck:** maple with rosewood fingerboard (bound from 1965), dot markers (blocks from 1966); 24-inch scale, 22 frets; truss-rod adjuster at body end; one string-guide.
- **Body:** contoured offset-waist; sunburst or colors.
- **Electronics:** two rectangular white six-polepiece pickups, each with metal 'sawtooth' sides; two controls (volume, tone) and jack, all on lower metal plate adjoining pickguard; slide-switch and two roller controls (volume, tone), all on upper metal plate adjoining pickguard; three slide-switches on metal plate inset into pickguard.
- **Hardware:** ten-screw white or tortoiseshell laminated plastic pickguard; six-saddle bridge, spring-loaded string mute, vibrato tailpiece.

Some examples with gold-plated hardware.

■ **1962** Jaguar

JAGUAR (MIJ) 1986–onward

Replica of early 1960s-period U.S. original
(see 1962 listing). Gold-plated hardware option (1994).
Foto Flame fake figured wood finish option (1994–96).
Also ANTIGUA JAGUAR, with white/brown shaded body
finish and matching pickguard (2004).

AMERICAN VINTAGE '62 JAGUAR 1999–current

Replica of 1962-period original (see 1962 listing).

ANTIGUA JAGUAR (MIJ) 2004

Replica of early 1960s-period U.S. original
(see 1962 listing), with white/brown shaded body
finish and matching pickguard.

■ 1996 Jaguar

JAGUAR 1986-2004

■ **1964** Jaguar

■ **1966** Jaguar

■ **1964** catalog

■ **1964** catalog

■ **2004** American Vintage
'62 Jaguar

JAGUAR
2004-2008

JAGUAR BARITONE CUSTOM (MIJ) 2004–06
Model name on headstock, long-scale neck.
Similar to JAGUAR (see 1986 listing) except:
- **Neck:** 21 frets, 28.5-inch scale; truss-rod
  adjuster at headstock end.
- **Body:** sunburst only.
- **Hardware:** nine-screw tortoiseshell laminated
  plastic pickguard; six-saddle bridge, bar tailpiece.
Known as JAGUAR BASS VI CUSTOM *(see 2006 listing).*

JAGUAR BARITONE HH (MIJ) 2005–current
*Black-face headstock, long-scale neck, two metal-cover
humbuckers, one metal control plate.*
Similar to JAGUAR BARITONE CUSTOM
(see 2004 listing) except:
- **Neck:** black-face headstock.
- **Body:** black only.
- **Electronics:** two metal-cover humbuckers;
  two controls (volume, tone) and jack, all on
  metal plate adjoining pickguard: three-way
  selector on pickguard.
- **Hardware:** 11-screw black laminated plastic
  pickguard; six saddle slimmer bridge,
  bar tailpiece.

JAGUAR HH (MIJ) 2005–current
*Special on black-face headstock, two metal-cover
humbuckers, three metal control plates.*
Similar to JAGUAR (see 1986 listing) except:
- **Neck:** truss-tod adjuster at headstock end;
  black-face headstock.
- **Body:** black only.
- **Electronics:** two metal-cover humbuckers.
- **Hardware:** nine-screw black plastic pickguard.

■ **2005** Limited Edition
Jaguar HH

CLASSIC PLAYER JAGUAR SPECIAL
2008-current

Six-saddle slimmer bridge, re-positioned vibrato.
Similar to AMERICAN VINTAGE '62 JAGUAR (see listing in earlier Other US-made Models section), except:

- **Body:** sunburst or red.
- **Hardware:** six-saddle slimmer bridge, re-positioned vibrato tailpiece.

■ **2007** Classic Player Jaguar Special HH

JAGUAR 2008

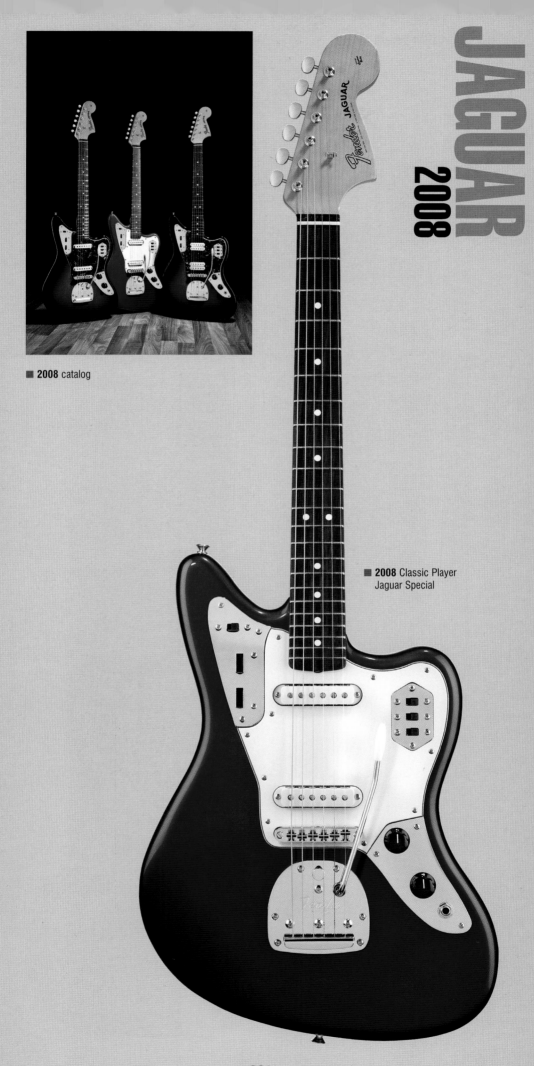

JAGUAR 2008

2008 catalog

2008 Classic Player
Jaguar Special

CLASSIC PLAYER JAGUAR SPECIAL HH (MIM)
2008-current

Six-saddle slimmer bridge, re-positioned vibrato,
two white humbuckers.

Similar to CLASSIC PLAYER JAGUAR SPECIAL
(see previous listing), except:

- **Body:** sunburst or white.
- **Electronics:** two white coverless humbuckers;
  two roller controls (pickup-coil blend) on upper
  metal plate adjoining pickguard.
- **Hardware:** nine-screw tortoiseshell laminated
  plastic pickguard.

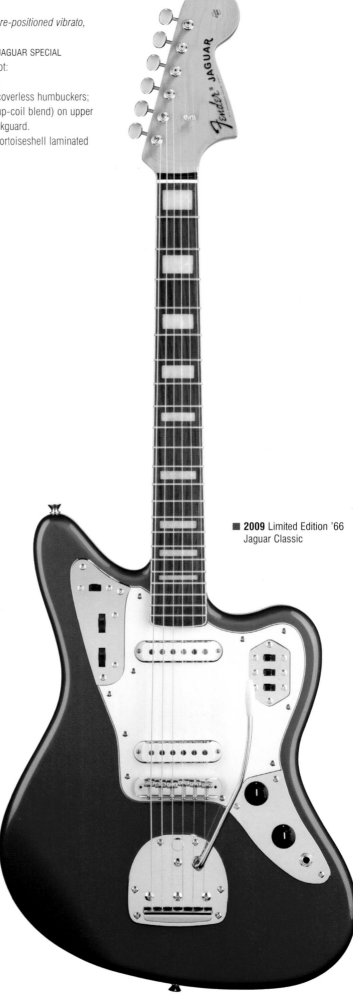

■ **2009** Limited Edition '66
Jaguar Classic

JAGUAR 2008

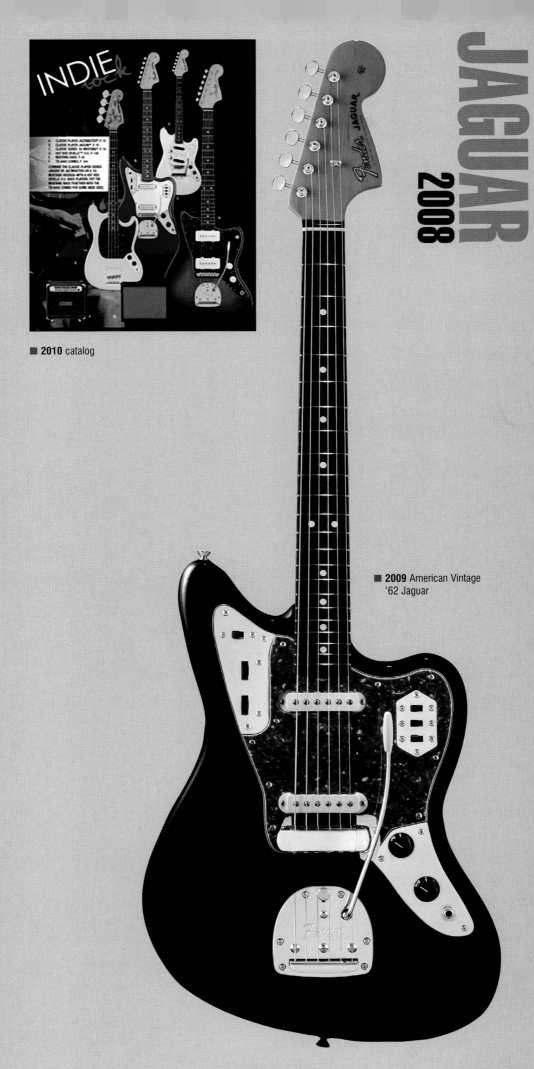

2010 catalog

2009 American Vintage
'62 Jaguar

■ **1965** catalog

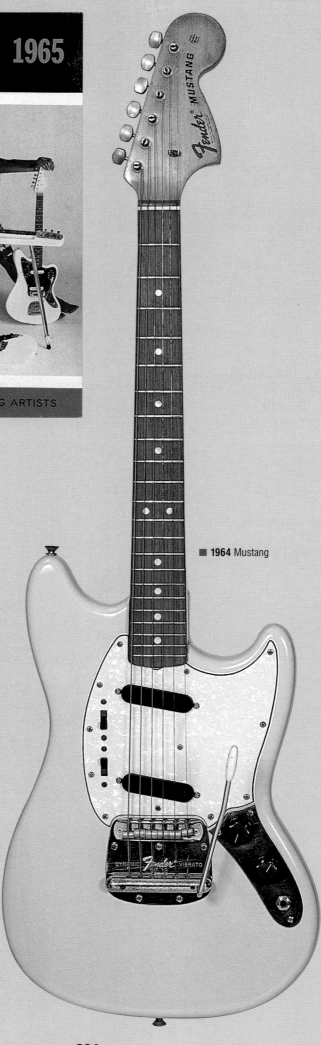

■ **1964** Mustang

MUSTANG
1964-2006

MUSTANG 1964–81

*Model name on headstock, two angled pickups,
two slide switches, vibrato tailpiece.*
- **Neck:** maple with rosewood fingerboard
  (fretted maple option from 1970); 22.5-inch
  scale and 21 frets (1964–69) or 24-inch scale
  and 22 frets; truss-rod adjuster at body end;
  plastic tuner buttons (metal from 1975);
  one string-guide (two from 1975).
- **Body:** contoured offset-waist; sunburst or colors.
- **Electronics:** two white or black plain-top pickups
  (both angled); two controls (volume, tone) and jack,
  all on metal plate adjoining pickguard; two selector
  slide-switches on pickguard.
- **Hardware:** 12-screw white pearl or tortoiseshell
  laminated plastic pickguard (black laminated plastic
  from 1975); six-saddle bridge with vibrato tailpiece.
Early examples with slab body.

ANTIGUA MUSTANG 1977–79

As MUSTANG of the period (see 1964 listing) but with
white/brown shaded body finish and matching-color
laminated plastic pickguard.

MUSTANG (MIJ) 1986–onward

Replica of 1969-period U.S. original with 24-inch
scale (see 1964 listing). Also COMPETITION MUSTANG,
with stripes on body (2002–03).

COMPETITION MUSTANG (MIJ) 2002–03

Reproduction of 24-inch scale MUSTANG
(see 1964 listing) except:
- **Body:** stripes on body.

'65 MUSTANG REISSUE (MIJ) 2006–current

Replica of 1965-period original with
24-inch scale (see MUSTANG 1964 listing).

MUSTANG 1964-2006

■ **2005** Limited Edition
'65 Mustang

■ **2005** catalog

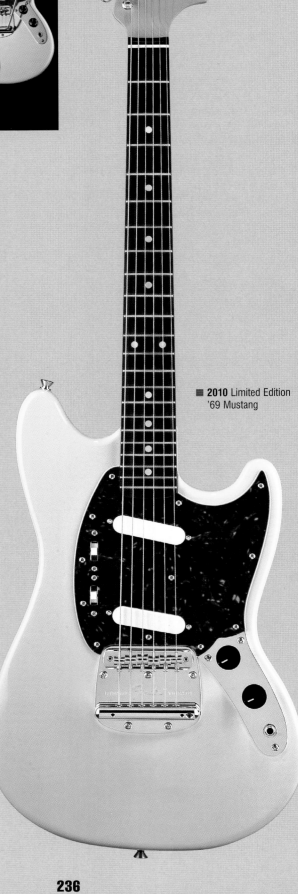

■ **2010** Limited Edition
'69 Mustang

ELECTRIC XII 12-string 1965–69

Model name on 12-string 'hockey-stick' headstock.

- **Neck:** maple with rosewood fingerboard (bound from 1965), dot markers (blocks from 1966); truss-rod adjuster at body end; one 'bracket' string-guide; six-tuners-per-side 'hockey-stick' headstock.
- **Body:** contoured offset-waist; sunburst or colors.
- **Electronics:** two black plain-top split pickups; two controls (volume, tone) and jack, all on metal plate adjoining pickguard; four-way rotary selector on pickguard.
- **Hardware:** 17-screw white pearl or tortoiseshell laminated plastic pickguard; 12-saddle bridge with through-body stringing.

■ **1965** Electric XII

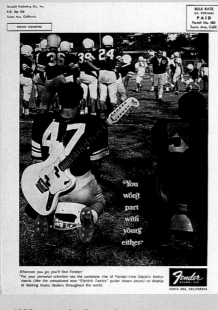

1966 Electric XII
(selector switch not original)

ELECTRIC XII
1968-1969

1965 catalog

1966 Electric XII

CORONADO I 1966–69

Model name on headstock, hollow twin-cutaway body,
one pickup.

- **Neck:** maple with rosewood fingerboard; truss-rod
  adjuster at body end; plastic tuner buttons; single
  string-guide.
- **Body:** hollow twin-cutaway bound; long f-holes;
  sunburst or colors.
- **Electronics:** one metal-cover black-center
  six-polepiece pickup (at neck); two controls
  (volume, tone) on body; side-mounted jack.
- **Hardware:** white or gold laminated plastic
  pickguard; single-saddle wooden bridge, tailpiece;
  or six-saddle metal-top bridge, vibrato tailpiece.

CORONADO II 1966–69

Model name on headstock, hollow twin-cutaway body,
two pickups.

Similar to CORONADO I (see previous listing) except:
- **Neck:** bound fingerboard, block markers.
- **Body:** bound long f-holes.
- **Electronics:** two pickups; four controls
  (two volume, two tone) and three-way selector,
  all on body.
- **Hardware:** six-saddle metal-top bridge,
  tailpiece with F inlay; or six-saddle all-metal bridge,
  vibrato tailpiece.

Prototype examples with unbound dot-marker neck and
three-tuners-per-side headstock; truss-rod adjuster at
headstock end; unbound body; black laminated plastic
pickguard; six-section tailpiece.

CORONADO XII 12-string 1966–69

Model name on 12-string headstock,
hollow twin-cutaway body, two pickups.
Similar to CORONADO II (see previous listing) except:
- **Neck:** one 'bracket' string-guide; six-tuners-per-side
  'hockey stick' headstock.
- **Hardware:** six-saddle metal-top bridge;
  tailpiece with F inlay.

■ **1966** Coronado XII

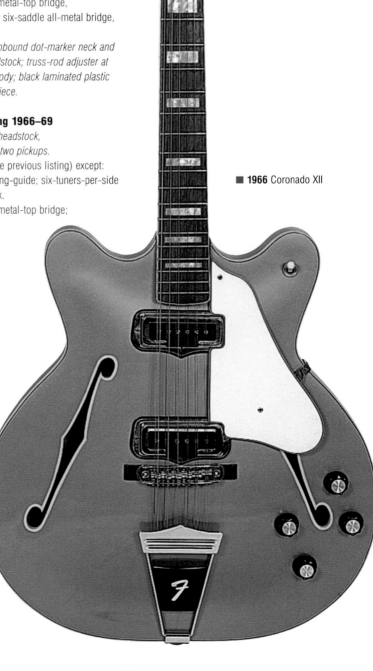

■ **1966** Wildwood Coronado II

■ **1968** Wildwood Coronado XII

CORONADO II ANTIGUA 1967–71

White/brown shaded hollow twin-cutaway body,
two pickups.

Similar to CORONADO II (see 1966 listing) except:

• **Body:** white/brown shaded finish.
• **Hardware:** pearl tuner buttons; 'Antigua' on
  matching-color laminated plastic pickguard;
  six-saddle all-metal bridge, vibrato tailpiece only.

CORONADO XII ANTIGUA (12-string) 1967–71

12-string headstock, white/brown shaded hollow
twin-cutaway body, two pickups.

Similar to CORONADO XII 12-string
(see 1966 listing) except:

• **Body:** white/brown shaded finish.
• **Hardware:** pearl tuner buttons; 'Antigua' on
  matching-color laminated plastic pickguard.

CORONADO II WILDWOOD 1967–69

Colored wood hollow twin-cutaway body, two pickups.
Similar to CORONADO II (see 1966 listing) except:

• **Body:** six dye-injected color combinations.
• **Hardware:** pearl tuner buttons; 'Wildwood' on white
  laminated plastic pickguard; six-saddle all-metal
  bridge, vibrato tailpiece only.

CORONADO XII WILDWOOD (12-string)
1967–69

12-string headstock, colored wood hollow twin-cutaway
body, two pickups.

Similar to CORONADO XII 12-string
(see 1966 listing) except:

• **Body:** six dye-injected color combinations.
• **Hardware:** pearl tuner buttons; 'Wildwood'
  on white laminated plastic pickguard.

LTD 1968–74

Hollow single-cutaway body, metal tailpiece, one floating pickup.

- **Neck:** maple with bound ebony fingerboard, 'diamond-in-block' markers; 20 frets; truss-rod adjuster at body end; three-tuners-per-side headstock.
- **Body:** hollow single-cutaway bound; carved top; sunburst or natural.
- **Electronics:** one metal-cover six-polepiece humbucker (mounted on neck-end); two controls (volume, tone) and jack, all on pickguard.
- **Hardware:** gold-plated; tortoiseshell laminated plastic pickguard; single-saddle wooden bridge, tailpiece with F inlay.

■ **1968** LTD

LTD&MONTEGO 1968

MONTEGO I 1968–74

*Hollow single-cutaway body, one pickup,
metal tailpiece.*

- **Neck:** maple with bound ebony
  fingerboard, 'diamond-in-block' markers;
  20 frets; truss-rod adjuster at body end;
  three-tuners-per-side headstock.
- **Body:** hollow single-cutaway bound;
  bound f-holes; finished in sunburst or natural.
- **Electronics:** one metal-cover six-polepiece
  humbucker (at neck); two controls (volume, tone)
  on body; side-mounted jack.
- **Hardware:** black laminated plastic pickguard;
  single-saddle wooden bridge, tailpiece with F inlay.

MONTEGO II 1968–74

Hollow single-cutaway body, two pickups, metal tailpiece.
Similar to MONTEGO I (see previous listing) except:
- **Electronics:** two humbuckers; four controls
  (two volume, two tone) and three-way selector,
  all on body.

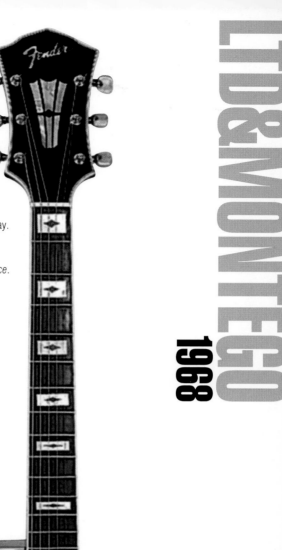

■ **1968** Montego II

243

■ **1969** Maverick

CUSTOM 1969–70
Model name on 'hockey stick' headstock.
- **Neck:** maple with bound rosewood fingerboard, block markers; truss-rod adjuster at body end; one 'bracket' string-guide; three-tuners-per-side 'hockey stick' headstock.
- **Body:** contoured offset-waist with pointed base; sunburst only.
- **Electronics:** two black plain-top split pickups; two controls (volume, tone) and jack, all on metal plate adjoining pickguard; four-way rotary selector on pickguard.
- **Hardware:** 17-screw tortoiseshell laminated plastic pickguard; six-saddle bridge with vibrato tailpiece.

Made using modified ELECTRIC XII parts, some with purpose-built necks. Some examples with MAVERICK model name, not Custom, on headstock.

MAVERICK 1969–70
See earlier CUSTOM listing this year.

■ **1969** Custom

■ **1976** press advertisement

SWINGER 1969

Arrow-head-shape headstock, one angled pickup.

- **Neck:** maple with rosewood fingerboard;
  22.5-inch scale, 21 frets; truss-rod adjuster at body
  end; one string-guide; 'arrow-head' shape headstock.
- **Body:** contoured offset-waist with 'scoop' in base;
  various colors.
- **Electronics:** one black plain-top pickup
  (angled at neck); two controls (volume, tone)
  and jack, all on metal plate adjoining pickguard.
- **Hardware:** 12-screw white pearl or tortoiseshell
  laminated plastic pickguard; three-saddle
  bridge/tailpiece.

*Made from modified Musicmaster
and Mustang parts. Many examples
have no Swinger logo on headstock.
Also unofficially known as ARROW
or MUSICLANDER.*

■ **1969** Swinger

SWINGER 1969-1979

246

STARCASTER 1976–80

Model name on 'hooked' headstock with black edging, semi-acoustic offset-waist body.

- **Neck:** fretted maple; 22 frets; 'bullet' truss-rod adjuster at headstock end; one 'bracket' string-guide; three-screw neckplate; black edging on headstock.
- **Body:** Semi-acoustic offset-waist bound; f-holes; sunburst or colors.
- **Electronics:** two metal-cover split-polepiece humbuckers; five controls (two volume, two tone, master volume) and three-way selector, all on body; side-mounted jack.
- **Hardware:** Black laminated plastic pickguard; six-saddle bridge with through-body stringing.

LEAD I 1979–82

Model name on headstock, one humbucker pickup, two switches.

- **Neck:** fretted maple, or maple with rosewood fingerboard; truss-rod adjuster at body end; two string-guides.
- **Body:** sunburst or colors.
- **Electronics:** one black or white 12-polepiece humbucker (at bridge); two controls (volume, tone), two two-way selectors, and jack, all on pickguard.
- **Hardware:** 11-screw black or white laminated plastic pickguard; six-saddle bridge with through-body stringing.

LEAD II 1979–82

Model name on headstock, two single-coils, two switches.

Similar to LEAD I (see previous listing) except:

- **Electronics:** two black or white six-polepiece pickups (both angled); one two-way selector, one three-way selector.

■ **1976** Starcaster

BULLET (first version) 1981–83

Model name on headstock, single-cutaway body,
bridge on metal pickguard.

- **Neck:** fretted maple, or maple with rosewood
  fingerboard; truss-rod adjuster at body end;
  one string-guide; Telecaster-style headstock.
- **Body:** slab single-cutaway; red or white.
- **Electronics:** two black or white plain-top pickups
  (neck pickup angled); two controls (volume, tone),
  three-way selector and jack, all situated on pickguard.
- **Hardware:** six-screw (plus four at bridge) white or
  black-painted metal pickguard; six-saddle bridge,
  raised 'lip' of pickguard forms tailpiece.

Earliest examples use some Korean-made components.

BULLET DELUXE 1981–83

Model name on headstock, single-cutaway body,
separate bridge.

Similar to BULLET FIRST VERSION (see previous listing)
except:

- **Hardware:** eight-screw white or black laminated
  plastic pickguard; separate six-saddle bridge with
  through-body stringing.

BULLET (second version) 1983

Model name on headstock, offset-cutaway body,
two single-coils, bridge on metal pickguard.

- **Neck:** fretted maple; truss-rod adjuster at body end;
  one string-guide; Telecaster-style headstock.
- **Body:** slab offset-cutaway; red or white.
- **Electronics:** two white plain-top pickups
  (neck pickup angled); two controls (volume, tone),
  three-way selector and jack, all on pickguard.
- **Hardware:** six-screw (plus four at bridge)
  white-painted metal pickguard; six-saddle bridge,
  raised 'lip' of pickguard forms tailpiece.

BULLET H1 1983

'Bullet' name on headstock, offset-cutaway body,
one humbucker, bridge on metal pickguard.

Similar to BULLET SECOND VERSION
(see previous listing) except:

- **Electronics:** one white plain-top
  humbucker (at bridge);
  pushbutton coil-switch replaces
  three-way selector.

■ **1981** Bullet
(first version)

BULLET 1981-1985

BULLET H2 1983

'Bullet' name on headstock, offset-cutaway body, two humbuckers, separate bridge.
Similar to BULLET SECOND VERSION
(see earlier listing this year) except:
- **Body:** sunburst or colors.
- **Electronics:** two white plain-top humbuckers; three-way selector, plus two pushbutton coil-switches.
- **Hardware:** nine-screw white laminated plastic pickguard; six-saddle separate bridge with through-body stringing.

BULLET S2 1983

'Bullet' name on headstock, offset-cutaway body, two single-coils, separate bridge.
Similar to BULLET SECOND VERSION
(see earlier listing this year) except:
- **Body:** sunburst or colors.
- **Hardware:** nine-screw white laminated plastic pickguard; six-saddle separate bridge with through-body stringing.

BULLET S3 1983

'Bullet' name on headstock, offset-cutaway body, three single-coils, separate bridge.
Similar to BULLET SECOND VERSION
(see earlier listing this year) except:
- **Body:** sunburst or colors.
- **Electronics:** three black or white plain-top pickups (bridge pickup angled); five-way selector.
- **Hardware:** nine-screw white laminated plastic pickguard; six-saddle separate bridge with through-body stringing.

ESPRIT STANDARD (MIJ) 1984

Three-tuners-per-side headstock, twin-cutaway body, two humbuckers.
- **Neck:** maple glued-in, with bound rosewood fingerboard; 24.75-inch scale, 22 frets; truss-rod adjuster at headstock end; three-tuners-per-side headstock; neck matches body color.
- **Body:** semi-solid twin-cutaway bound; sunburst or black.
- **Electronics:** two black 12-polepiece humbucker pickups; two controls (volume, tone) and three-way selector, all on body; side-mounted jack.
- **Hardware:** six-saddle bridge, tailpiece.

ESPRIT ELITE (MIJ) 1984

Three-tuners-per-side headstock, 'Elite' on truss-rod cover, twin-cutaway body, two humbuckers.
Similar to ESPRIT STANDARD (see next listing) except:
- **Neck:** snowflake position markers; pearl tuner buttons; Elite on truss-rod cover.
- **Body:** sunburst or colors.
- **Electronics:** four controls (two volume, two tone), three-way selector and coil-switch, all on body.
- **Hardware:** fine-tuner tailpiece.

ESPRIT ULTRA (MIJ) 1984

Three-tuners-per-side headstock, 'Ultra' on truss-rod cover, twin-cutaway body, two humbuckers.
Similar to ESPRIT STANDARD (see previous listing) except:
- **Neck:** bound ebony fingerboard, split-block position markers; ebony tuner buttons; Ultra on truss-rod cover.
- **Body:** sunburst or colors.
- **Electronics:** four controls (two volume, two tone), three-way selector and coil-switch, all situated on body.
- **Hardware:** gold-plated; fine-tuner tailpiece.

FLAME STANDARD (MIJ) 1984

Three-tuners-per-side headstock, offset-cutaway body, two humbuckers.
Similar to ESPRIT STANDARD (see earlier listing this year) except:
- **Body:** smaller, semi-solid offset-cutaway.

KATANA (MIJ) 1985–86

Model name on headstock, wedge-shape body.
- **Neck:** maple glued-in with bound rosewood fingerboard, offset triangle markers; 24.75-inch scale, 22 frets; truss-rod adjuster at headstock end; string clamp; arrow-head-shape headstock; neck matches body color.
- **Body:** bevelled-edge wedge; various colors.
- **Electronics:** two black coverless humbuckers; two controls (volume, tone) and three-way selector, all on body; side-mounted jack.
- **Hardware:** two-pivot bridge/vibrato unit.

■ 1985 Katana

D'AQUISTO ELITE (MIJ) 1984, 1989–94

Hollow single-cutaway body, one pickup,
wooden tailpiece.

Similar to D'AQUISTO STANDARD (see next listing) except:
- **Neck:** bound ebony fingerboard, block markers;
  ebony tuner buttons.
- **Electronics:** one black 12-polepiece humbucker
  pickup (one metal-cover six-polepiece humbucker
  1989–94); two controls (volume, tone) on body.
- **Hardware:** gold-plated.

D'AQUISTO STANDARD (MIJ) 1984

Hollow single-cutaway body, two pickups,
wooden tailpiece.

- **Neck:** maple glued-in, with bound rosewood
  fingerboard; 24.75-inch scale, 20 frets; truss-rod
  adjuster at headstock end; pearl tuner buttons;
  three-tuners-per-side headstock.
- **Body:** hollow archtop single-cutaway bound;
  f-holes; sunburst, natural or black.
- **Electronics:** two black 12-polepiece humbuckers;
  four controls (two volume, two tone) and three-way
  selector, all on body; side-mounted jack.
- **Hardware:** bound floating wooden pickguard;
  single-saddle wooden bridge, wooden tailpiece.

■ **1995** D'Aquisto Custom Ultra
(Custom Shope one-off)

D'AQUISTO 1984-2001

D'AQUISTO ELITE 1994–95, 2000–01

*Hollow single-cutaway body, one floating pickup,
wooden tailpiece.*
Similar to D'AQUISTO DELUXE (see 1995 listing)
except:
- **Neck:** split-block markers; ebony tuner buttons.
- **Body:** sunburst or natural.
- **Electronics:** floating humbucker.

Custom Shop production.

D'AQUISTO DELUXE 1995–2001

*Hollow single-cutaway body, one pickup,
wooden tailpiece.*
- **Neck:** maple glued-in, with bound ebony
  fingerboard, block markers; 25.125-inch scale,
  22 frets; truss-rod adjuster at headstock end;
  three-tuners-per-side headstock.
- **Body:** hollow archtop single-cutaway bound;
  f-holes; sunburst, natural, or red.
- **Electronics:** one metal-cover six-polepiece
  humbucker (at neck); two controls (volume, tone)
  on body; side-mounted jack.
- **Hardware:** gold-plated; bound wooden pickguard;
  single-saddle wooden bridge, wooden tailpiece.

Custom Shop production.

■ **1995** D'Aquisto Deluxe

PERFORMER (MIJ) 1985–86
Model name on headstock, two angled white plain-top pickups.

- **Neck:** maple with rosewood fingerboard; 24 frets; truss-rod adjuster at headstock end; string clamp; 'arrow-head' shape headstock.
- **Body:** contoured offset-waist with 'hooked' horns; sunburst or colors.
- **Electronics:** two white plain-top humbuckers (both angled); two controls (volume, tone), three-way selector and coil-switch, all on pickguard; side-mounted jack.
- **Hardware:** ten-screw white laminated plastic pickguard; two-pivot bridge/vibrato unit.

■ **1985** Performer

PERFORMER
1985-1993

ELAN I (MIM) 1993

Three-tuners-per-side headstock, 'EL' on truss-rod cover, offset-cutaway body, two humbuckers.

- **Neck:** mahogany glued-in, with bound ebony fingerboard; 25.1-inch scale, 22 frets; truss-rod adjuster at headstock end; pearl tuner buttons; three-tuners-per-side headstock; neck matches body color; 'EL' on truss-rod cover.
- **Body:** offset-cutaway carved-top bound; sunburst or colors.
- **Electronics:** two black coverless humbuckers; two controls (volume, tone) and five-way selector, all on body; side-mounted jack.
- **Hardware:** six-saddle bridge with through-body stringing.

Previously with 'Heartfield' or 'Heartfield by Fender' on headstock as part of Elan series.

■ **1986** Performer

A PRODIGY FROM MEXICO

A new Fender factory based just over the California border in Mexico had been making amplifiers and cabinets for a few years, but during 1991 its first guitar products became evident, including the Standard Strat, Tele, P-Bass and Jazz. More signature models were built at the US factory, for Robert Cray (above) and Jeff Beck, while another superstrat-style instrument came along, known as the Prodigy.

Fender U.S. came up with a new design in 1991 called the Prodigy, another shortlived attempt to compete with superstrats and their progeny. The Prodigy had an offset-waist body with sharper horns than a Stratocaster, the requisite two single-coils and a humbucker, and an optional locking vibrato. There was a matching bass, too.

Significantly, the Prodigy was among the first Fender guitars to receive attention at the company's new factory in Ensenada, Mexico, which had been established in 1987. Ensenada is some 180 miles south of Los Angeles and is situated just across the California/Mexico border. Fender amps started to appear from Mexico in 1989, with guitars following soon after. The factory would be entirely rebuilt in 1994 after a disastrous fire.

By early 1992 the Mexican factory was assembling around 175 Fender Standard Stratocasters per day, and by 1995 had a capacity for producing 600 instruments a day. Bodies and necks for the Made In Mexico guitars were produced at the U.S. factory in Corona and sent down to the Mexican plant. There they were sanded, painted, buffed, and assembled with Mexican-made hardware and pickups. The factory also produced all Fender's strings.

By late 1997, Mexico would be assembling around 150,000 Fender guitars a year, compared to some 85,000 at Corona, with a workforce of around 1,000 at the Mexico factory and 700 at Corona.

The chief advantage to Fender of its Mexican and some offshore production sites is the cheapness of the labor. Fender has like many Western companies searched far and wide for this expediency. In addition to continuing products from Korea, the lowest-price Squier-brand Fender guitars were by 1999 being made at two factories in China, a source the company had used since the start of the 1990s.

New models from the U.S. factory included two signature Jeff Beck and Robert Cray Strats. Set Neck Teles were launched, with a Country Artist (pictured opposite) added in 1992.

An Associated Press wire report for 21st March marked a sad occasion: "Clarence Leo Fender, whose revolutionary Stratocaster was the guitar of choice for rock stars from Buddy Holly to Jimi Hendrix, died today. He was 82. Fender was found unconscious in his Fullerton home by his wife, Phyllis, and died on the way to hospital. Fender had suffered Parkinson's disease for decades but continued to work on guitar designs." Leo had been at his bench at his G&L company just the day before, tinkering with yet another guitar improvement.

RR-58 (MIJ) 1993

RR on truss-rod cover, two humbuckers, fixed bridge.
- **Neck:** mahogany glued-in, with rosewood fingerboard; 24.75-inch scale, 22 frets; truss-rod adjuster at headstock end; neck matches body color; RR on truss-rod cover.
- **Body:** blonde, green or red
- **Electronics**: two black plain-top humbuckers; two controls (volume, tone) and five-way selector, all on body; side mounted jack.
- **Hardware:** four-screw black laminated plastic pickguard; six-saddle bridge with through-body stringing.

Previously with 'Heartfield' or 'Heartfield by Fender' on headstock as part of RR series.

ROBBEN FORD ELITE 1994–2001

Signature on headstock, unbound fingerboard, twin-cutaway body.
- **Neck:** mahogany glued-in, with unbound ebony fingerboard (pao ferro from 1997); 24.625-inch scale, 22 frets; truss-rod adjuster at headstock end; three-tuners-per-side headstock.
- **Body:** twin-cutaway bound; sunburst, black, or red.
- **Electronics**: two metal-cover six-polepiece humbuckers; four controls (two volume, two tone), three-way selector and coil-switch, all on body; side-mounted jack.
- **Hardware:** six-saddle bridge, fine-tuner tailpiece.

Custom Shop production.

ROBBEN FORD ULTRA FM 1994–2001

Signature on headstock, bound fingerboard, twin-cutaway body.
Similar to ROBBEN FORD ELITE (see previous listing) except:
- **Neck:** bound ebony fingerboard with split-block position markers.

Custom Shop production.

ROBBEN FORD ULTRA SP 1994–2001

Signature on headstock, bound fingerboard, twin-cutaway body, gold-plated hardware.
Similar to ROBBEN FORD ELITE (see earlier listing this year) except:
- **Neck:** bound ebony fingerboard with split-block position markers; ebony tuner buttons.
- **Body:** semi-solid.
- **Hardware:** gold-plated.

Custom Shop production.

PRODIGY 1991–93

Prodigy on headstock, two single-coils and one humbucker, six-pivot bridge/vibrato unit.

- **Neck:** fretted maple, or maple with rosewood fingerboard; 22 frets; truss-rod adjuster at headstock end; one string-guide.
- **Body:** contoured offset-waist; various colors.
- **Electronics:** two black six-polepiece pickups and one black coverless humbucker (at bridge); two controls (volume, tone), five-way selector and jack, all on pickguard.
- **Hardware:** eight-screw black laminated plastic pickguard; six-pivot bridge/vibrato unit.

PRODIGY II 1991–92

Prodigy on headstock, two single-coils and one humbucker, locking vibrato system.

Similar to PRODIGY (see previous listing) except:

- **Neck:** no string-guide; locking nut.
- **Hardware:** chrome-plated or black-plated; two-pivot locking bridge/vibrato unit.

■ **1991** Prodigy II

PRODIGY
1993-1994

JAG-STANG (MIJ) 1996–onward
Model name on headstock, angled single-coil and humbucker.

- **Neck:** maple with rosewood fingerboard; 24-inch scale, 22 frets; truss-rod adjuster at body end; one string-guide.
- **Body:** contoured offset-waist; blue or red.
- **Electronics:** one white six-polepiece pickup (at neck) and one white coverless humbucker (at bridge), both angled; two controls (volume, tone) and jack, all on metal plate adjoining pickguard; two selector slide-switches on pickguard.
- **Hardware:** ten-screw white pearl laminated plastic pickguard; six-saddle bridge with vibrato unit.

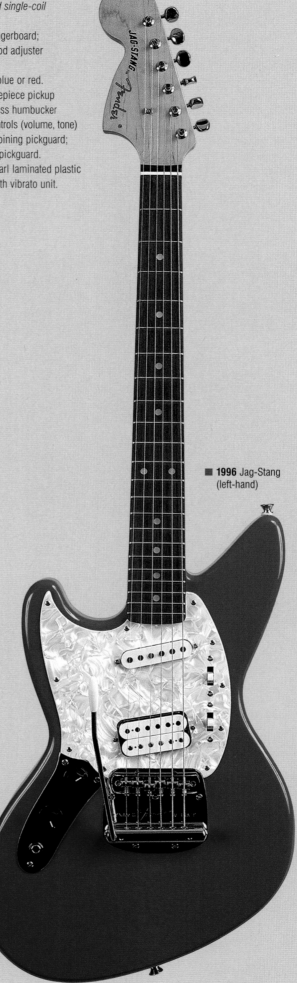

■ **1996** Jag-Stang (left-hand)

JAG-STANG 1968-1969

JAG-SHAPED STANG

Fenders beyond the ubiquitous Strats and Teles were proving popular with so-called grunge guitarists: Seattle supremo Kurt Cobain of Nirvana had played Jaguars and Mustangs; Steve Turner in Mudhoney opted for a Mustang; J. Mascis of Dinosaur Jr. was often seen with his Jazzmaster. And the reason was relatively straightforward. These guitars had the comforting Fender logo on the head, but could be bought more cheaply secondhand than Strats or Teles. The ethics suited grunge perfectly.

Back in 1993, Cobain decided to take cut-up photos of his Jag and Mustang and stick them together, this way and that, trying combinations to see what they would look like. Larry Brooks of the Custom Shop took Cobain's paste-ups, assembled the design, and added a contour or two to improve balance and feel.

After Cobain's untimely death in 1994, his family collaborated with Fender to release a Japanese-made production version of the instrument, named the Fender Jag-Stang. Cobain's guitar hit the market in 1996.

The Lone Star Stratocaster, also launched in 1996, was one example of how the Fender R&D department worked. What it called the core products were taken and subtly (and not-so-subtly) modified to create 'new' models based on players' changing tastes. Thus the Lone Star (renamed the American Fat Strat Texas Special in 2000) took an American Standard Strat and changed the pickup configuration to a Seymour Duncan Pearly Gates Plus humbucker at the bridge, plus two of Fender's 'hot' Texas Special single-coils.

■ **2004** Jag-Stang

■ **2006** Artist Series Jag-Stang

257

CYCLONE (MIM) 1998–2006

Name on headstock, one angled single-coil and one humbucker.

- **Neck:** maple with rosewood fingerboard; 24.75-inch scale, 22 frets; truss-rod adjuster at headstock end; one string-guide.
- **Body:** contoured offset-waist; sunburst or colors.
- **Electronics:** one white six-polepiece pickup (angled at neck) and one white/black coverless humbucker (at bridge); two controls (volume, tone) and jack, all on metal plate adjoining pickguard; three-way selector on pickguard.
- **Hardware:** nine-screw white pearl laminated plastic pickguard; six-pivot bridge/vibrato unit.

■ **1998** Cyclone

CYCLONE II (MIM) 2002–2006

Name on headstock, three angled single-coils.
Similar to CYCLONE (see 1998 listing) except:
- **Body:** blue or red, with stripes.
- **Electronics:** three rectangular white six-polepiece
  pickups, each with metal 'sawtooth' sides, all angled;
  two controls (volume, tone) and jack, all on metal
  plate adjoining pickguard; three slide-switches on
  metal plate inset into pickguard.

CYCLONE HH (MIM) 2003–05

Name on headstock, two humbuckers.
Similar to CYCLONE (see 1998 listing) except:
- **Electronics:** two black coverless humbuckers.
- **Hardware:** nine-screw white pearl or black
  laminated plastic pickguard.

■ **2004** catalog

■ **2004** Cyclone

■ **2004** Cyclone II

259

SHOWMASTER FMT 1998–2005

Model name on headstock, 22 frets, figured carved body top, two single-coils and one humbucker.

- **Neck:** fretted maple, or maple with rosewood fingerboard; 22 frets; truss-rod adjuster at headstock end; staggered height locking tuners; roller nut.
- **Body:** with figured carved top; sunburst or colors.
- **Electronics:** two black six-polepiece pickups and one black coverless humbucker (at bridge); two controls (volume, tone) and five-way selector, all on body; side-mounted jack.
- **Hardware:** no pickguard; two-pivot bridge/vibrato unit (or two-pivot locking bridge/vibrato unit 1998–99).

Custom Shop production.

SHOWMASTER SET NECK FMT 1999–2005

Model name on headstock, 22 frets, glued-in neck, two single-soils and one humbucker.

Similar to SHOWMASTER FMT (see previous listing) except:
- **Neck:** maple glued-in, with rosewood fingerboard only.
- **Hardware:** two-pivot locking bridge/vibrato unit only.

Custom Shop production.

SHOWMASTER SET NECK FMT HARD-TAIL 1999–2005

Model name on headstock, 22-frets, glued-in neck, two-section wrapover bridge/tailpiece.

Similar to SHOWMASTER SET NECK FMT (see previous listing) except:
- **Hardware:** no roller nut; two-section wrapover bridge/tailpiece.

Custom Shop production.

SHOWMASTER STANDARD 1999–2005

Model name on headstock, 22 frets, carved body top.

Similar to SHOWMASTER FMT (see 1998 listing) except:
- **Body:** with carved top; various colors.
- **Hardware:** two-pivot bridge/ vibrato unit only.

Custom Shop production.

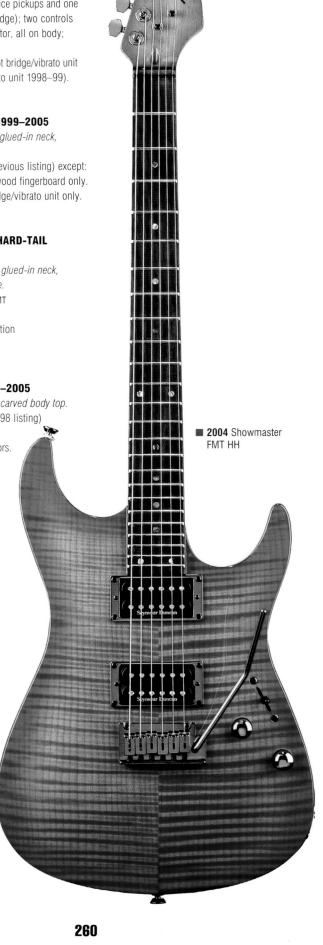

■ **2004** Showmaster FMT HH

SHOWMASTER 1998-2003

SHOWMASTER 7-STRING 2000–01
Model name on seven-string headstock.
Similar to SHOWMASTER FMT (see 1998 listing) except:
- **Neck:** maple with rosewood fingerboard only; no roller nut; seven-string headstock.
- **Body:** with carved top; various colors.
- **Hardware:** two-pivot bridge/vibrato unit only.

SHOWMASTER 7-STRING HARD-TAIL 2000–01
Model name on seven-string headstock, six-saddle bridge.
Similar to SHOWMASTER FMT (see 1998 listing) except:
- **Hardware:** two-section wrapover bridge/tailpiece.

FLAT HEAD SHOWMASTER 2003–04
Name on headstock, 22 frets, one humbucker.
- **Neck:** maple with ebony fingerboard; 22 frets; truss-rod adjuster at headstock end; staggered height locking tuners; no position markers except 'crossed pistons' inlay at 12th fret; Flat Head on headstock.
- **Body:** various colors.
- **Electronics:** one black coverless humbucker; one control (volume) on body; side-mounted jack.
- **Hardware:** black-plated; no pickguard; six-saddle small bridge with through-body stringing.
Custom Shop production.

HIGHWAY ONE SHOWMASTER HH 2003–04
Name on headstock, 24 frets, two humbuckers.
- **Neck:** maple with rosewood fingerboard; 24 frets; truss-rod adjuster at headstock end; single-bar string-guide; locking nut.
- **Body:** black, pewter, or silver, satin finish.
- **Electronics:** two black coverless humbuckers; two controls (volume, tone) and three-way selector, all situated on the guitar's body; side-mounted jack.
- **Hardware:** No pickguard; two-pivot locking bridge/vibrato unit.

HIGHWAY ONE SHOWMASTER HSS 2003–04
Name on headstock, 24 frets, two single-coils and one humbucker.
Similar to HIGHWAY ONE SHOWMASTER HH (see previous listing) except:
- **Electronics:** two black six-polepiece pickups and one black coverless humbucker; two controls (volume, tone) and five-way selector, all on body.

■ **2004** Showmaster H

SHOWMASTER CELTIC H (MIK) 2003

Celtic design inlay at 12th fret, offset cutaway body.
- **Neck:** maple glued-in, with rosewood fingerboard; 24 frets; truss-rod adjuster at headstock end; two string-guides; locking tuners; no front markers except Celtic design inlay at 12th fret.
- **Body:** silver only, satin finish.
- **Electronics:** one black coverless humbucker (at bridge); one control (volume) on body; side-mounted jack.
- **Hardware:** black-plated; no pickguard; six-saddle small bridge with through-body stringing.

SHOWMASTER DELUXE HH WITH TREMOLO (MIK) 2003

Glued-in neck, no front markers, bound gold body.
Similar to SHOWMASTER HH WITH TREMOLO (see later listing this year) except:
- **Body:** bound; gold only.
- **Electronics:** chrome-plated; two white coverless humbuckers.

■ **2004** Showmaster HH

SHOWMASTER H WITH TREMOLO (MIK) 2003

Glued-in neck, no fingerboard front markers,
one black humbucker.
- **Neck:** maple glued-in, with rosewood fingerboard, no front markers; 24 frets; truss-rod adjuster at headstock end; two string-guides; locking tuners.
- **Body:** silver only, satin finish.
- **Electronics:** one black coverless humbucker (at bridge); one control (volume) on body; side-mounted jack.
- **Hardware:** black-plated; no pickguard; two-pivot bridge/vibrato unit.

SHOWMASTER HH WITH TREMOLO (MIK) 2003

Glued-in neck, no fingerboard front markers,
two black humbuckers.
Similar to SHOWMASTER H (see previous listing) except:
- **Neck:** maple glued-in, with bound rosewood fingerboard.
- **Body:** bound; black only.
- **Electronics:** two black coverless humbuckers; two controls (volume, tone) and five-way selector, all on body.

SHOWMASTER SCORPION HH (MIK) 2003

'Scorpion' inlay at 12th fret, offset cutaway body.
- **Neck:** maple glued-in with bound rosewood fingerboard; 24 frets; truss-rod adjuster at headstock end; two string-guides; locking tuners; no fingerboard front markers except 'Scorpion' inlay at 12th fret.
- **Body:** bound; black only.
- **Electronics:** two black coverless humbuckers; two controls (volume, tone) and five-way selector, all on body; side-mounted jack.
- **Hardware:** black-plated; no pickguard; six-saddle small bridge with through-body stringing.

FLAT HEAD SHOWMASTER HH 2004–06

Name on headstock, 22 frets, two black plain-top
humbuckers.
Similar to FLAT HEAD SHOWMASTER (see 2003 listing) except:
- **Electronics:** two black plain top active humbuckers; one control (volume) and three-way selector, both on body.
Custom Shop production.

SHOWMASTER BLACKOUT (MIK) 2004–05

Glued-in neck, no front markers, two Seymour Duncan
humbuckers.
Similar to SHOWMASTER H (see 2003 listing) except:
- **Body:** black or blue.
- **Electronics:** two Seymour Duncan-logo black coverless humbuckers; two controls (volume, tone) and five-way selector, all on body.

SHOWMASTER ELITE 2004–08

Model name on headstock, 22 frets, glued-in neck,
two humbuckers, two-pivot vibrato.
Similar to SHOWMASTER FMT (see 1998 listing) except:
- **Neck:** mahogany glued-in, with ebony fingerboard, ornate markers; pearl tuner buttons; black-face Telecaster-style headstock.
- **Body:** brown or sunbursts.
- **Electronics:** two Seymour Duncan-logo black coverless humbuckers.
- **Hardware:** two-pivot bridge/vibrato unit.
Body with figured carved top in various woods
(FMT, LWT, QMT, SMT).
Custom Shop production.

■ **2008** catalog

SHOWMASTER ELITE HARD-TAIL 2004–08

Model name on headstock, 22 frets, glued-in neck,
two humbuckers, six-saddle wrapover bridge/tailpiece.
Similar to SHOWMASTER ELITE (see previous listing) except:
- **Neck:** no roller nut.
- **Hardware:** six-saddle wrapover bridge/tailpiece.
Custom Shop production.

SHOWMASTER FAT-HH (MIK) 2004–05

Glued-in neck, front markers, figured ash-top body,
two Seymour Duncan humbuckers.
Similar to SHOWMASTER H (see 2003 listing) except:
- **Neck:** fretboard position markers.
- **Body:** with figured ash top; sunburst only.
- **Electronics:** two Seymour Duncan-logo black coverless humbuckers; two controls (volume, tone) and five-way selector, all on body.
- **Hardware:** chrome-plated.

SHOWMASTER FAT-SSS (MIK) 2004–05

Glued-in neck, fingerboard front markers, figured
ash-top body, three Seymour Duncan single-coils.
Similar to SHOWMASTER FAT-HH (see previous listing) except:
- **Electronics:** three Seymour Duncan-logo black six-polepiece pickups (bridge pickup angled).

SHOWMASTER QBT-HH (MIK) 2004–07

Glued-in neck, fingerboard front markers, figured
bubinga-top body, two Seymour Duncan humbuckers.
Similar to SHOWMASTER H (see 2003 listing) except:
- **Neck:** fretboard position markers.
- **Body:** with figured bubinga top; brown only.
- **Electronics:** two Seymour Duncan-logo black coverless humbuckers; two controls (volume, tone) and five-way selector, all on body.
- **Hardware:** chrome-plated.

SHOWMASTER QBT-SSS (MIK) 2004–05

Glued-in neck, fingerboard front markers, figured bubinga-yop body, three Seymour Duncan single-coils. Similar to SHOWMASTER QBT-HH (see previous listing) except:

• **Electronics:** three Seymour Duncan-logo single-coils.

SHOWMASTER FMT-HH (MIK) 2005–07

Glued-in neck, fingerboard front markers, figured maple-top body, two Seymour Duncan humbuckers. Similar to SHOWMASTER H (see 2003 listing) except:

• **Neck:** dot position markers on fretboard.
• **Body:** with figured maple top; sunburst or natural.
• **Electronics:** two Seymour Duncan-logo black coverless humbuckers; two controls (volume, tone) and five-way selector, all on body.
• **Hardware:** chrome-plated.

SHOWMASTER QMT-HH (MIK) 2005–07

Glued-in neck, fingerboard front markers, figured maple-top body, two Seymour Duncan humbuckers. Similar to SHOWMASTER QBT-HH (see 2004 listing) except:

• **Body:** with figured maple top; sunbursts only.

■ **2004** Showmaster Blackout

SHOWMASTER

2004-2005

264

■ **2004** Showmaster Tie-Dye Hippie

■ **2004** Showmaster QBT-HH

■ **2006** Showmaster Fat HH Ash Top

TORONADO (MIM) 1998–2004

Model name on headstock, four controls,
two metal-cover humbuckers.

- **Neck:** maple with rosewood fingerboard;
  24.75-inch scale, 22 frets; truss-rod adjuster
  at headstock end; one string-guide.
- **Body:** contoured offset-waist; sunburst or colors.
- **Electronics:** two metal-cover humbuckers;
  four controls (two volume, two tone) on body;
  three-way selector on pickguard; side-mounted jack.
- **Hardware:** ten-screw tortoiseshell or white pearl
  laminated plastic pickguard; six-saddle bridge
  with through-body stringing.

CLASSIC ROCKER 2000–02

Hollow single-cutaway body, two pickups,
Bigsby vibrato tailpiece.

- **Neck:** maple glued-in, with bound rosewood
  fingerboard, diamond markers; truss-rod adjuster
  at headstock end; three-tuners-per-side headstock.
- **Body:** hollow single-cutaway bound, with bound
  f-holes; black or red.
- **Electronics:** two white-top six-polepiece pickups;
  four controls (three volume, one tone) and three-way
  selector, all on body; side-mounted jack.
- **Hardware:** white plastic pickguard; six-saddle
  metal-top bridge, Bigsby vibrato tailpiece.

Custom Shop production.

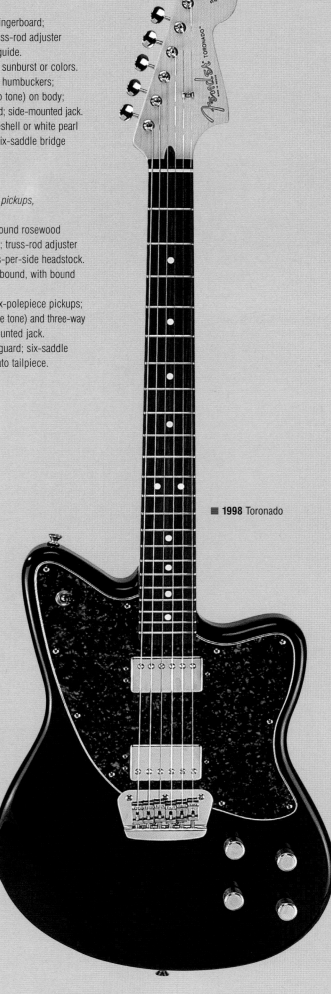

■ **1998** Toronado

TORONADO 1998-2002

■ **1998** press advertisement

TORONADO DVII 2002–04
Model name on black-face headstock, four controls,
two black six-polepiece pickups.
- **Neck:** maple with rosewood fingerboard; 24-inch scale, 22 frets; truss-rod adjuster at headstock end; one string-guide; black-face headstock.
- **Body:** contoured offset-waist; blonde or red.
- **Electronics:** two large black six-polepiece pickups; four controls (two volume, two tone) and three-way selector, all on body; side-mounted jack.
- **Hardware:** seven-screw black laminated plastic pickguard; six-saddle bridge, bar tailpiece.

TORONADO HH 2002–04
Model name on black-face
headstock, four controls,
two black coverless humbuckers.
Similar to TORONADO DVII
(see previous listing) except:
- **Electronics:** two black coverless humbuckers.

■ **2004** Toronado HH

HIGHWAY ONE TORONADO 2003–04

Model name on headstock, two controls,
two black coverless humbuckers.

- **Neck:** maple with rosewood fingerboard; 24.75-inch scale, 22 frets; truss-rod adjuster at headstock end; one string-guide.
- **Body:** contoured offset-waist; black, pewter or silver, satin finish.
- **Electronics:** two black coverless humbuckers; two controls (volume, tone) and three-way selector, all on body; side-mounted jack.
- **Hardware:** seven-screw black plastic pickguard; six-saddle bridge, bar tailpiece.
- **Hardware:** five-screw black plastic pickguard with decorative tooled leather overlay; three-saddle raised sides bridge with through-body stringing.

Custom Shop production.

TORONADO GT HH (MIK) 2005–06

Striped body, four controls, two Seymour Duncan black humbuckers.

- **Neck:** maple with rosewood fingerboard; 24.75-inch scale, 22 frets; truss-rod adjuster at headstock end; two string-guides; matching color headstock face.
- **Body:** contoured offset-waist; various colors, with stripes.
- **Electronics:** two Seymour Duncan-logo black coverless humbuckers; four controls (two volume, two tone) and three-way selector, all on body.
- **Hardware:** no pickguard; six-saddle bridge, bar tailpiece.

TORONADO HH (MIM) 2005–06

Model name on headstock, four controls,
two black coverless humbuckers.

Similar to TORONADO (see 1998 listing) except:
- **Body:** various colors.
- **Electronics:** two black coverless humbuckers; four controls (two volume, two tone) and three-way selector, all on body.
- **Hardware:** seven-screw black laminated plastic pickguard; six-saddle bridge, bar tailpiece.

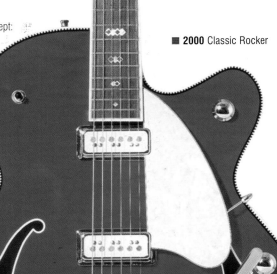

■ **2000** Classic Rocker

TORONADO
2003-2005

■ **2004** Toronado

■ **2004** Toronado GT HH

STRAT-O-SONIC DVI 2003–04

*Model name on headstock, one large black
six-polepiece pickup.*

- **Neck:** maple with rosewood fingerboard;
  22 frets; truss-rod adjuster at headstock end;
  staggered height locking tuners; black-face
  headstock.
- **Body:** semi-solid; sunburst, blonde, or red.
- **Electronics:** one large black six-polepiece
  pickup (at bridge); two controls (volume, tone)
  on body; side-mounted jack.
- **Hardware:** six-screw black laminated plastic
  pickguard; six-saddle wrapover bridge/tailpiece.

STRAT-O-SONIC DVII 2003–06

*Model name on headstock, two large black
six-polepiece pickups.*
Similar to STRAT-O-SONIC DVI (see previous listing)
except:

- **Electronics:** two large black six-polepiece pickups;
  two controls (volume, tone) and three-way selector,
  all on body.

STRAT-O-SONIC HH 2005–06

Model name on headstock, two black humbuckers.
Similar to STRAT-O-SONIC DVII (see 2003 listing) except:

- **Electronics:** two black coverless humbucker pickups.

TC-90 THINLINE (MIK) 2004–current

Twin-cutaway body with f-hole.

- **Neck:** maple glued-in, with rosewood fingerboard; 22 frets; truss-rod adjuster at headstock end; two string-guides; Telecaster style headstock with matching color face.
- **Body:** semi-solid slab twin-cutaway; f-hole; redburst or white.
- **Electronics:** two large black six-polepiece pickups; two controls (volume, tone) and three-way selector, all on body; side-mounted jack.
- **Hardware:** six-screw black laminated plastic pickguard; six-saddle bridge, bar tailpiece.

SO-CAL SPEED SHOP (MIK) 2005

So-Cal logo on body, red/white graphic finish.

- **Neck:** maple with rosewood fingerboard; 22 frets; truss-rod adjuster at headstock end; two string-guides; matching color headstock, neck and fingerboard.
- **Body:** red/white graphic finish only.
- **Electronics:** one black coverless humbucker (at bridge); one control (volume) on body; side-mounted jack.
- **Hardware:** no pickguard; six-saddle small bridge with through-body stringing.

■ **2004** American Special Toronado HH

CLASSIC ROCKER 2000-2005

■ **2004** Strat-O-Sonic HH

■ **2005** So-Cal Speed Shop

■ **2005** Tele-Sonic HH

ACKNOWLEDGMENTS

Owners' credits
Guitars photographed were owned at the time of
photography by the following individuals and organizations,
and we are most grateful for their help. Arbiter Group;
Scot Arch; Robin Baird; Mark Brend; Simon Carlton;
Chinery Collection; Paul Day; Dixie's Music; Jerry
Donahue; Malcolm Draper; John Entwistle; Fender
Great Britain & Ireland; Fender Japan; Fender Musical
Instruments Corporation; Paul Fischer; Rory Gallagher;
David Gilmour; Alex Gregory; Gruhn Guitars; Robin
Guthrie; George Harrison; Adrian Hornbrook; Steve
Howe; Steve Lewis; Mandolin Brothers; Graeme
Matheson; Paul Midgley; Music Ground; Carl Nielsen;
Alex Osborne; Tim Philips; Alan Rogan; Mike Slubwoski;
Bruce Welch.

Photographers
Garth Blore; Nigel Bradley; Matthew Chattle;
Miki Slingsby; William Taylor; Kelsey Vaughn.

Memorabilia
illustrated in this book came from the collections of:
Scot Arch; Tony Bacon; Paul Day; Fender Musical
Instruments Corporation; Martin Kelly; The Music
Trades; National Jazz Archive; Don Randall;
Alan Rogan; and Steve Soest.